Animal Skeletons & Anatomy

An Image Archive for Artists & Designers

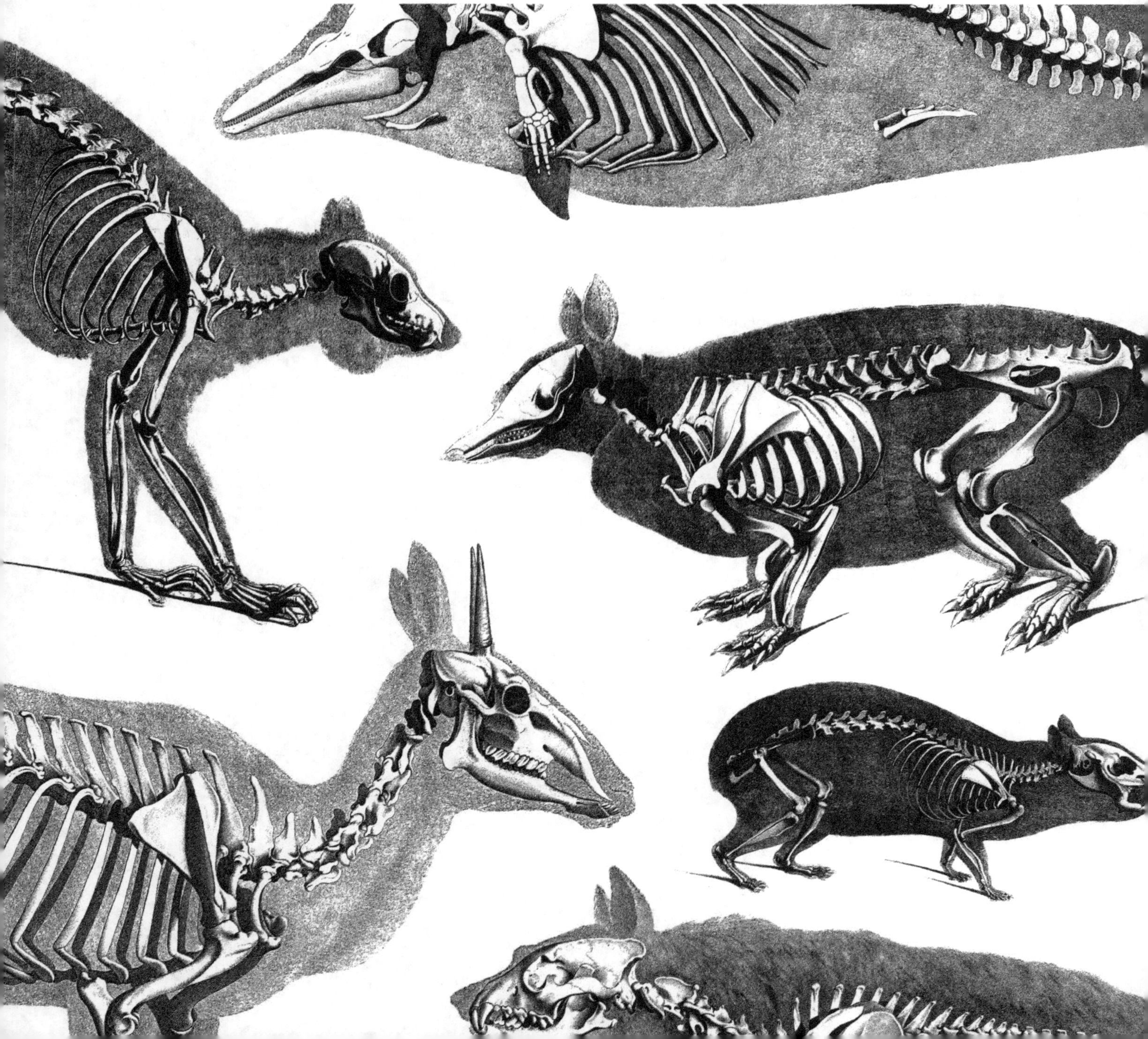

Introduction

This release has been one of our most ambitious projects yet. We have created a comprehensive and diverse pictorial archive of animal anatomical illustrations for the practical use of artists and designers, or to be appreciated by curious minds.

This title features hundreds of exquisitely crafted 17th and 18th-century etchings and engravings of animal skeletons and anatomical diagrams. Within this title, you will find a compelling collection of snakes, birds of prey, kangaroos, lions, mastodons, rabbits, walruses, bats, lizards, horses, giraffes, rhinoceros, deer, camels, whales and so much more.

With the aid of digital image editing technology, we have been able to restore incredibly rare 17th-century artwork into high-resolution images that are now suitable for use in graphic design projects, and many other creative applications.

We hope you enjoy this resource.

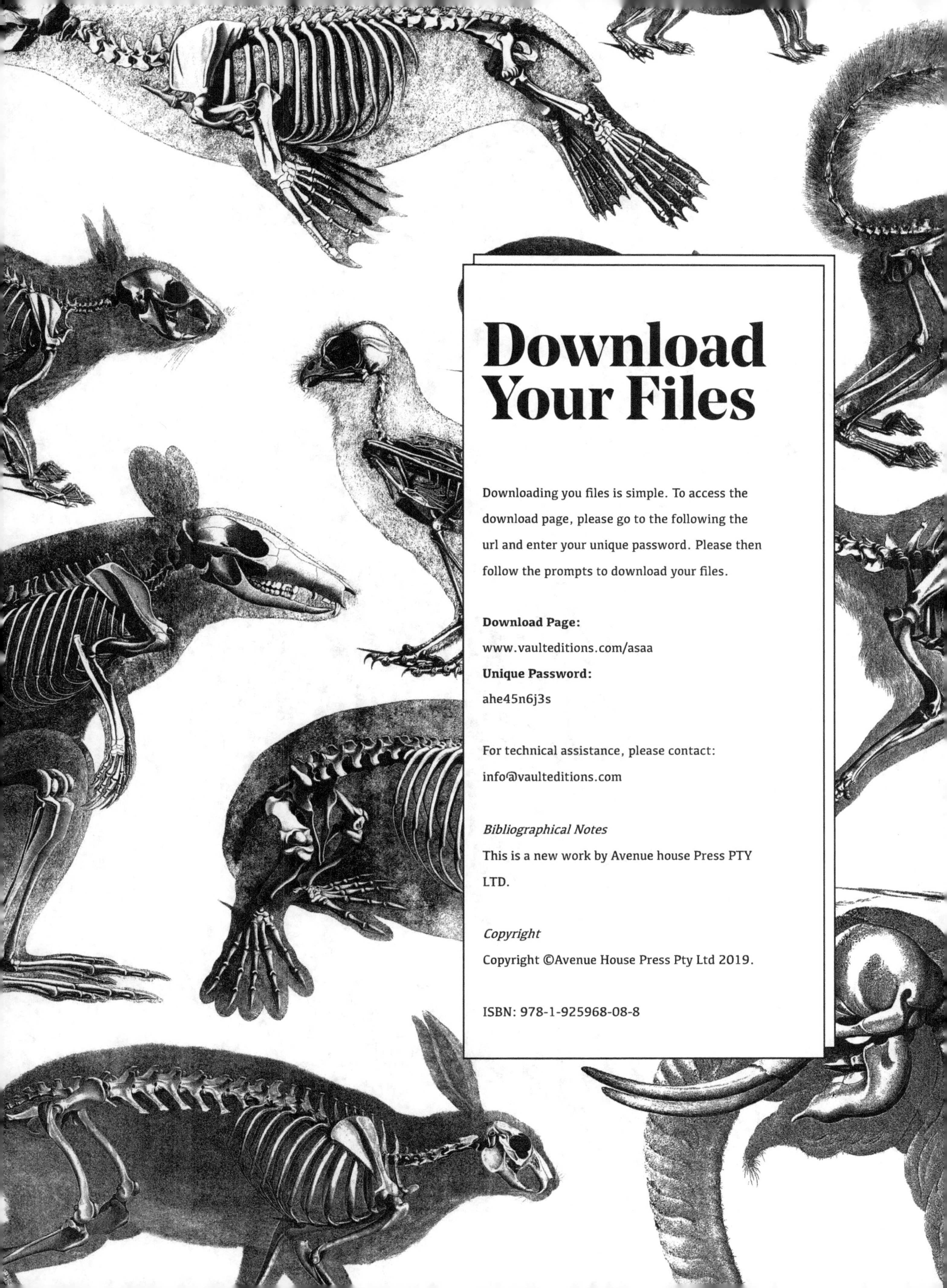

Download Your Files

Downloading you files is simple. To access the download page, please go to the following the url and enter your unique password. Please then follow the prompts to download your files.

Download Page:

www.vaulteditions.com/asaa

Unique Password:

ahe45n6j3s

For technical assistance, please contact:

info@vaulteditions.com

Bibliographical Notes

This is a new work by Avenue house Press PTY LTD.

Copyright

Copyright ©Avenue House Press Pty Ltd 2019.

ISBN: 978-1-925968-08-8

A01

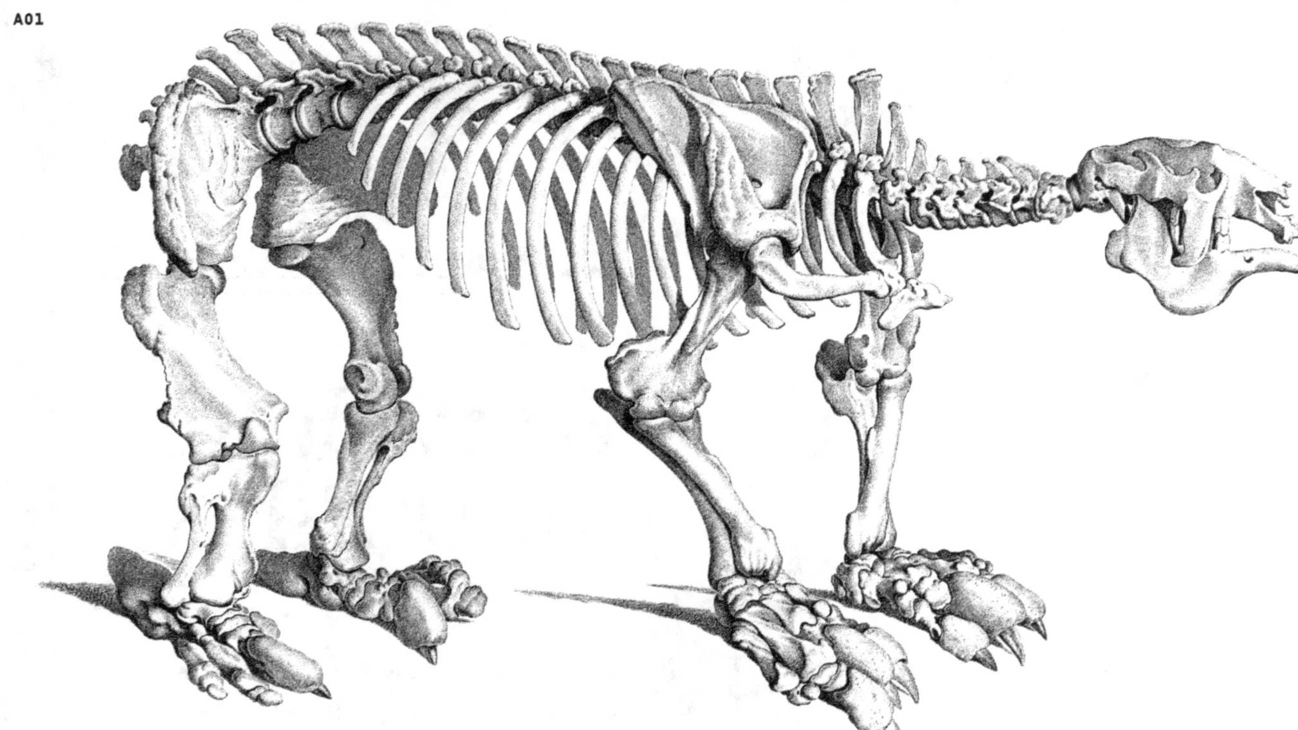

A02

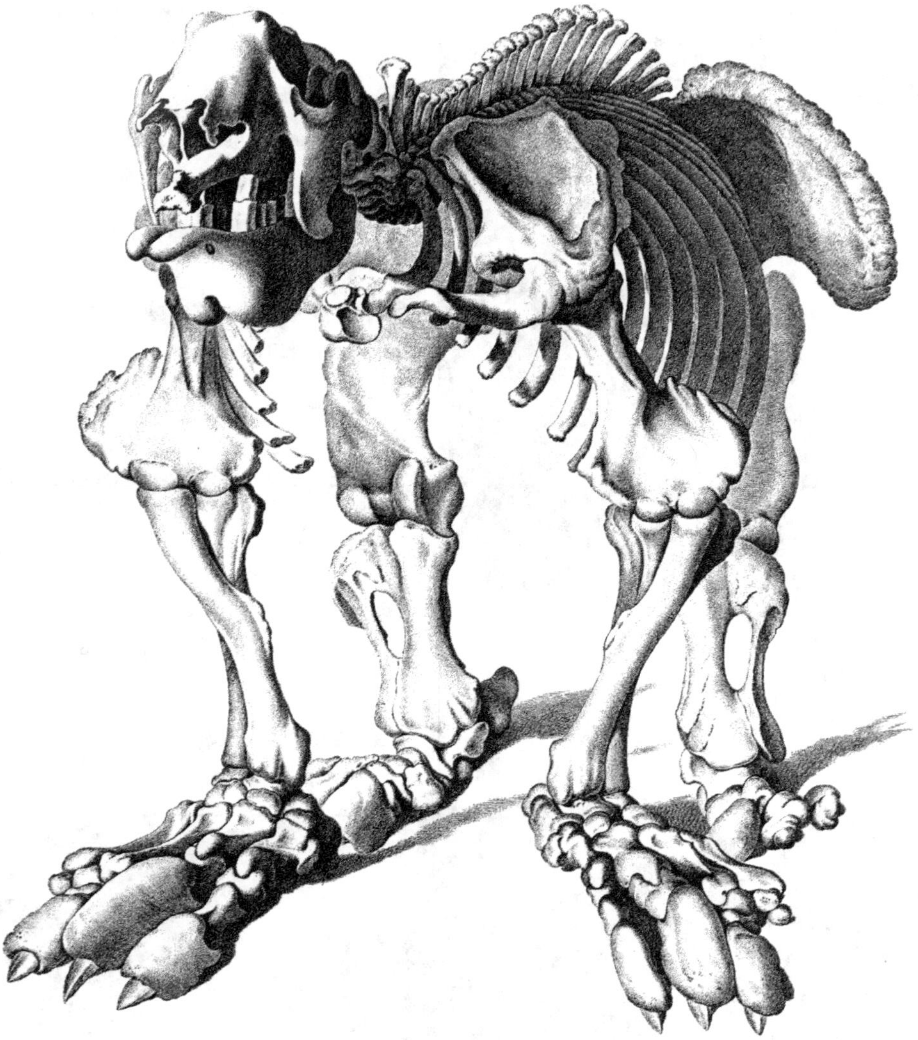

A03

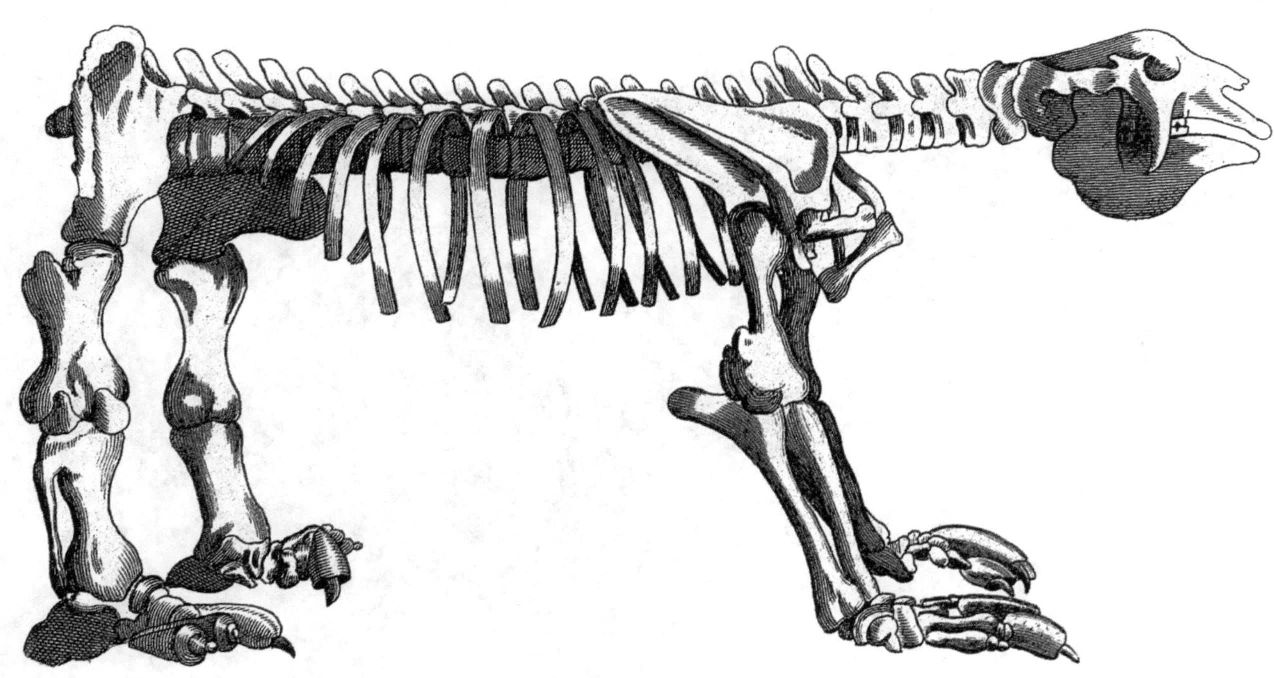

A04

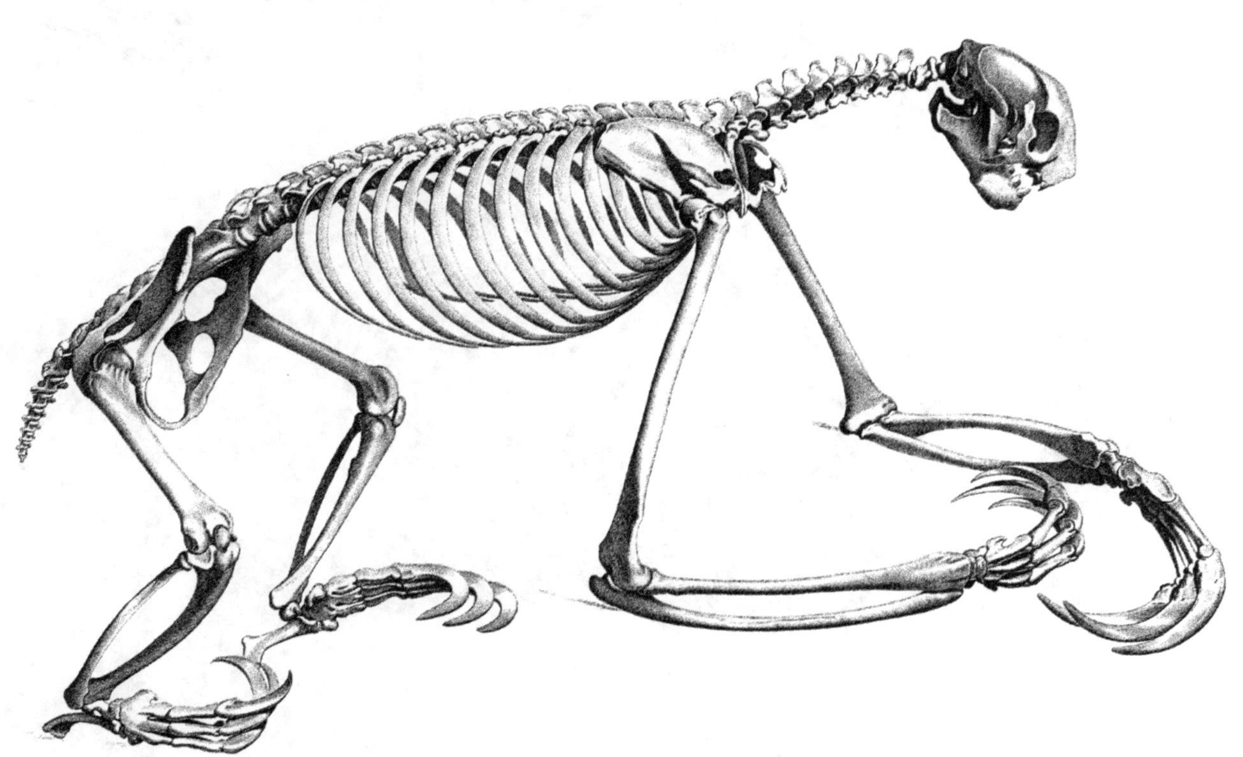

A05

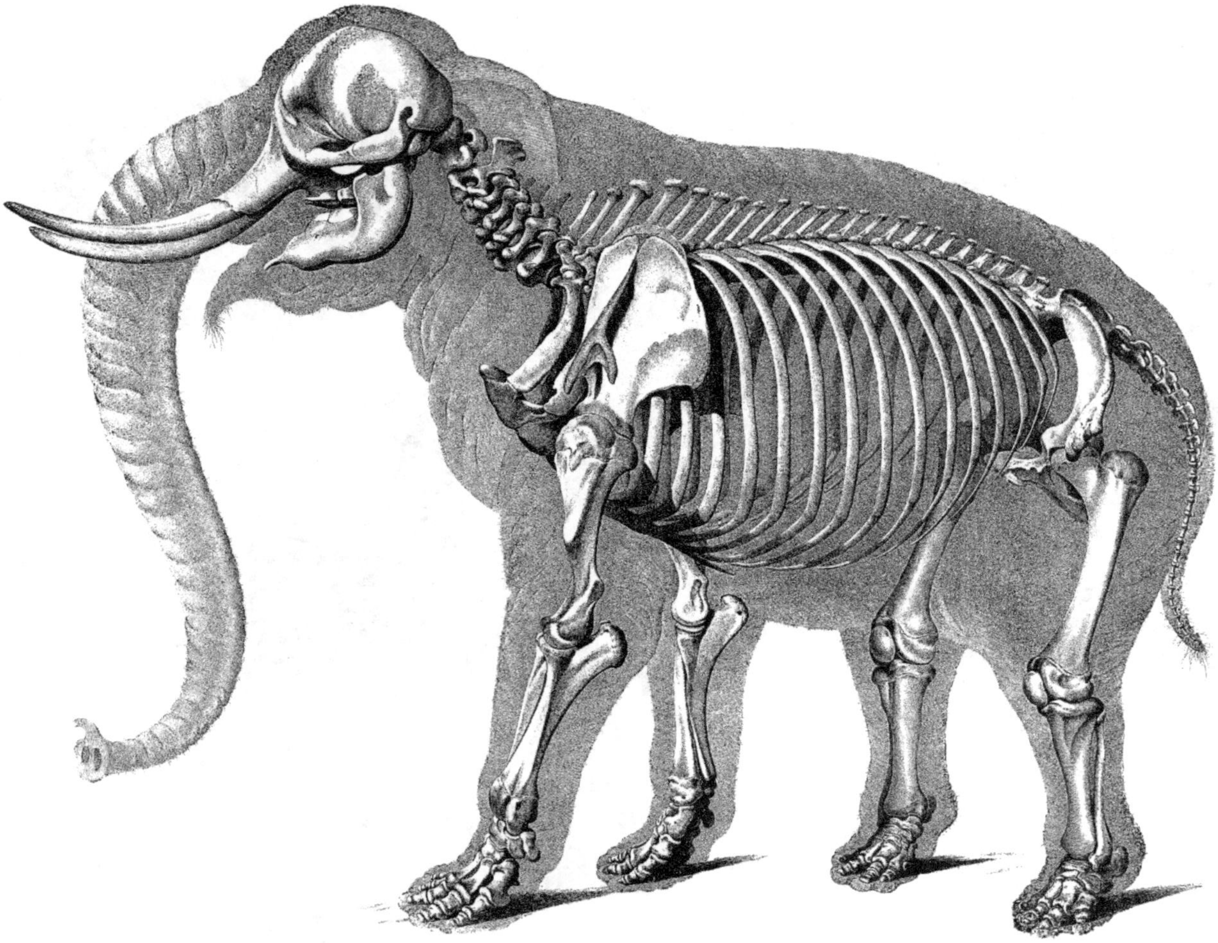

A06

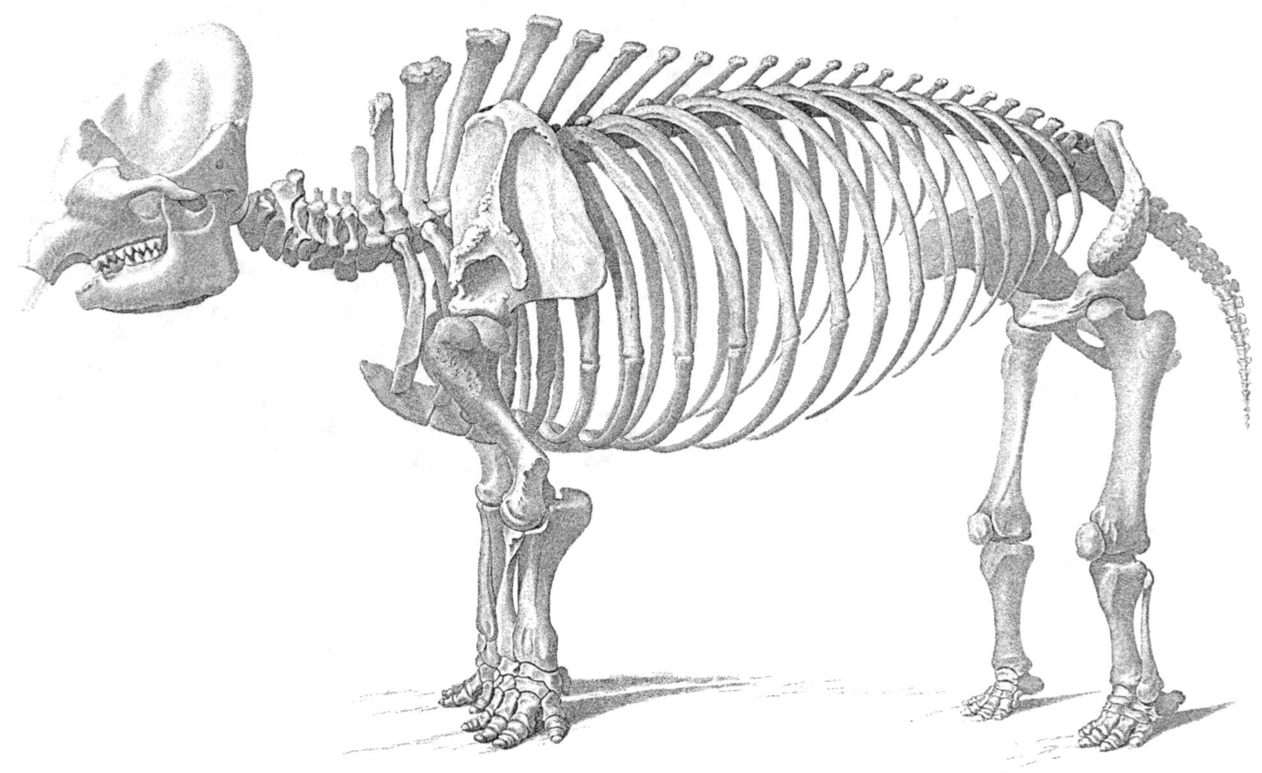

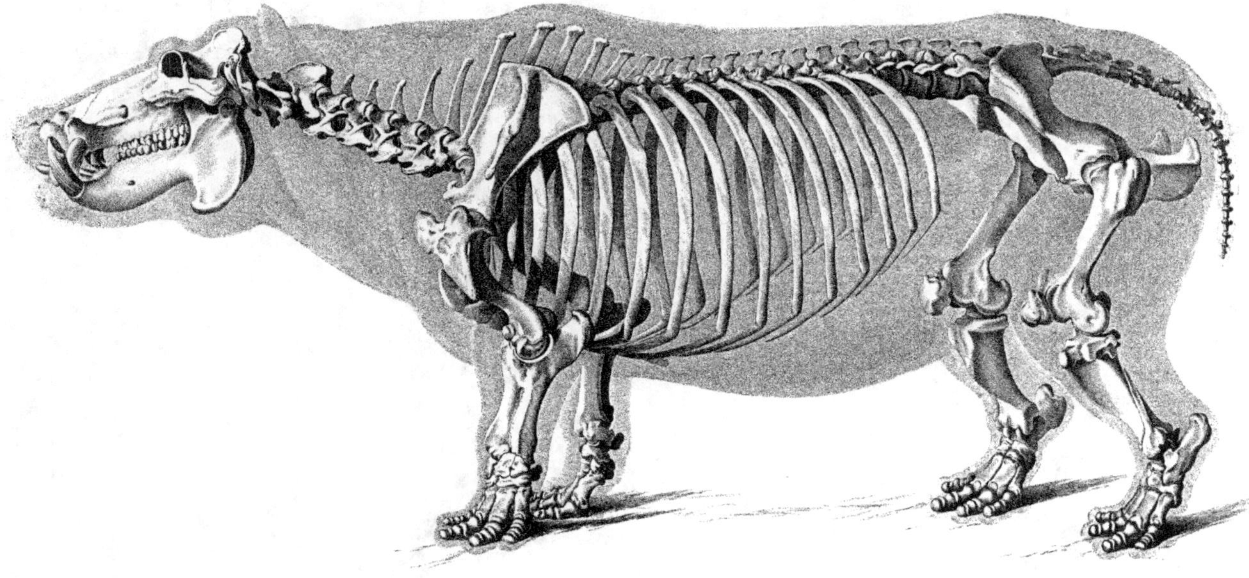

A08

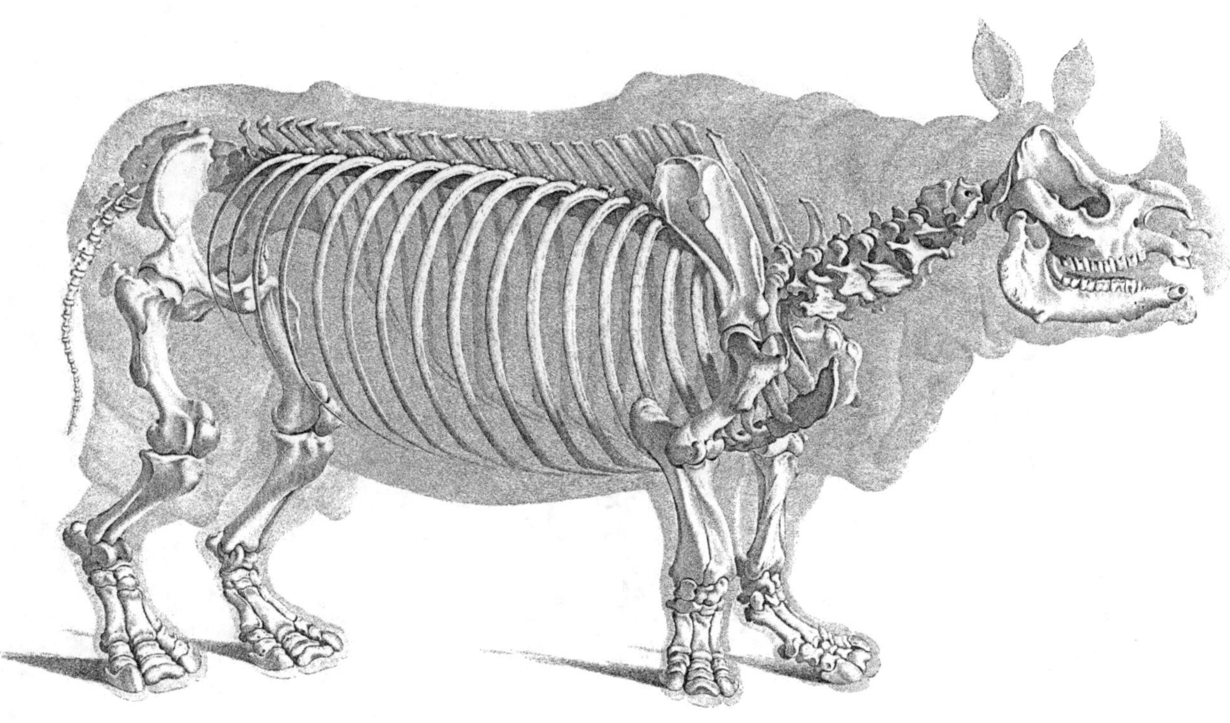

A09

ANIMAL SKELETONS & ANATOMY

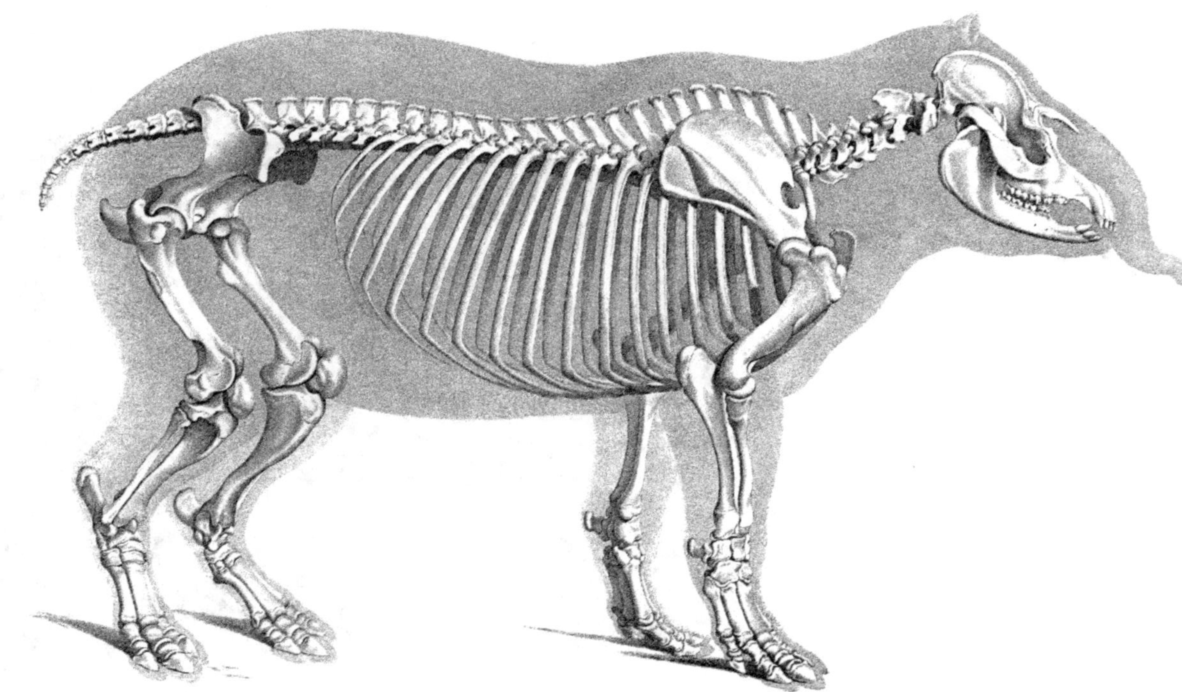

A10

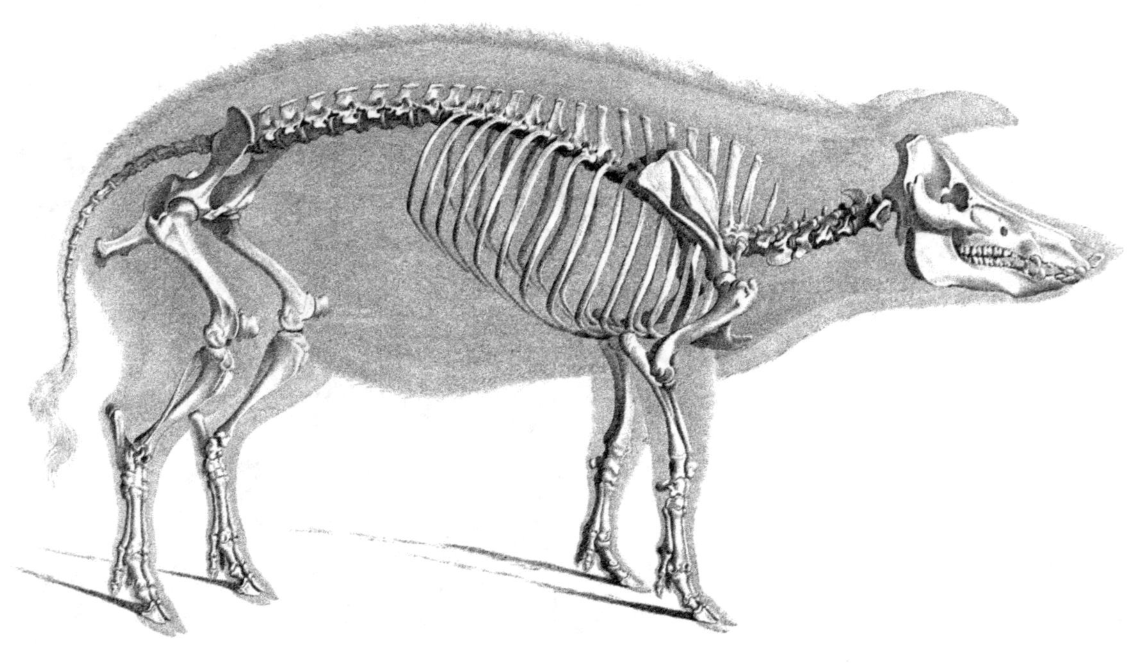

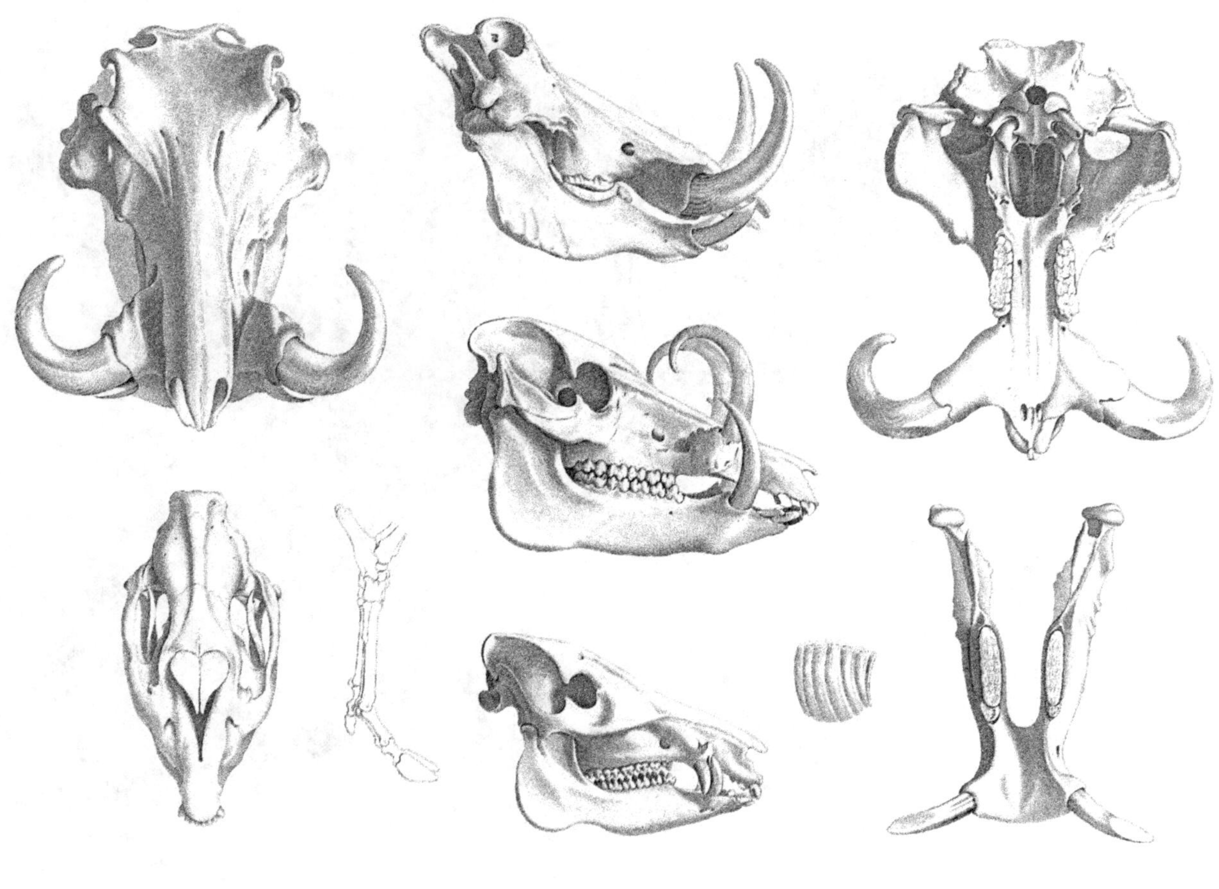

A12

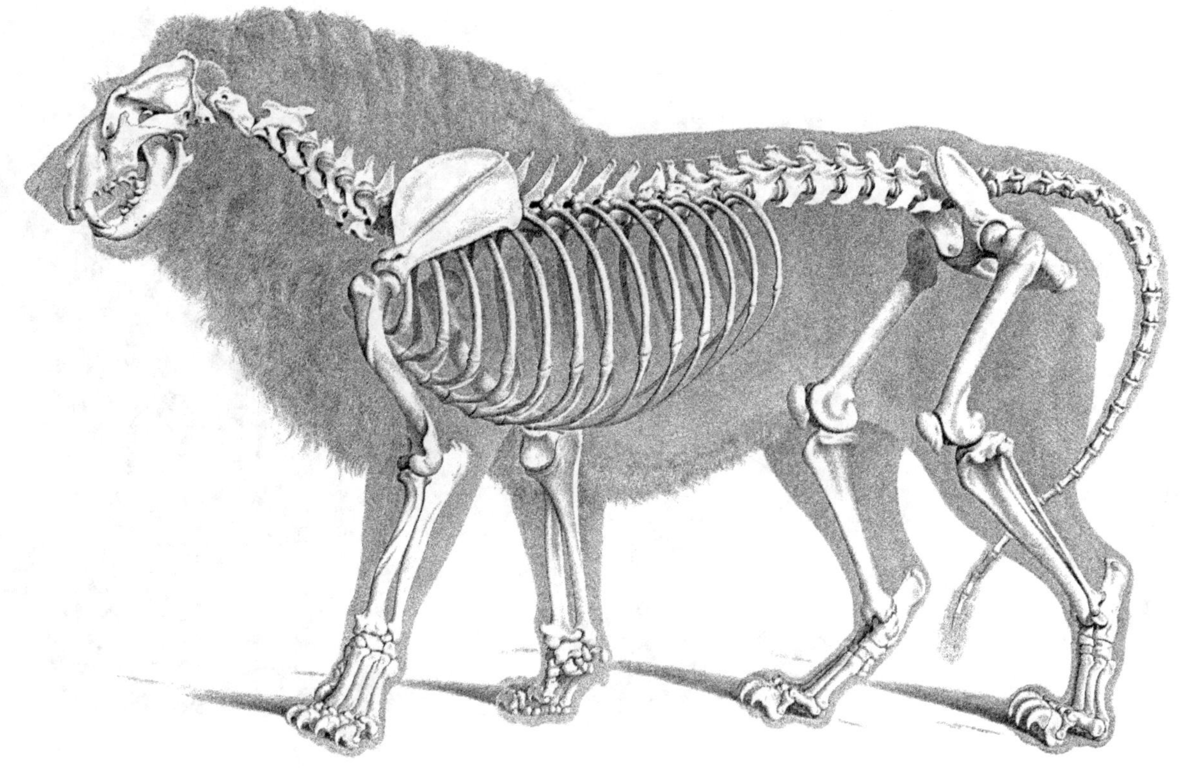

A13

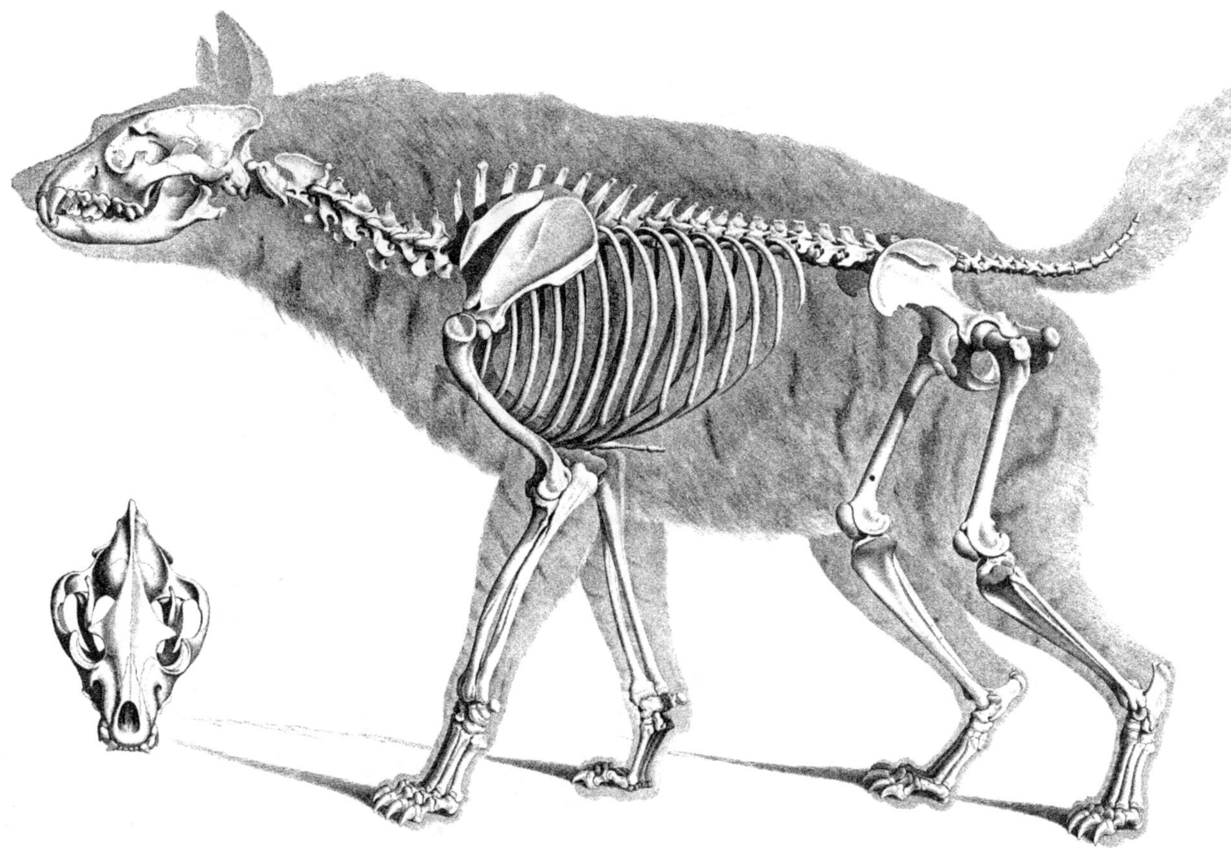

A14

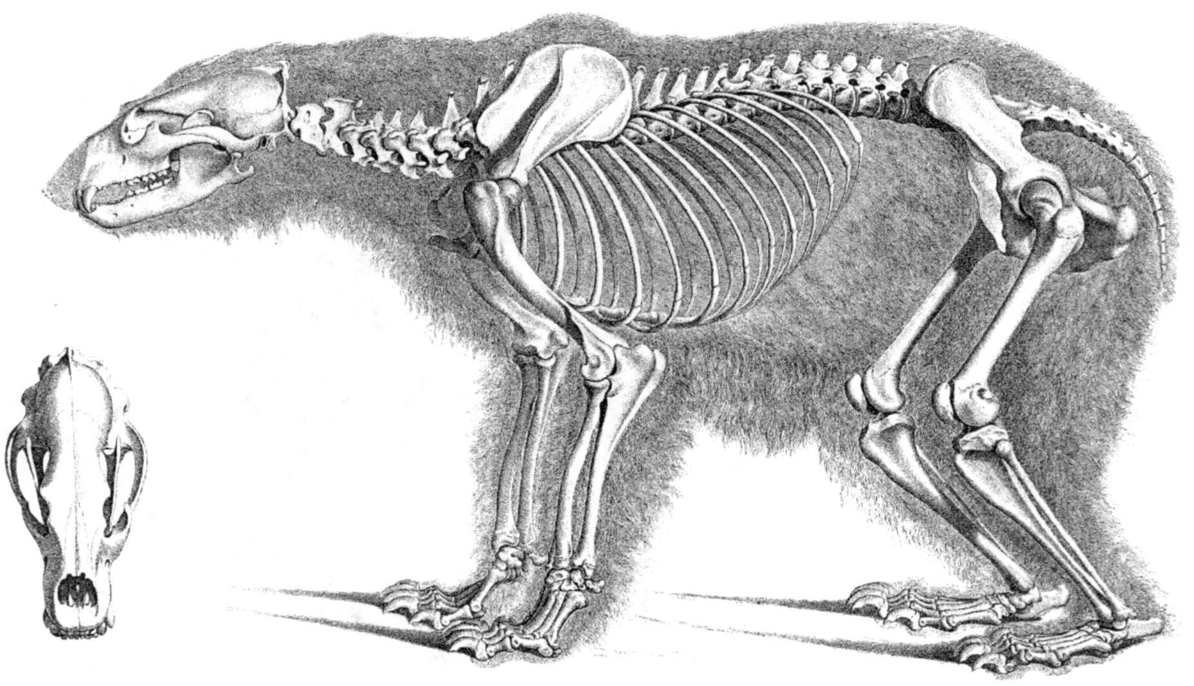

A15

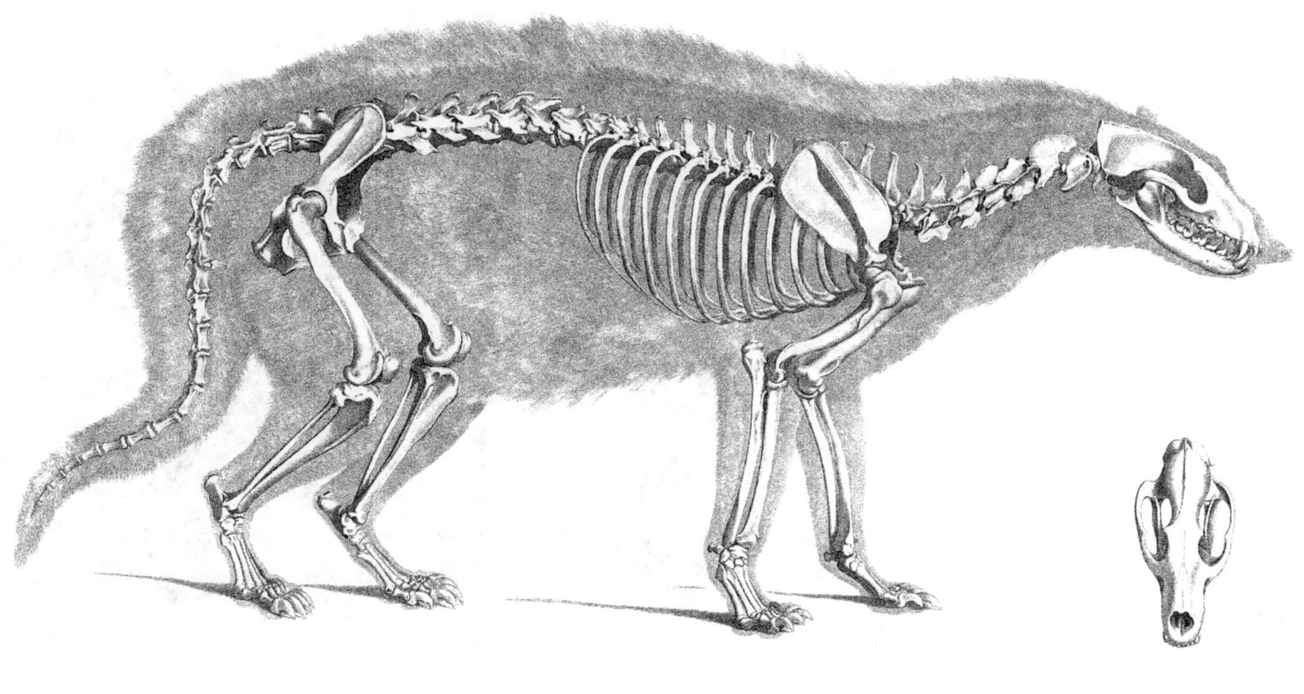

A16

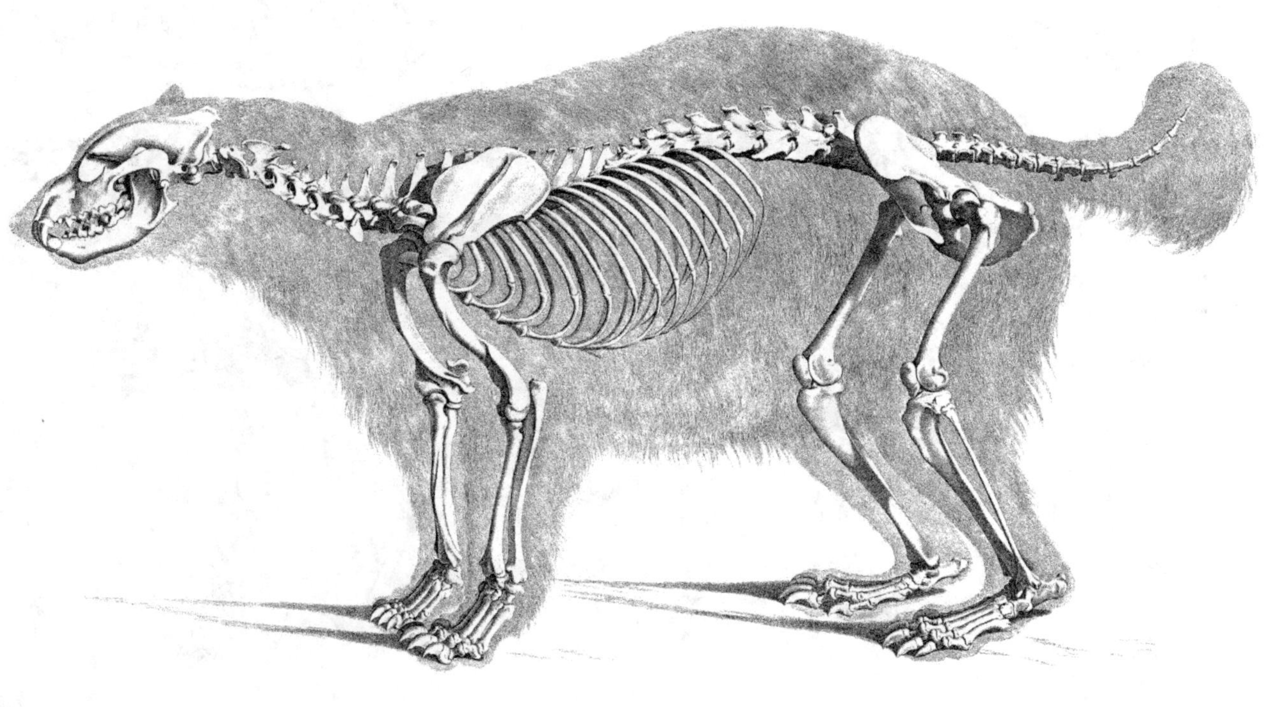

A17

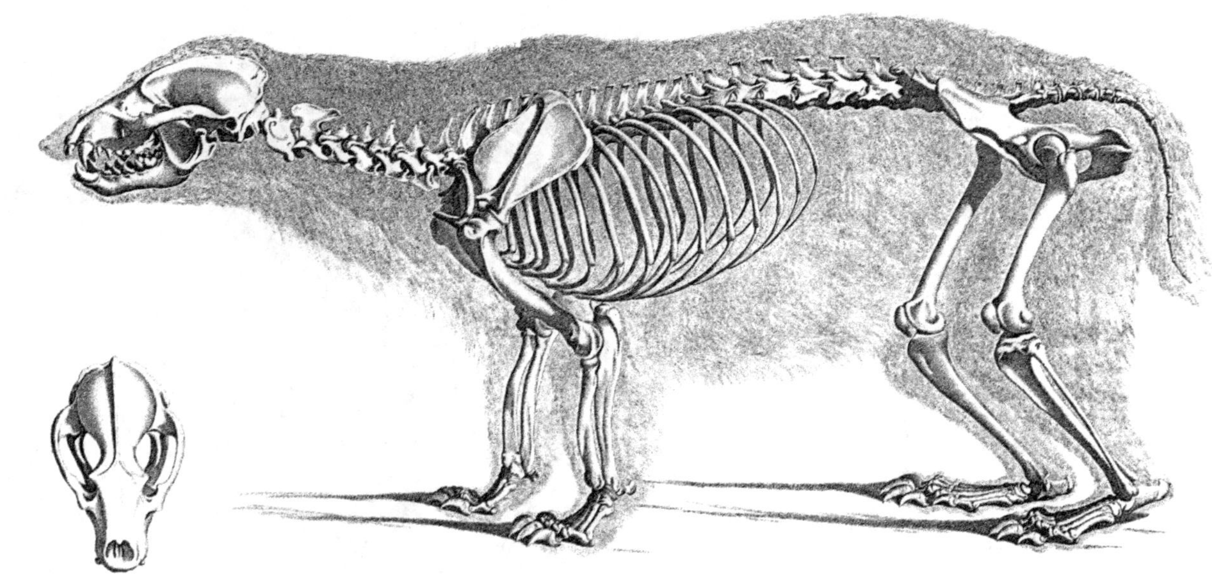

A18

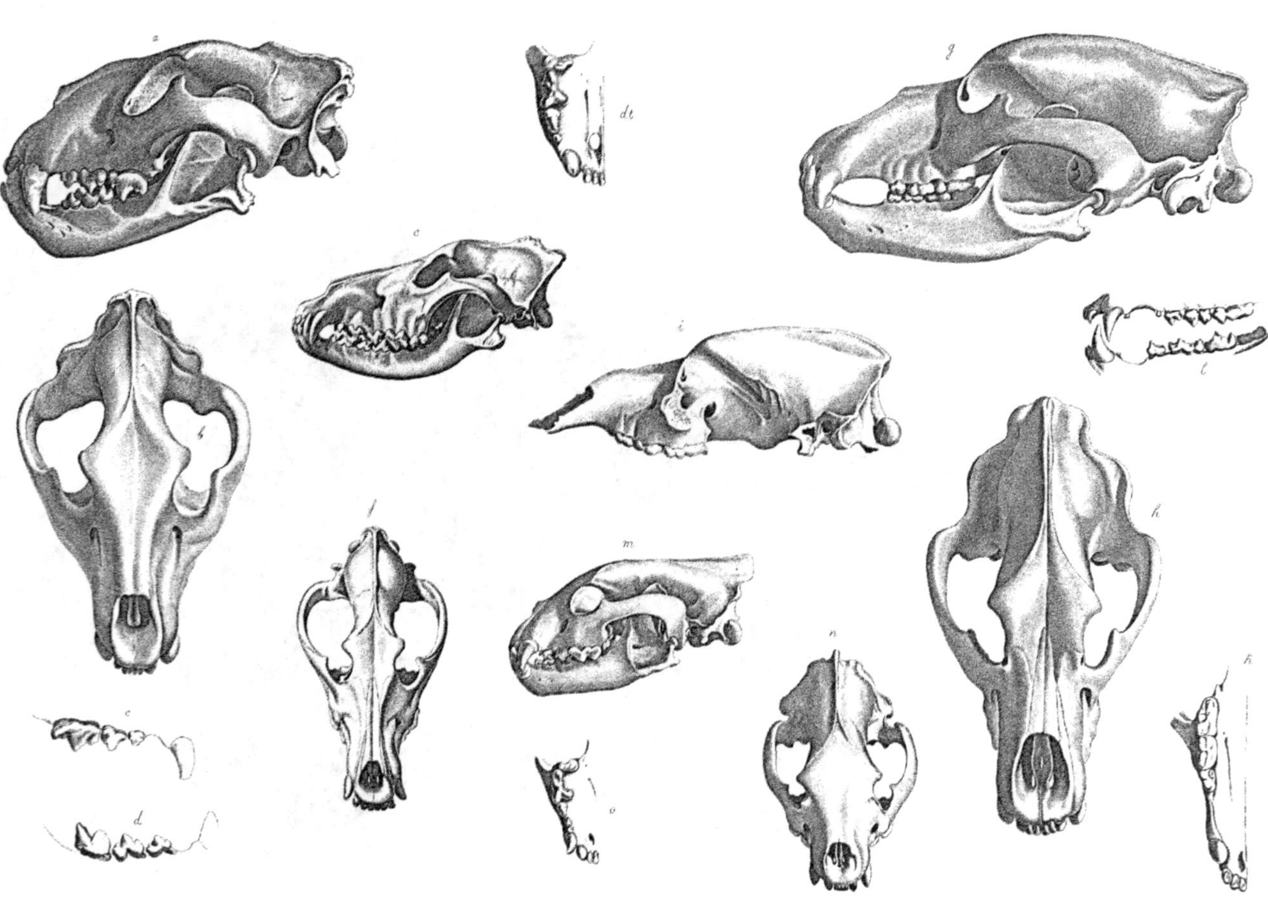

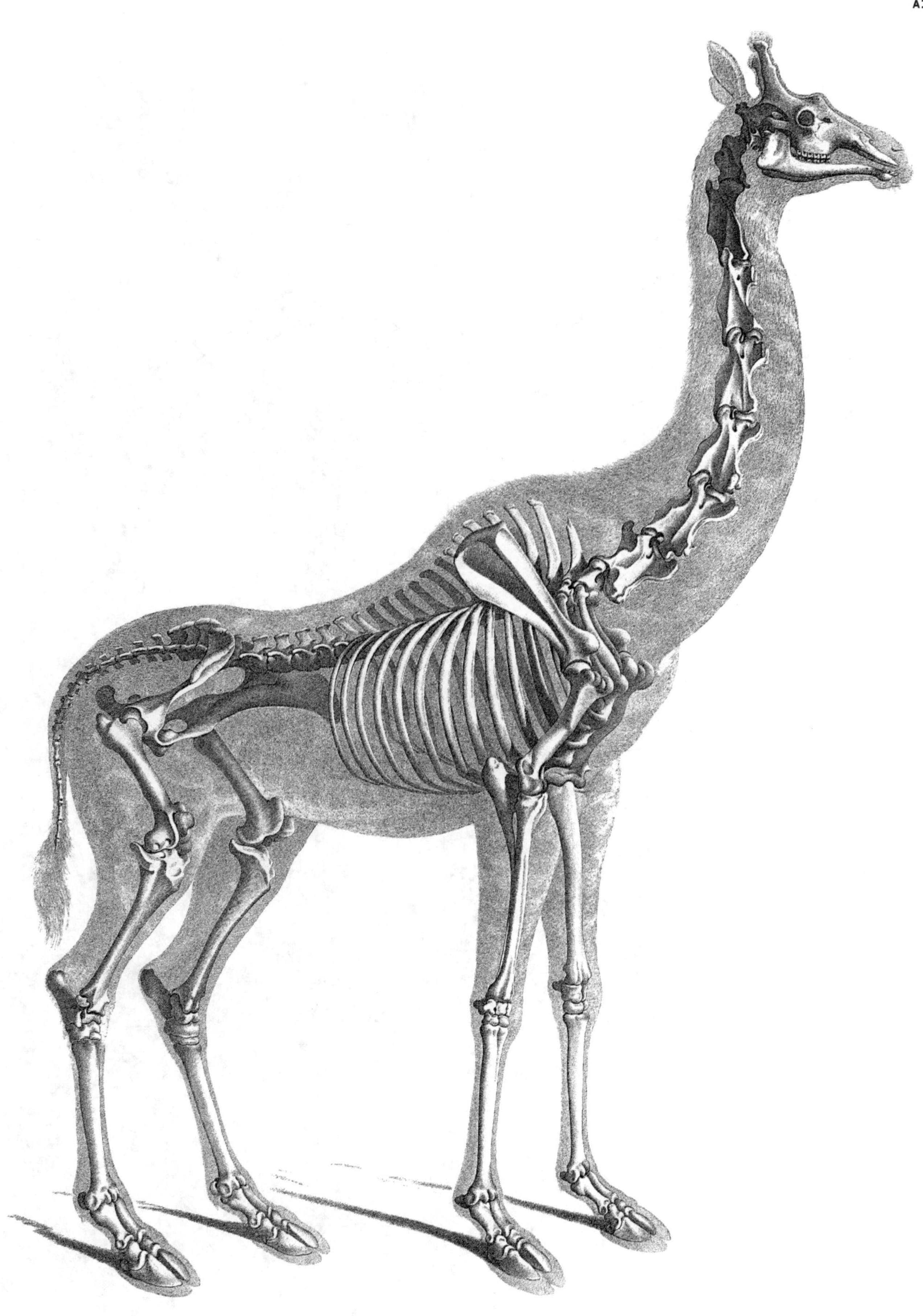

A20

A21

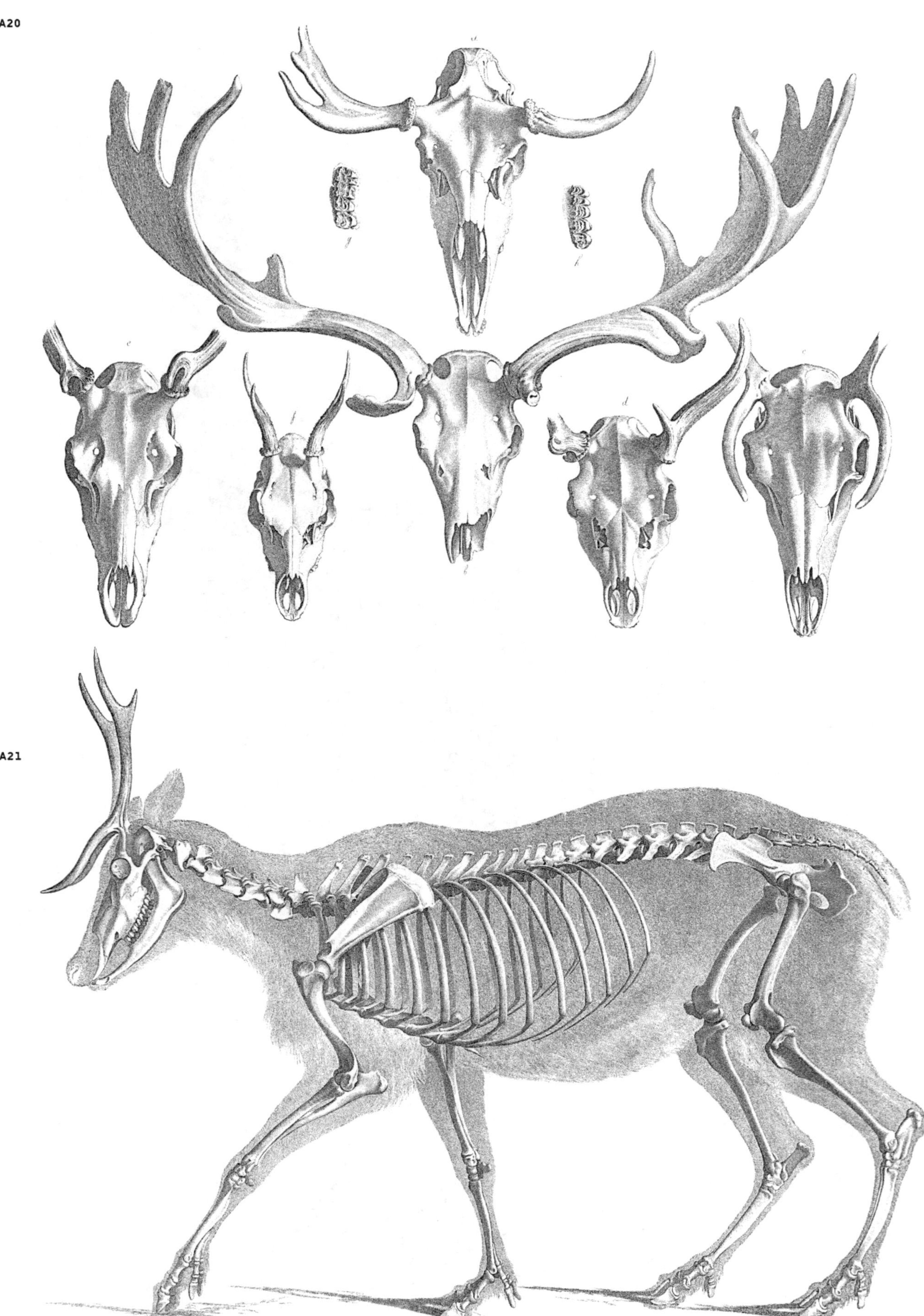

A22

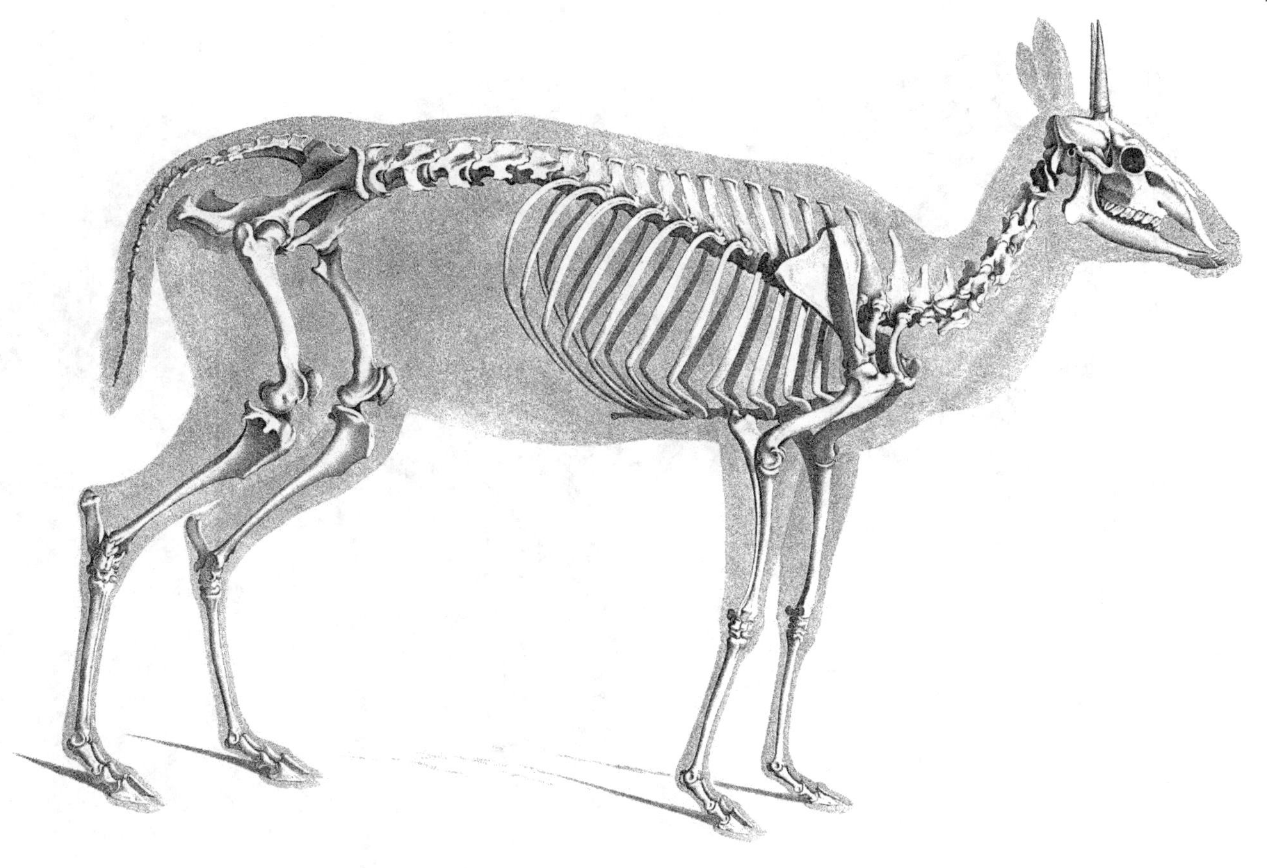

A23

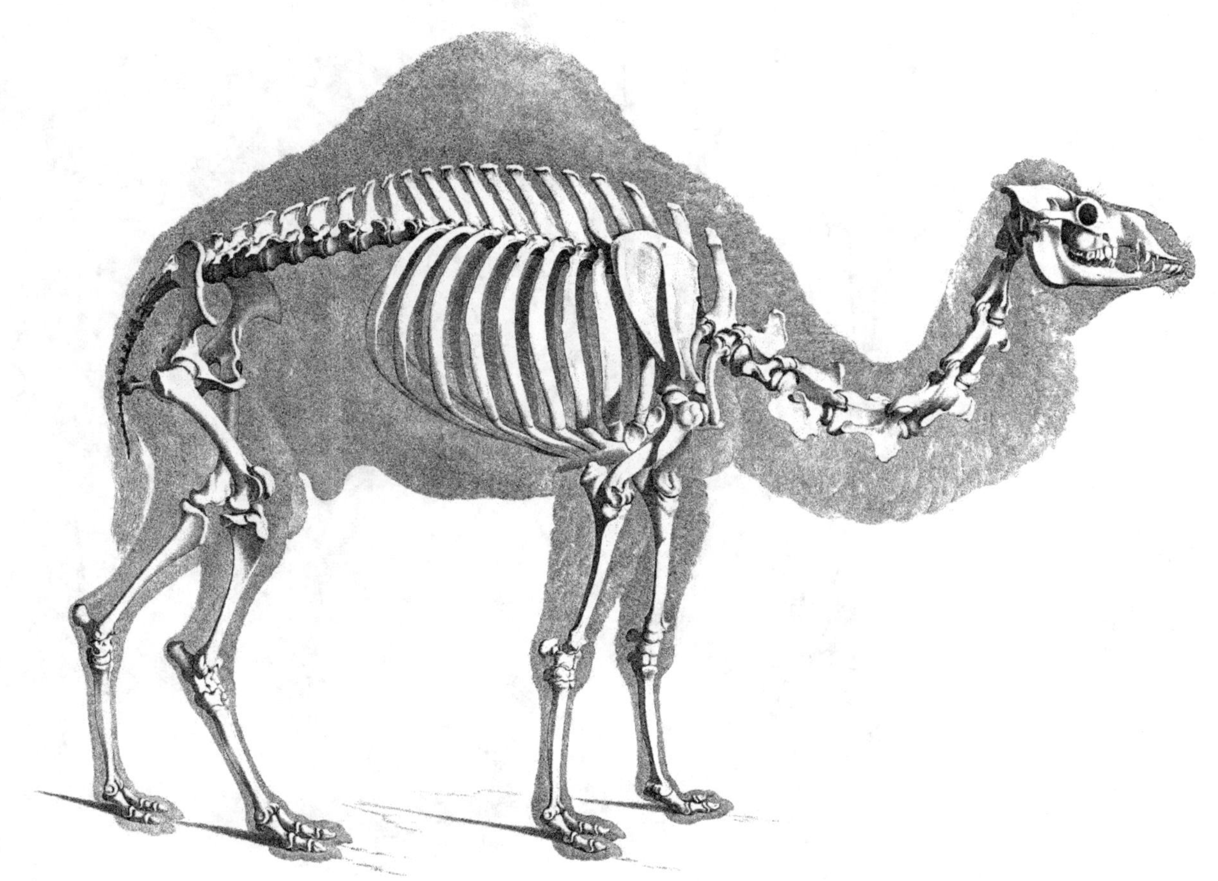

A24

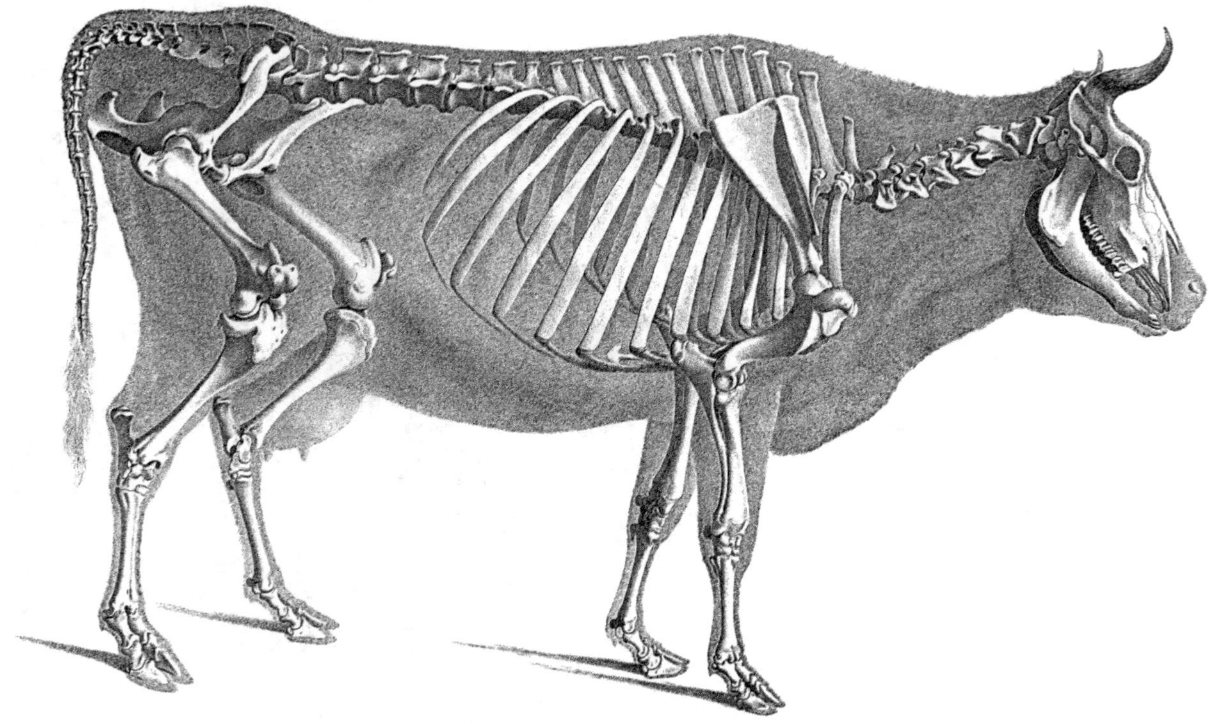

A25

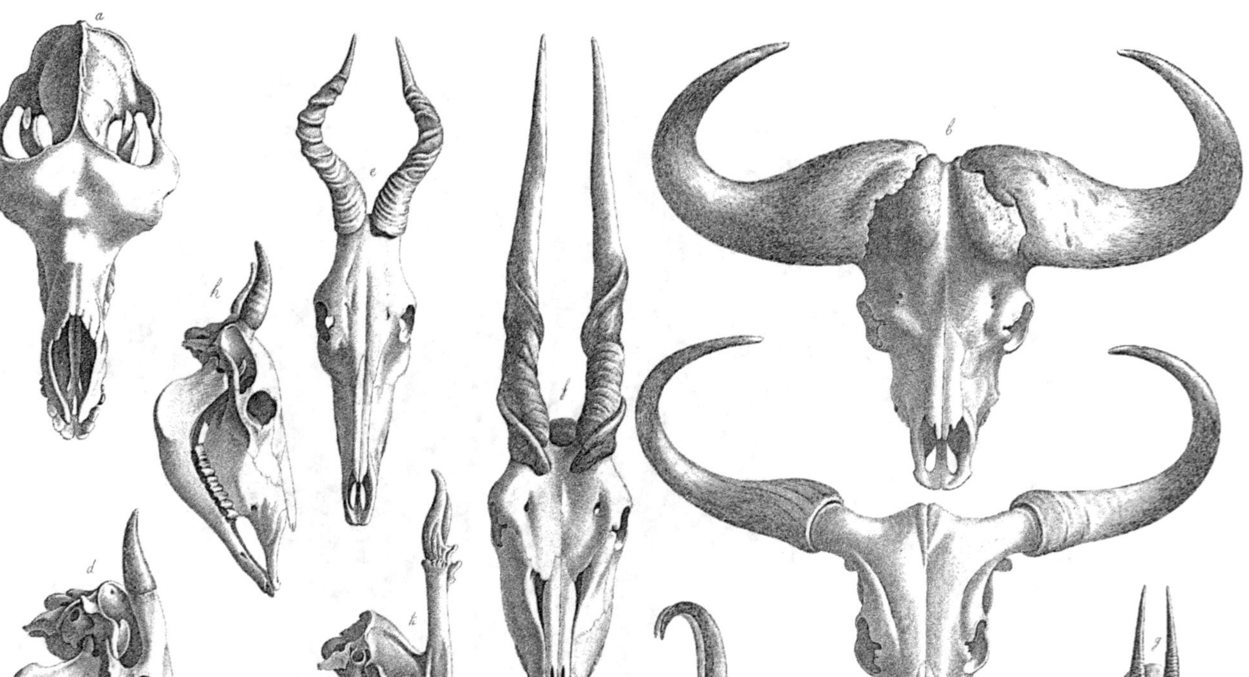

A26

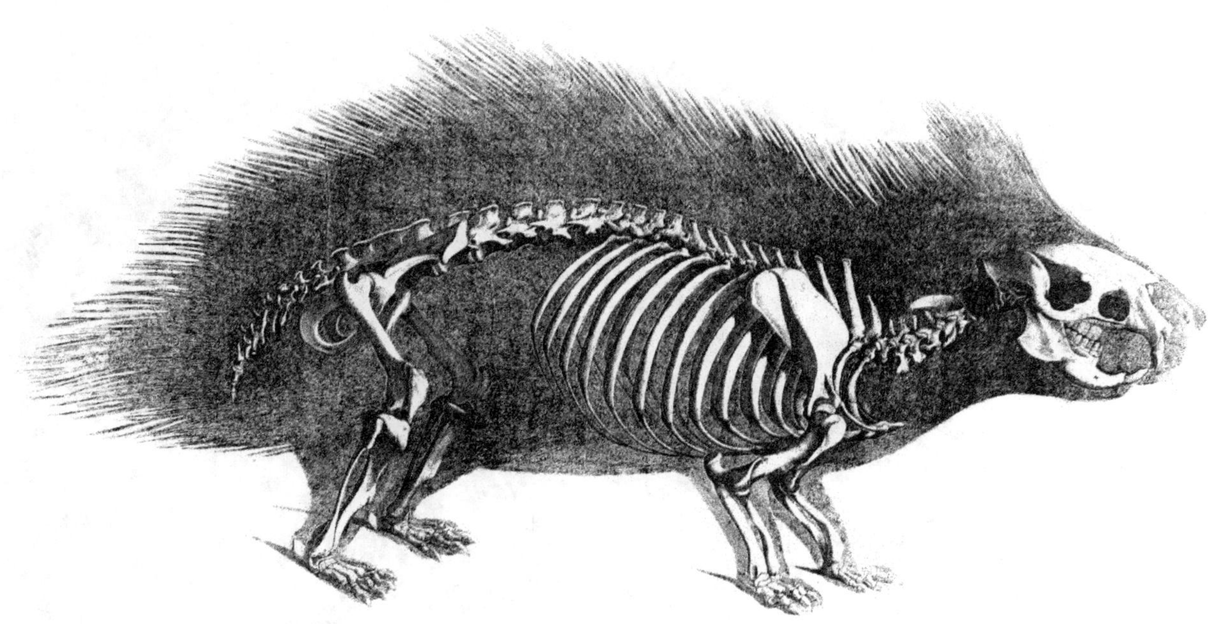

A27

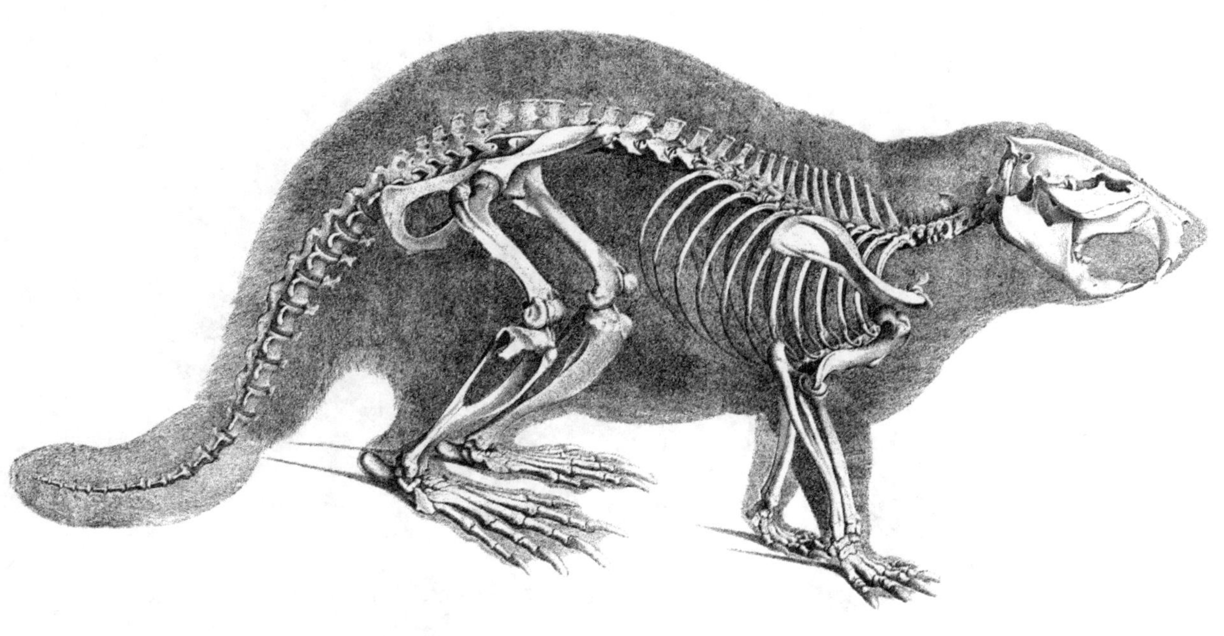

A28

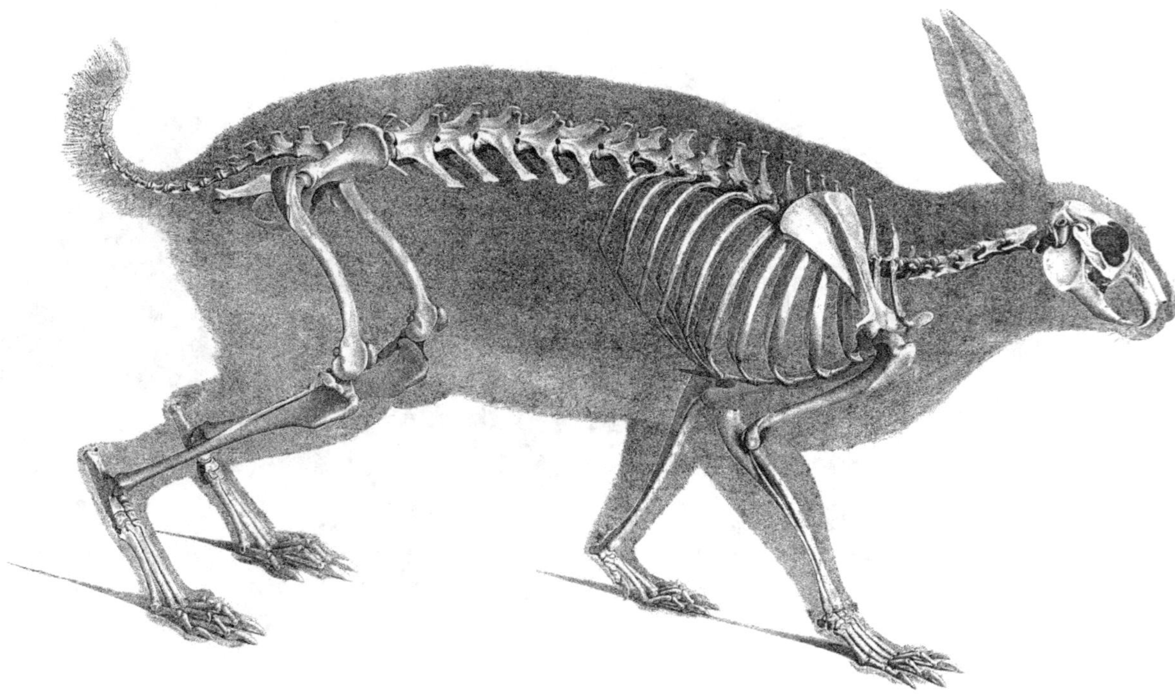

A29

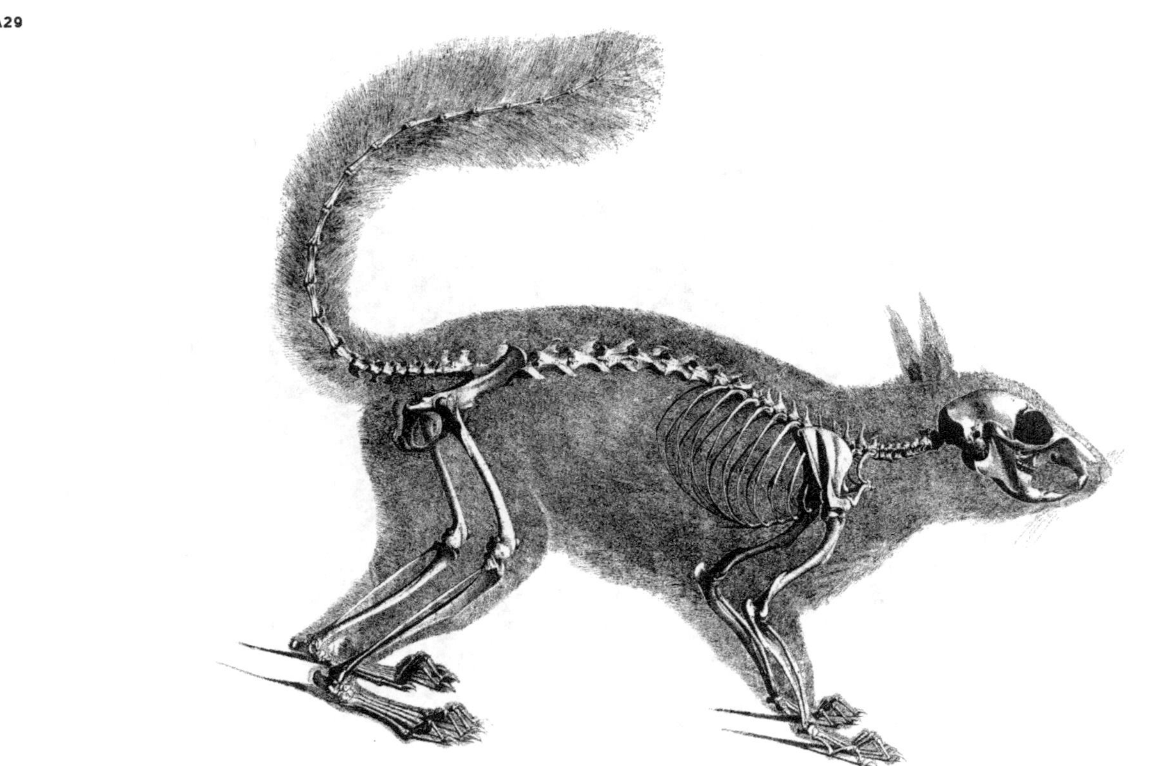

A30

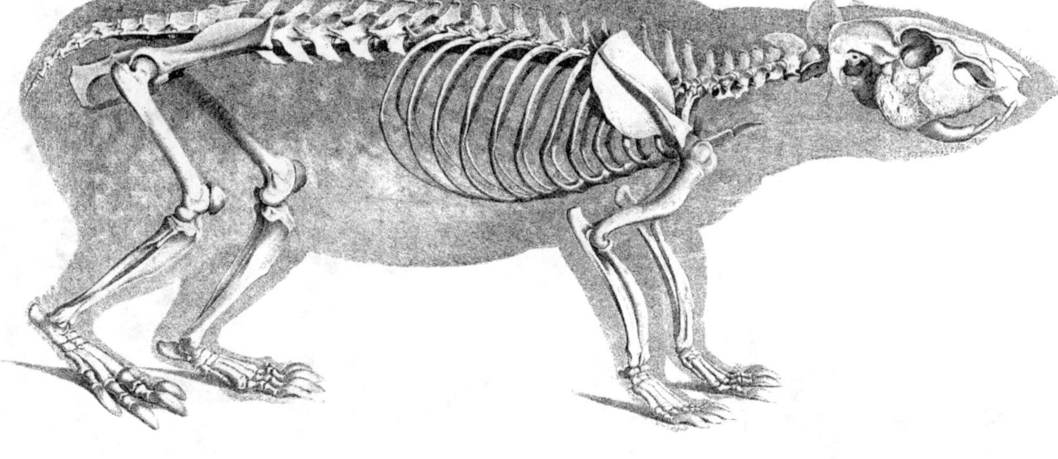

A31

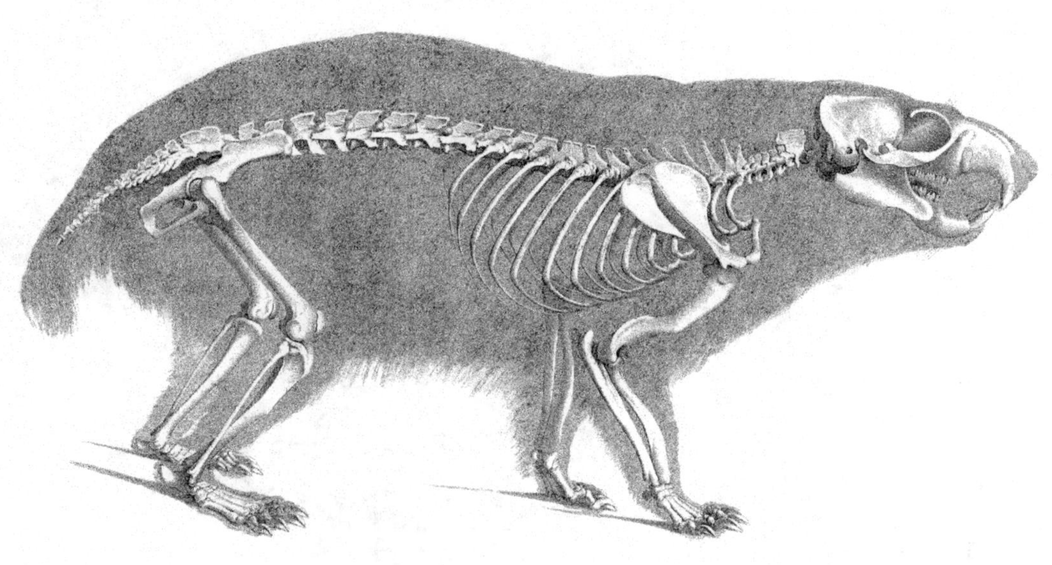

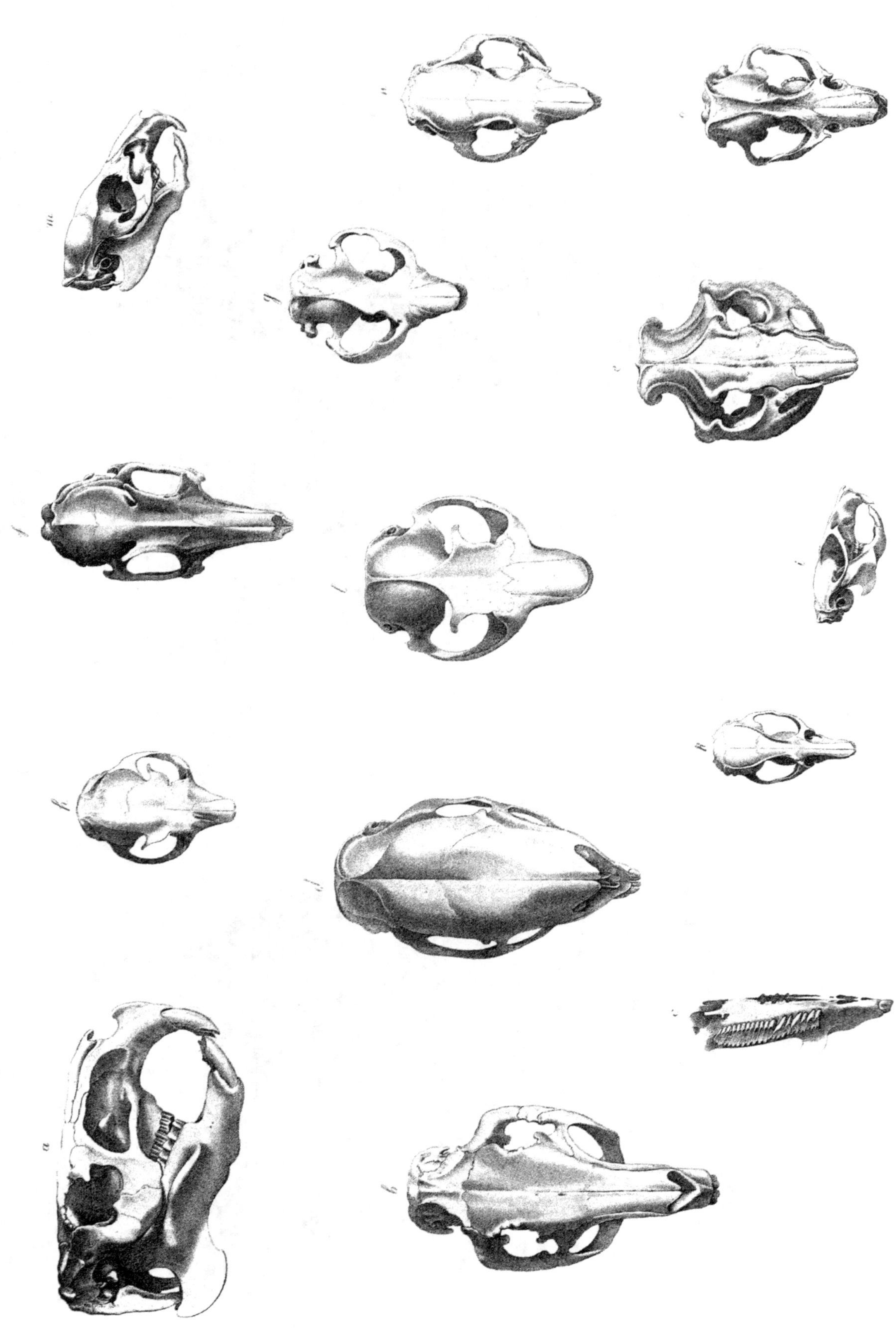

A33

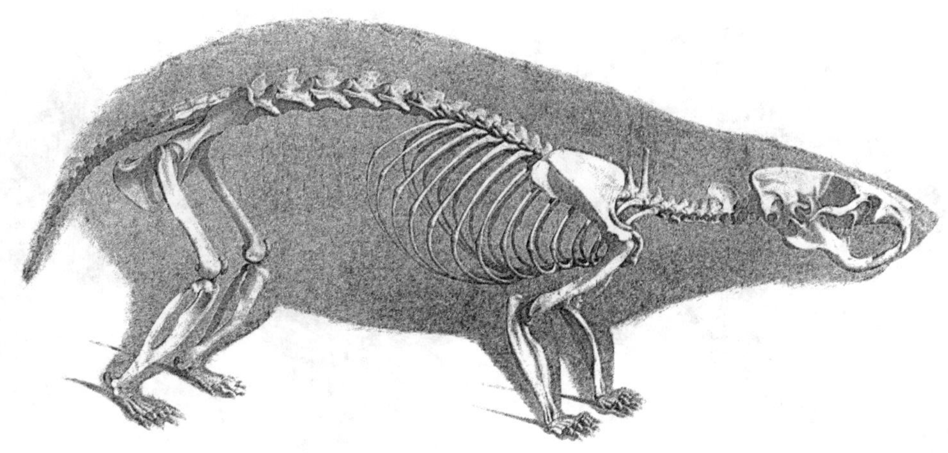

A34

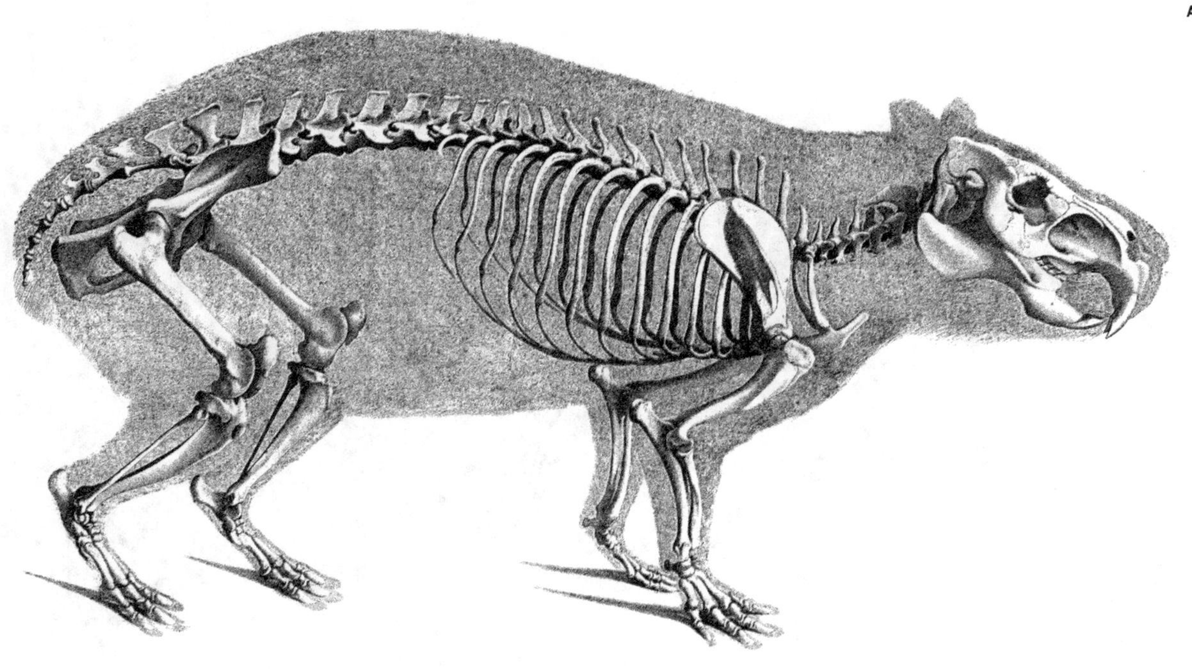

A35

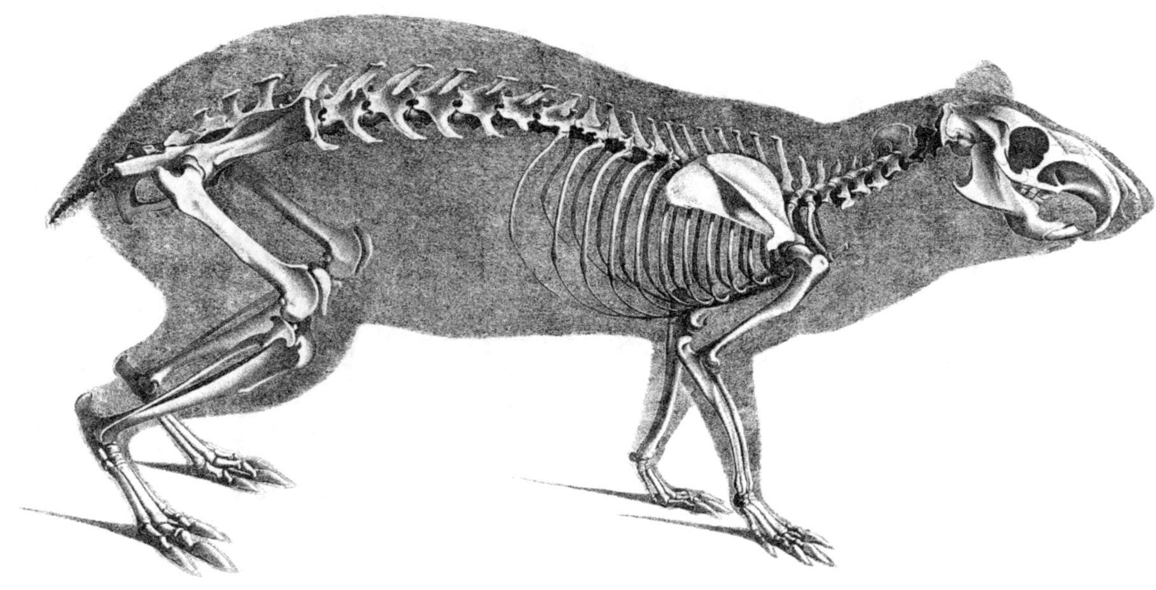

A36

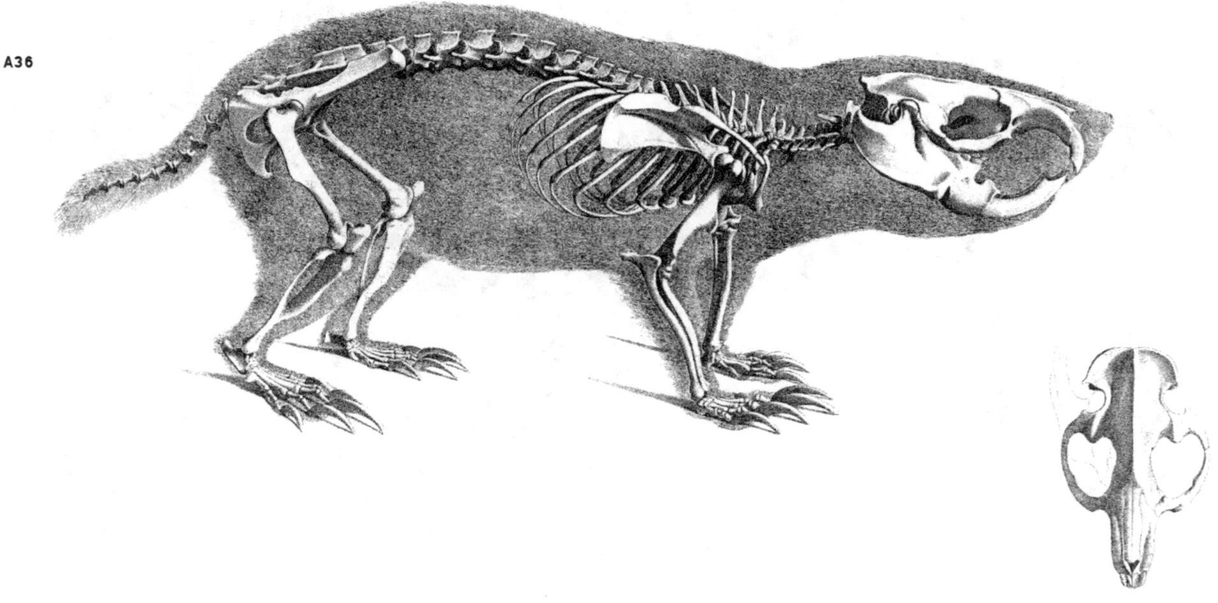

A37

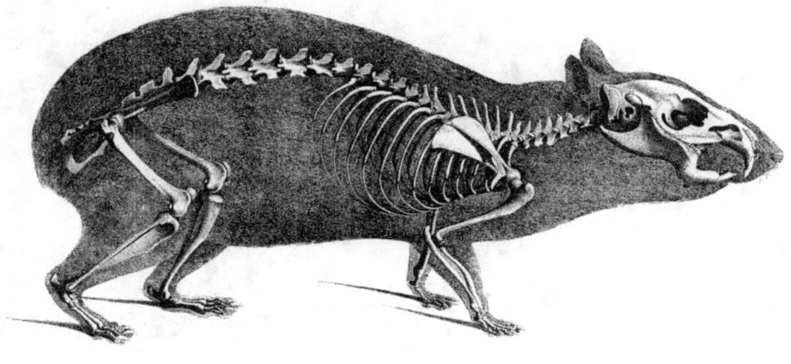

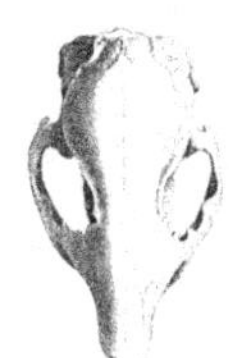

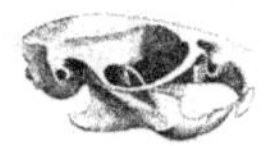

A38

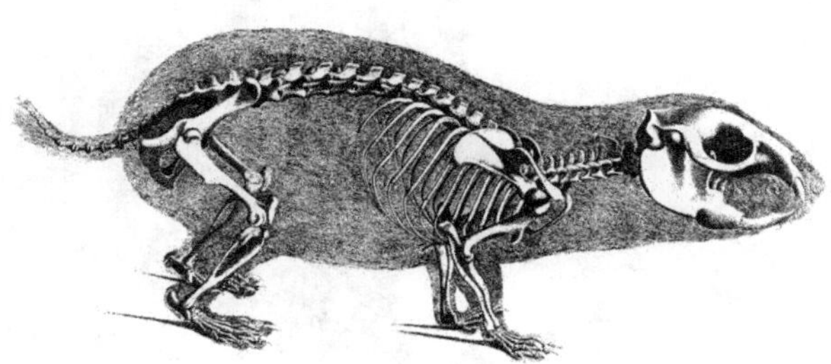

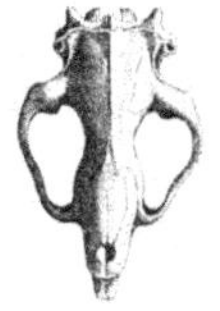

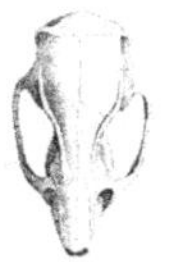

A39

ANIMAL SKELETONS & ANATOMY

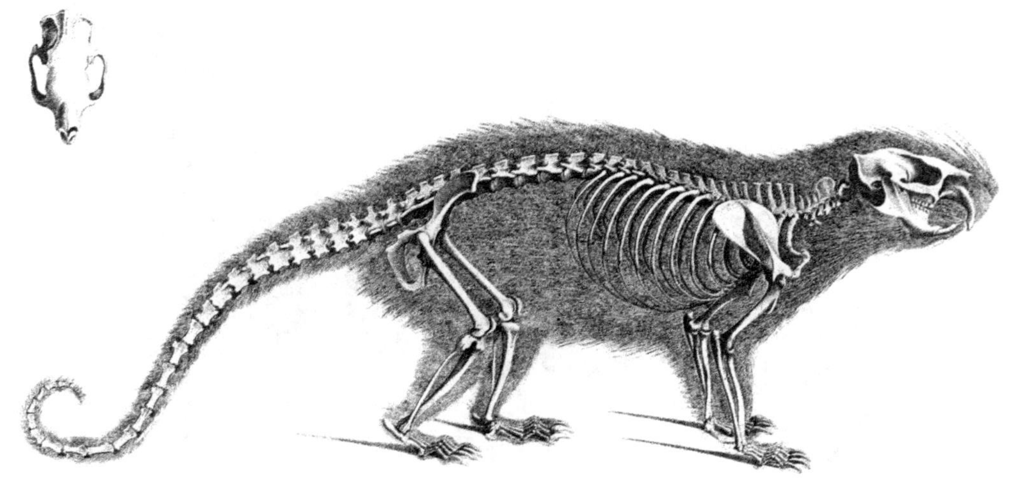

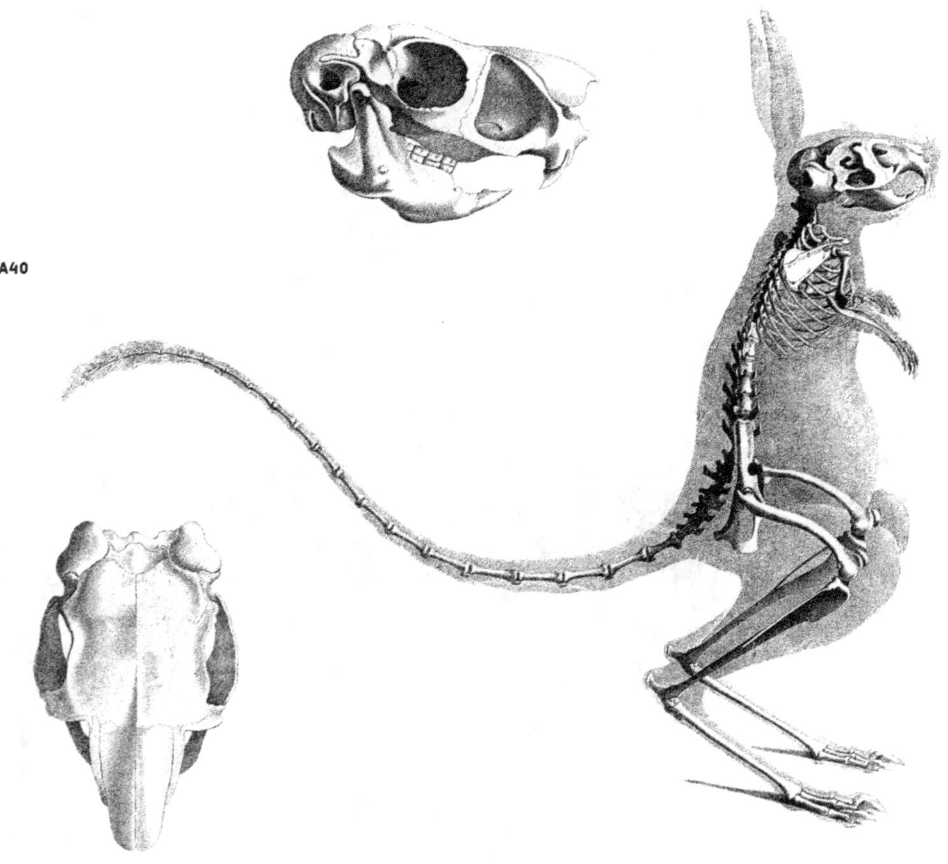

A40

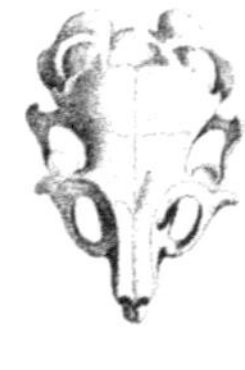

A41

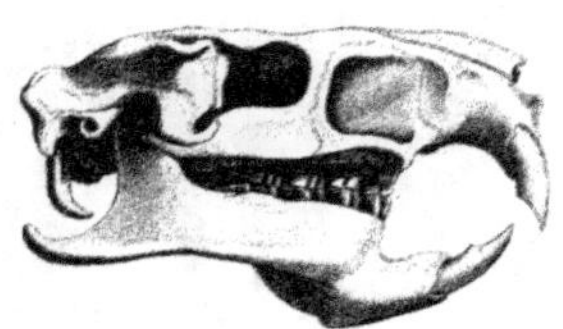

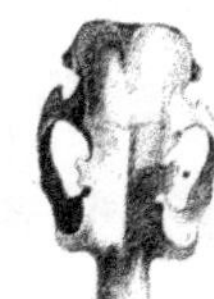

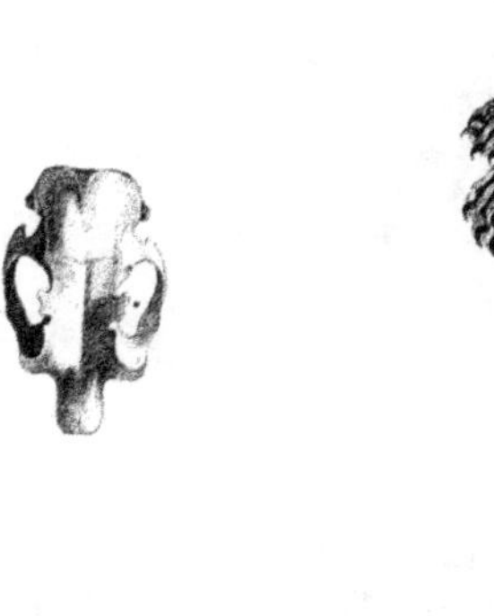

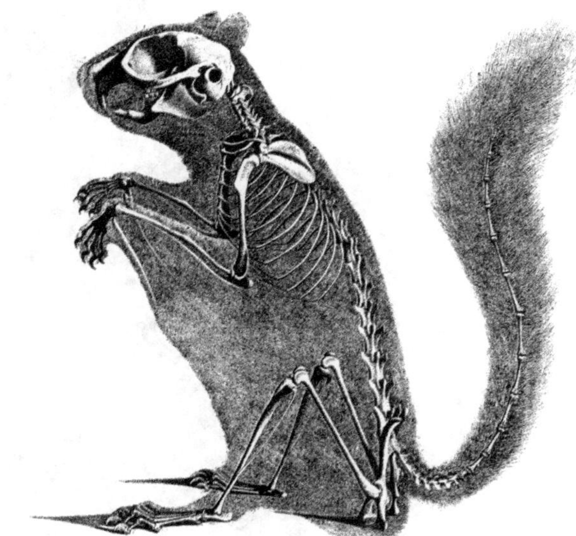

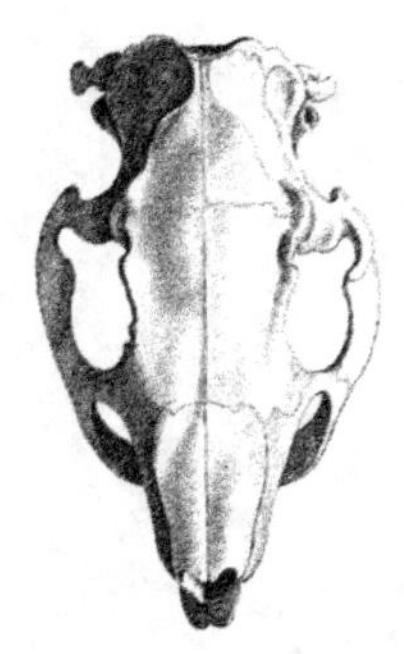

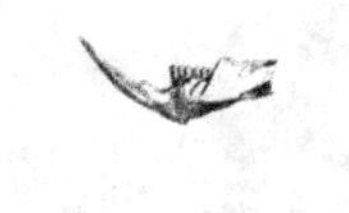

A42

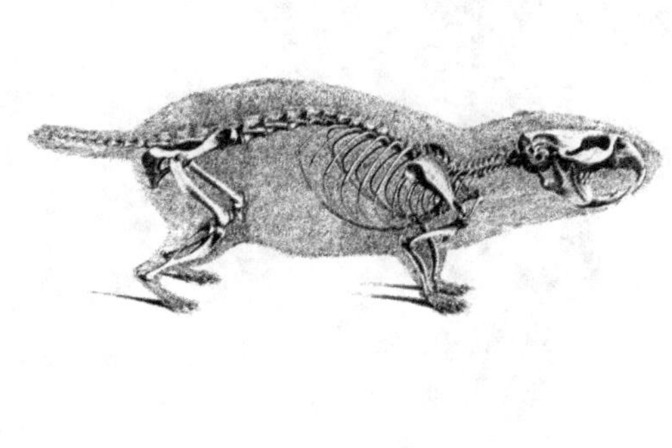

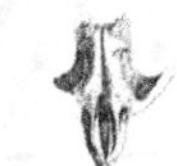

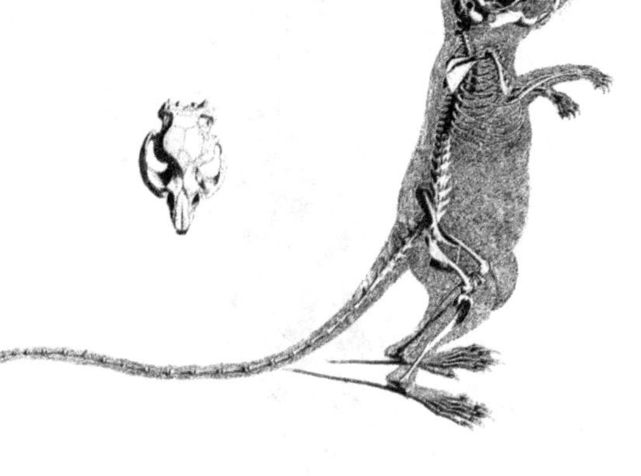

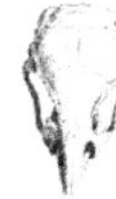

A43

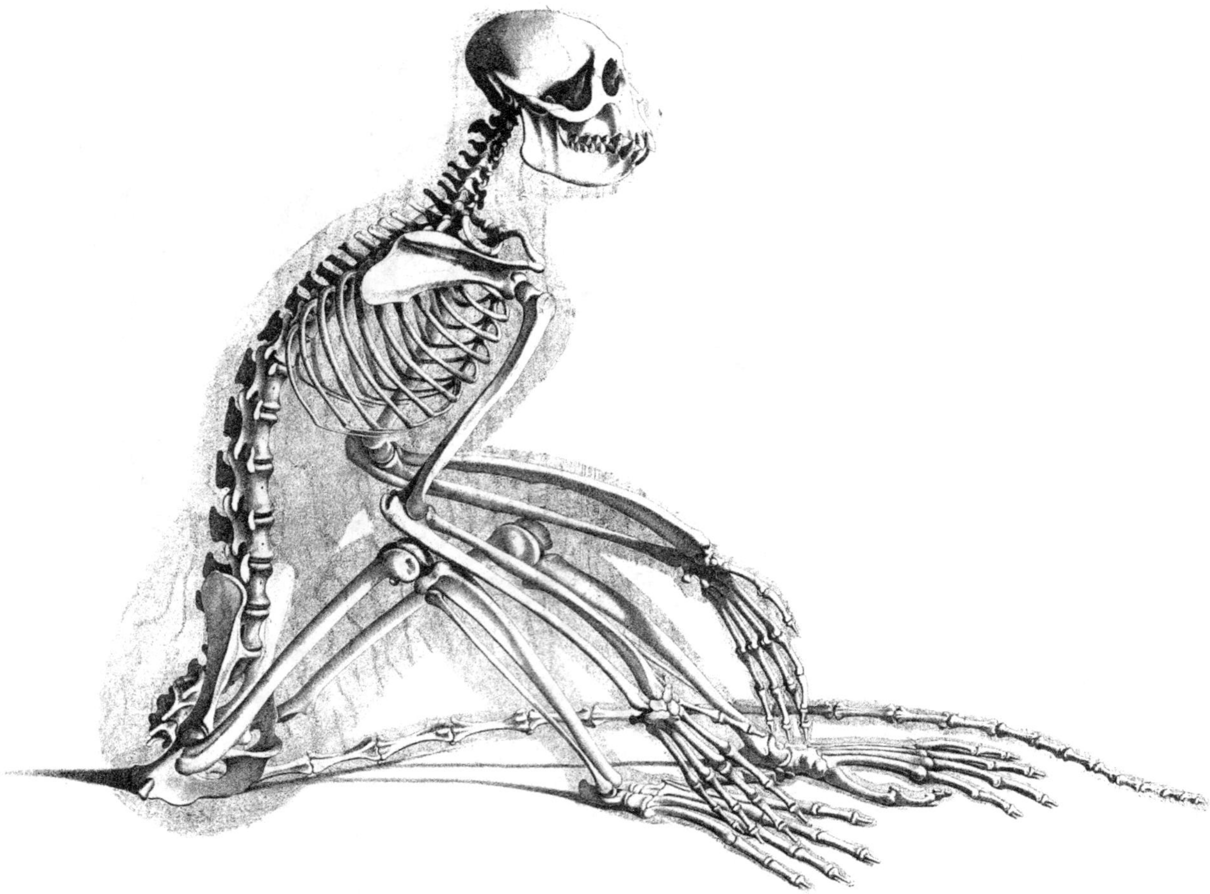

A44

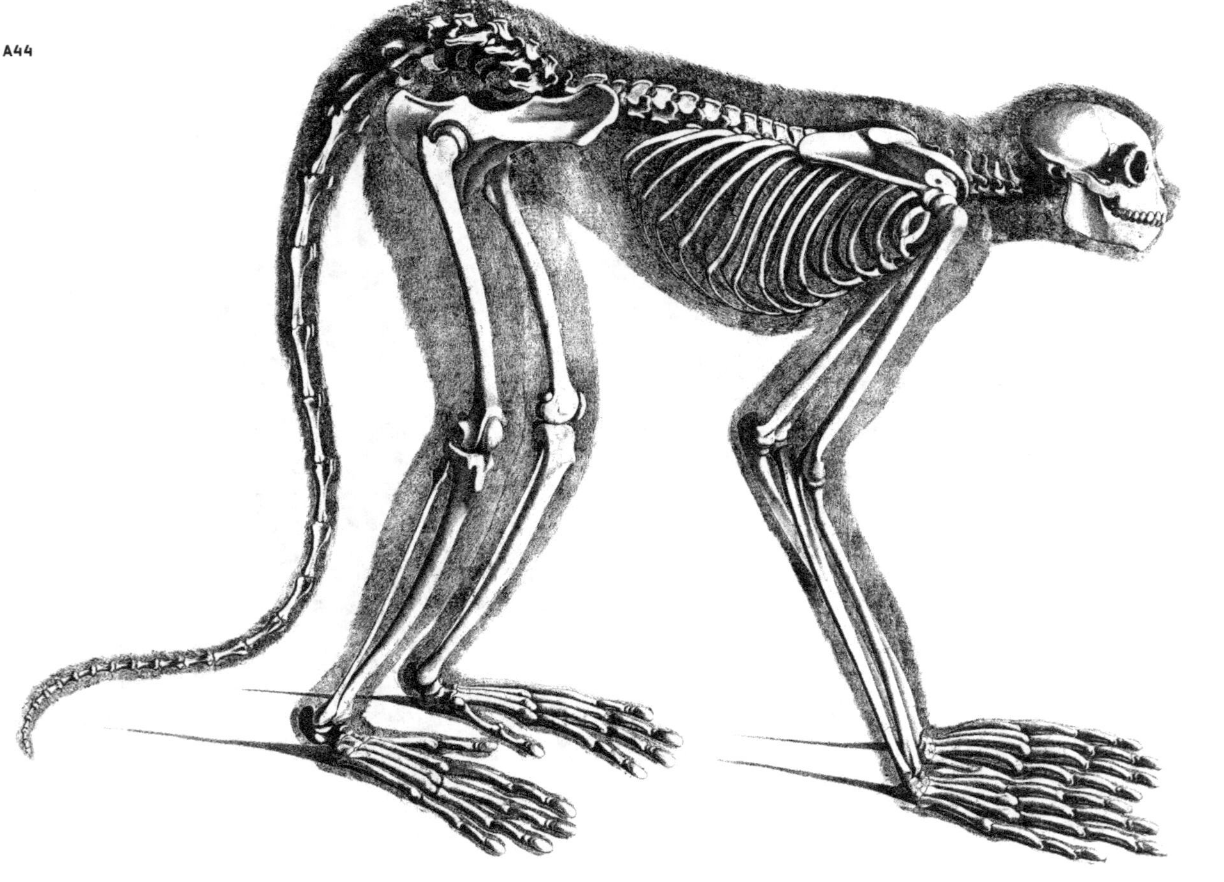

A45

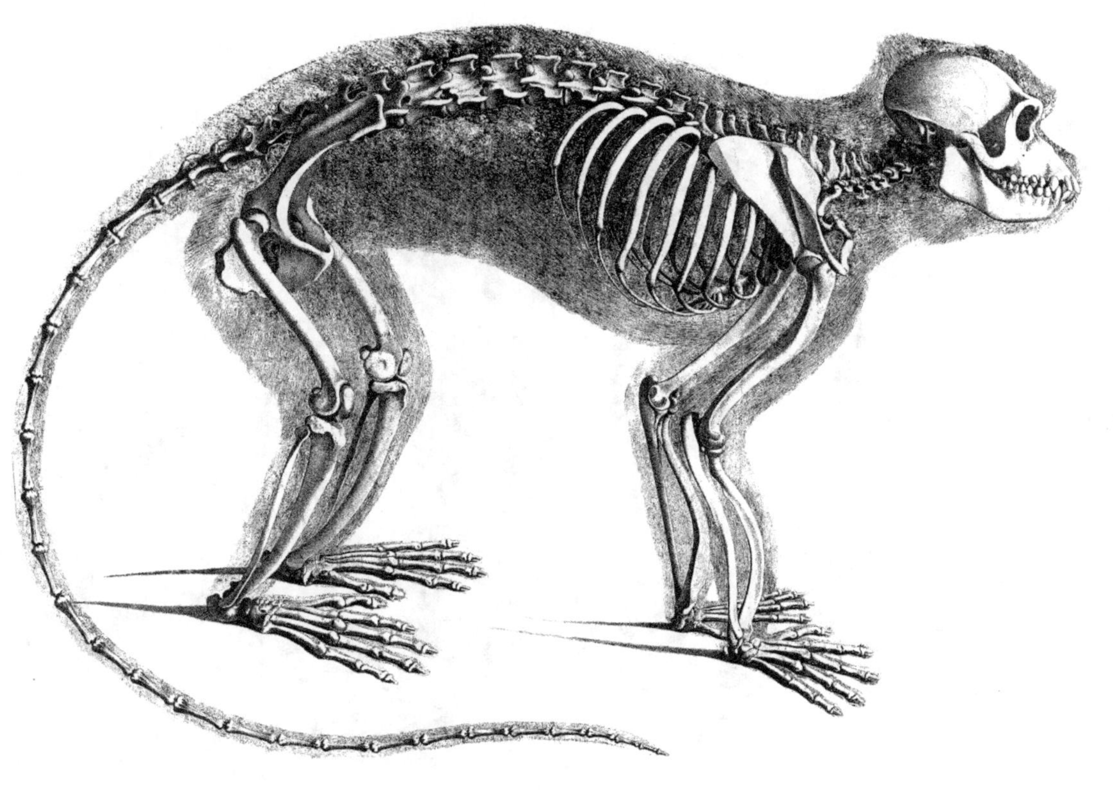

A46

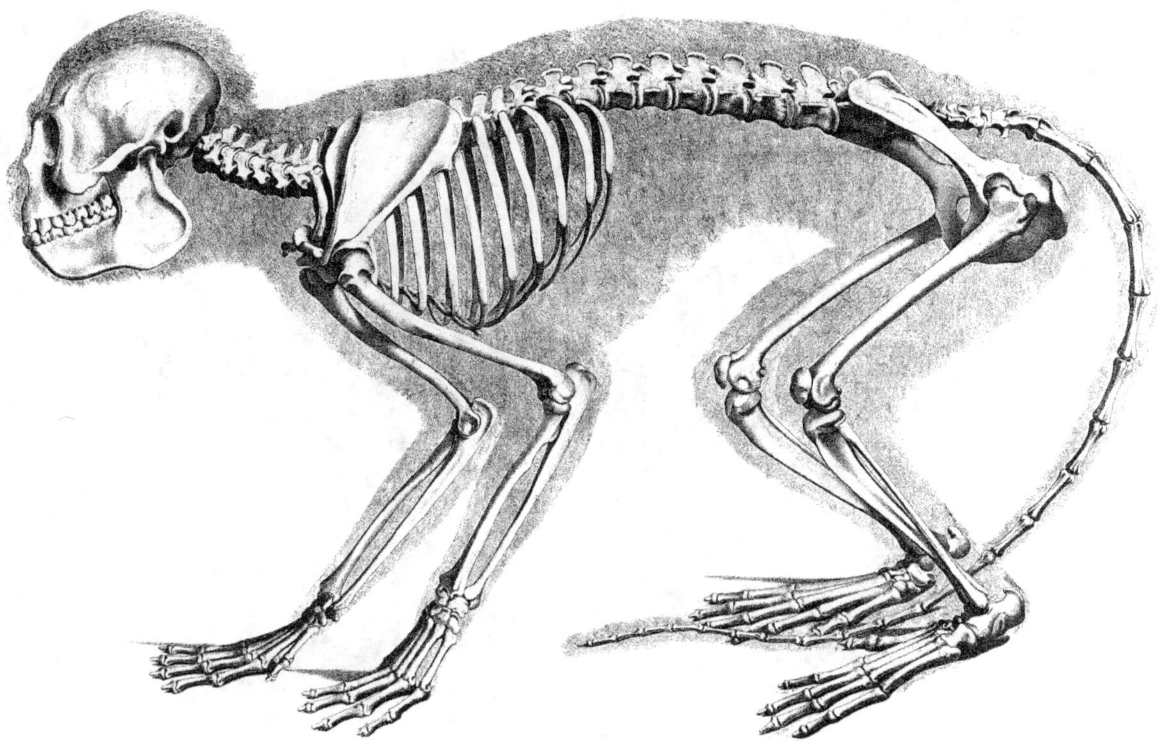

A47

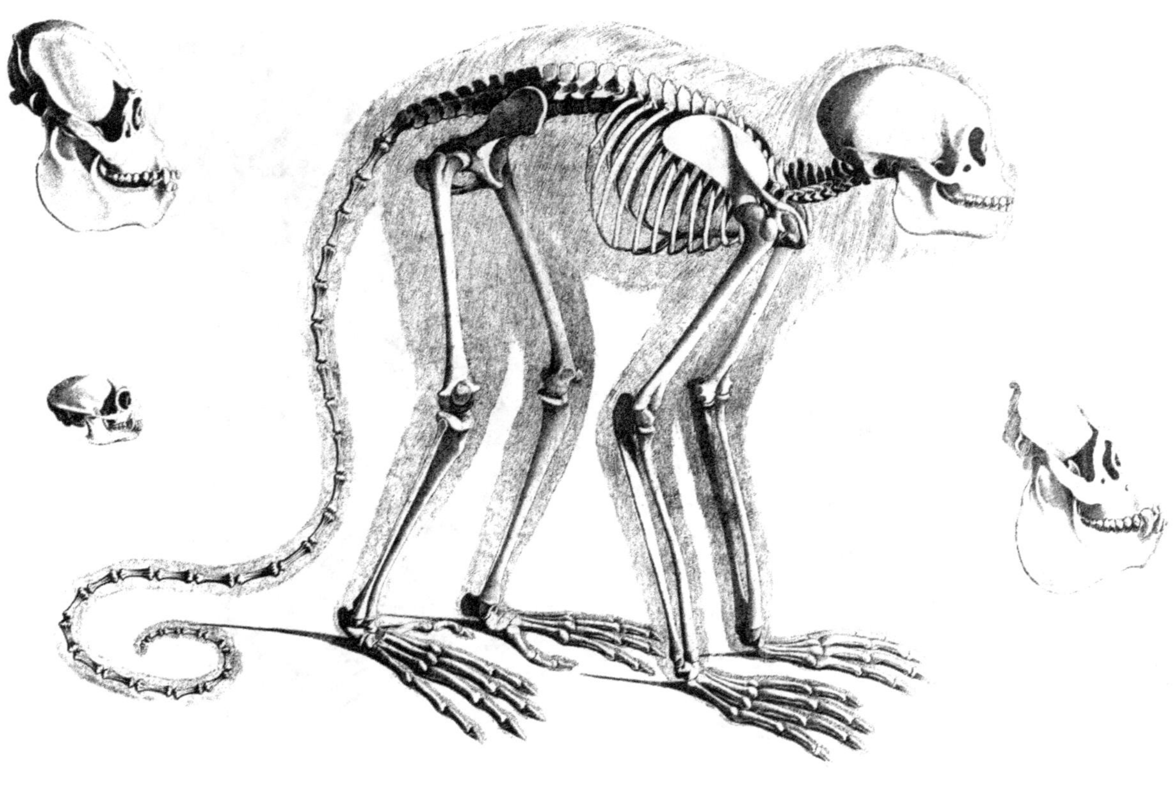

A48

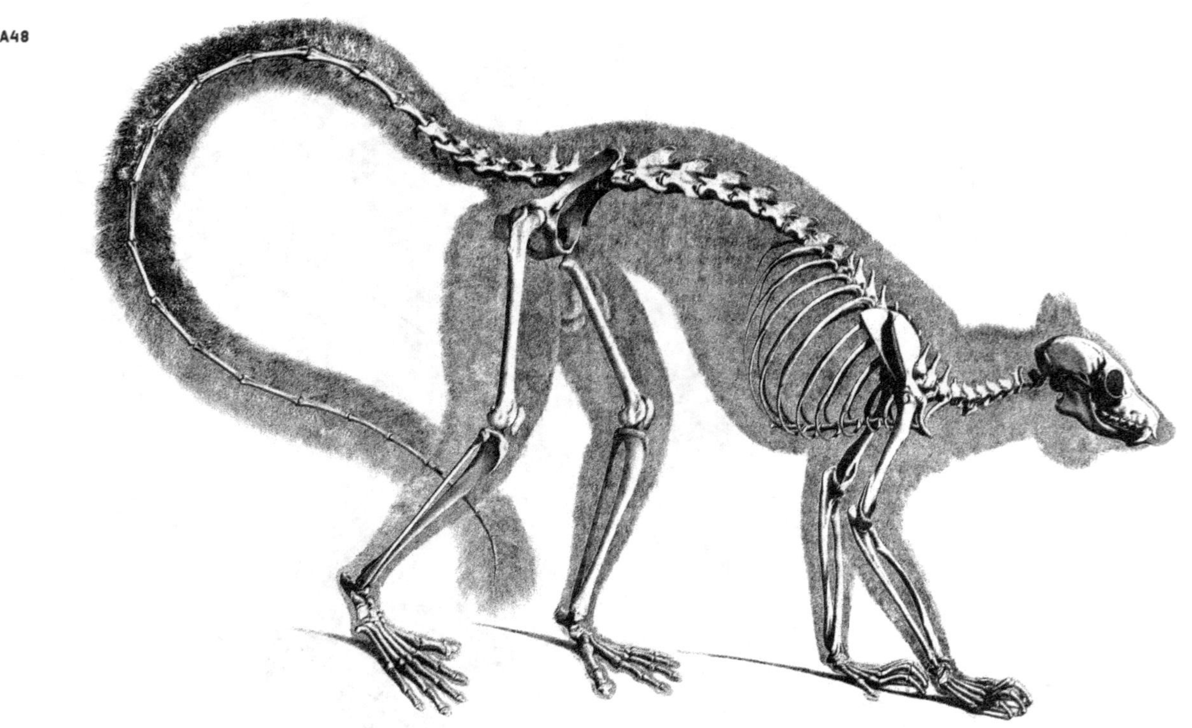

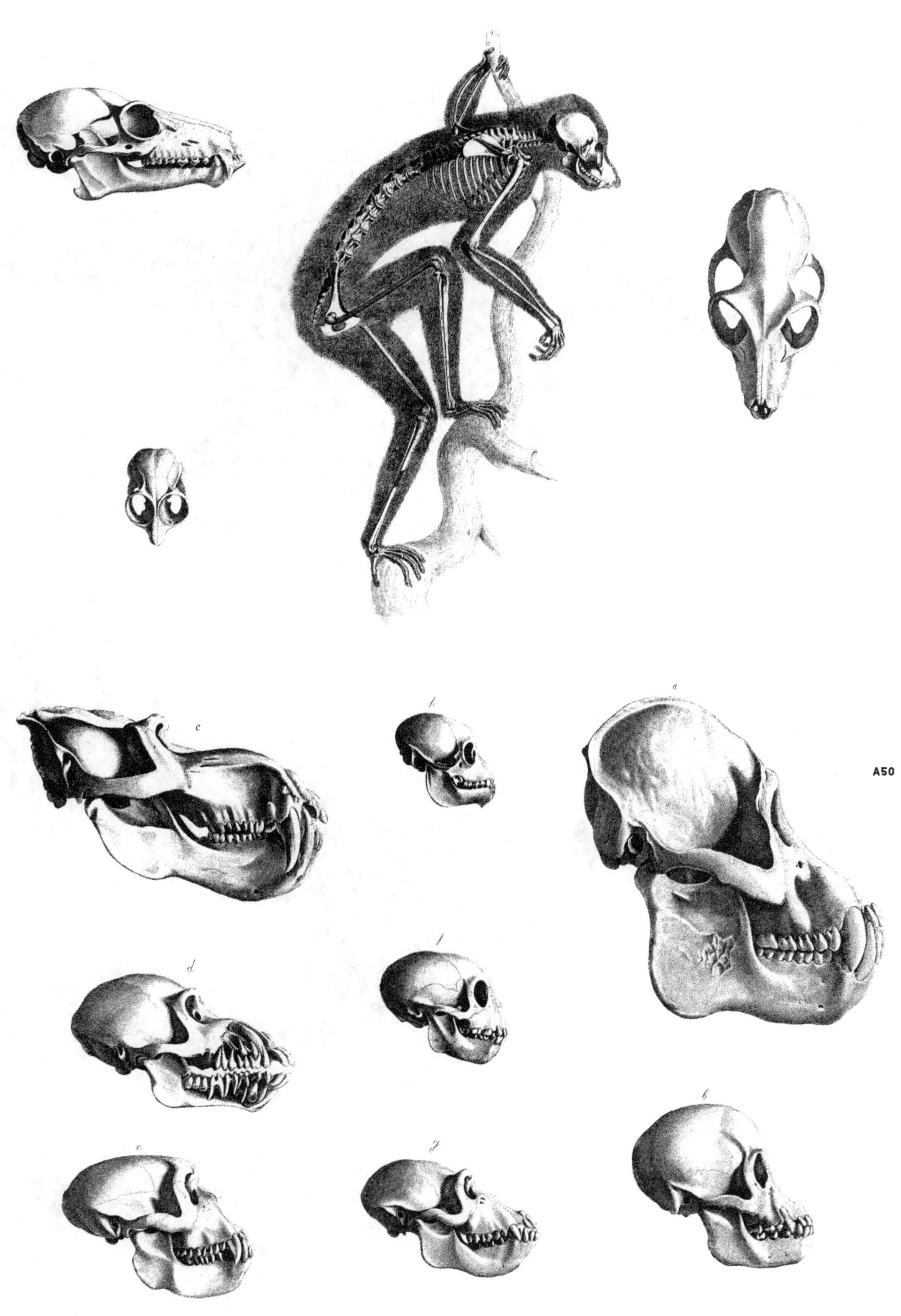

A51

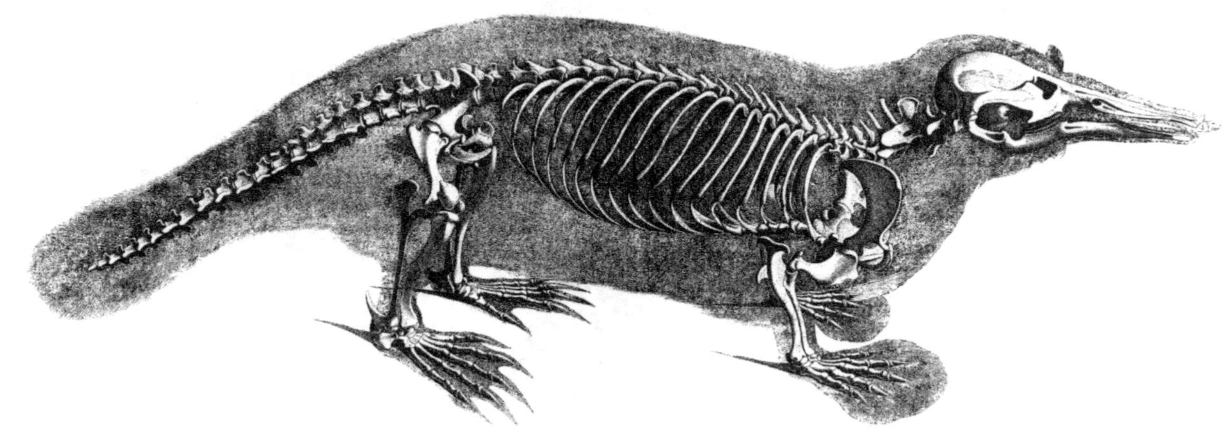

A52

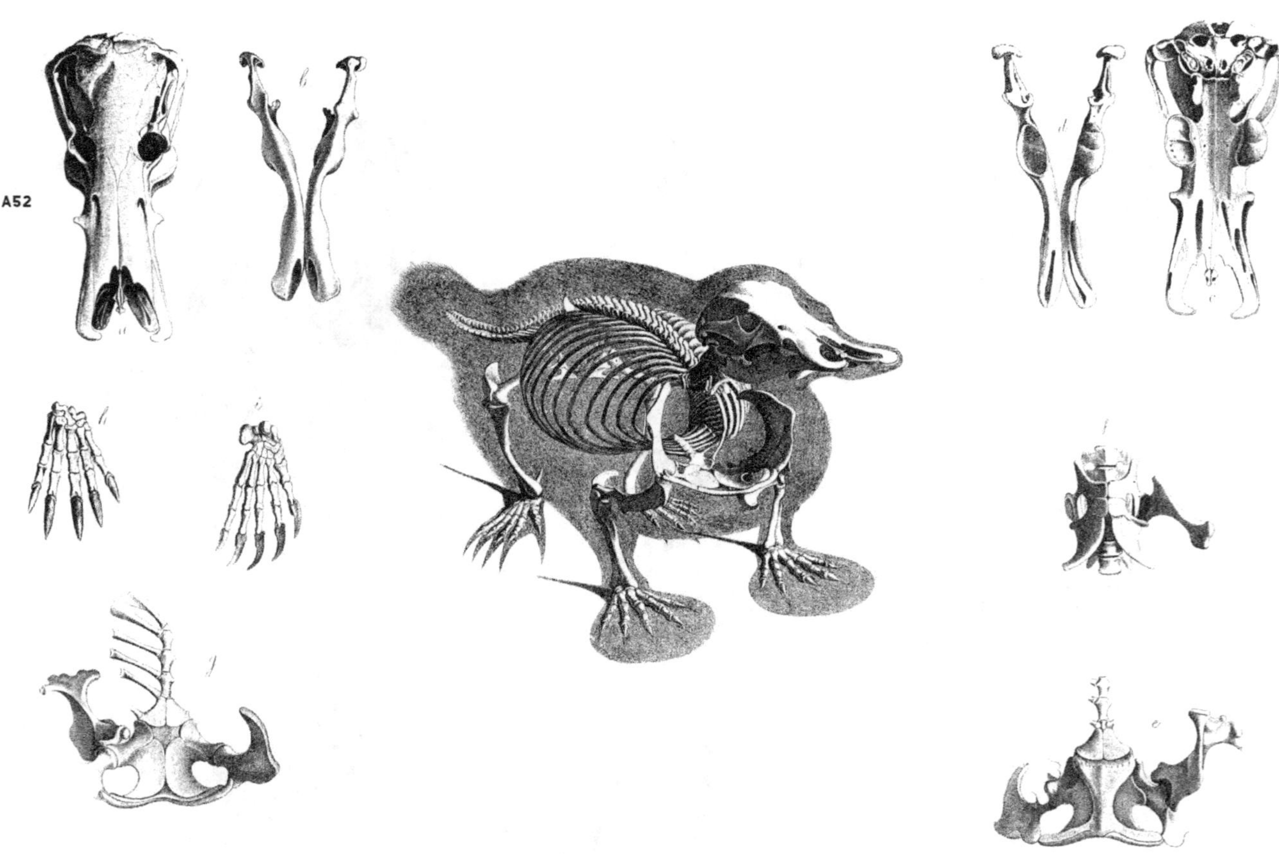

A53

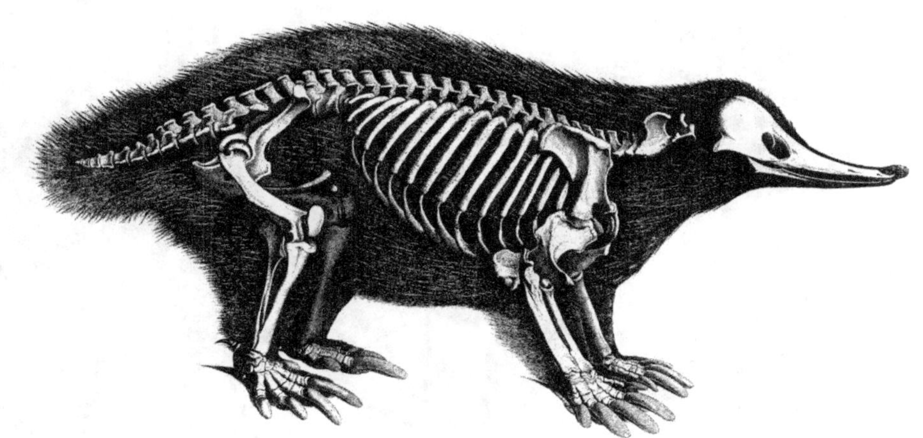

A54

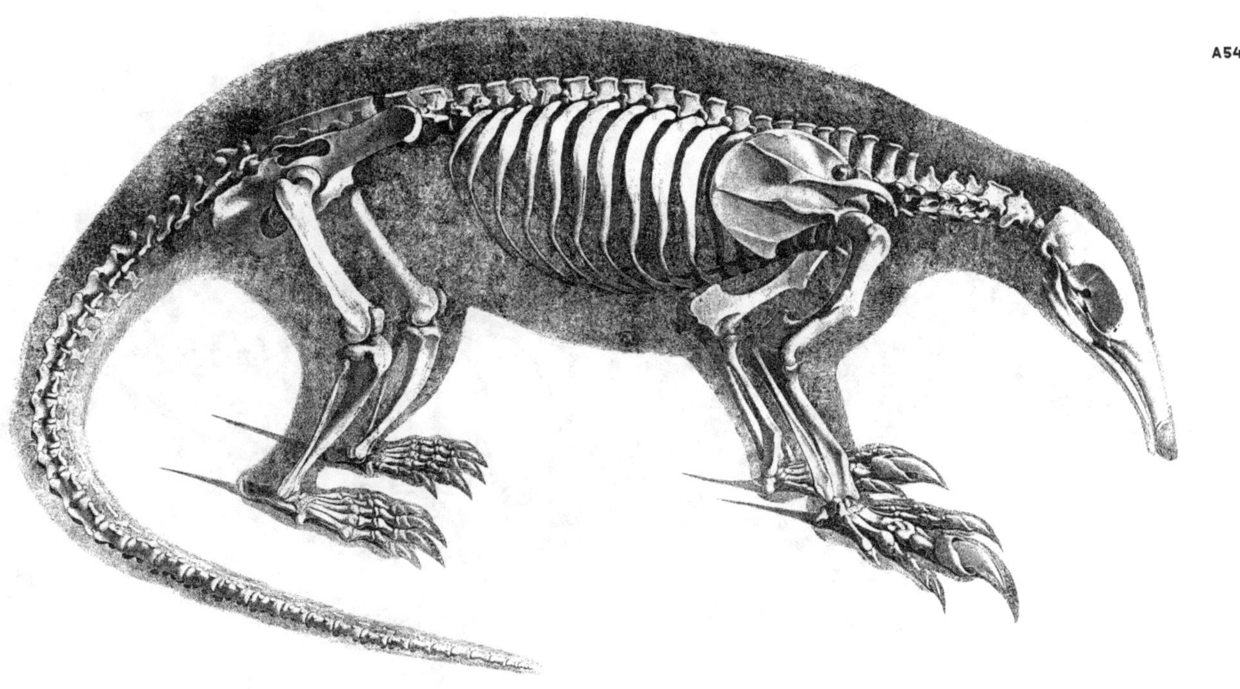

A55

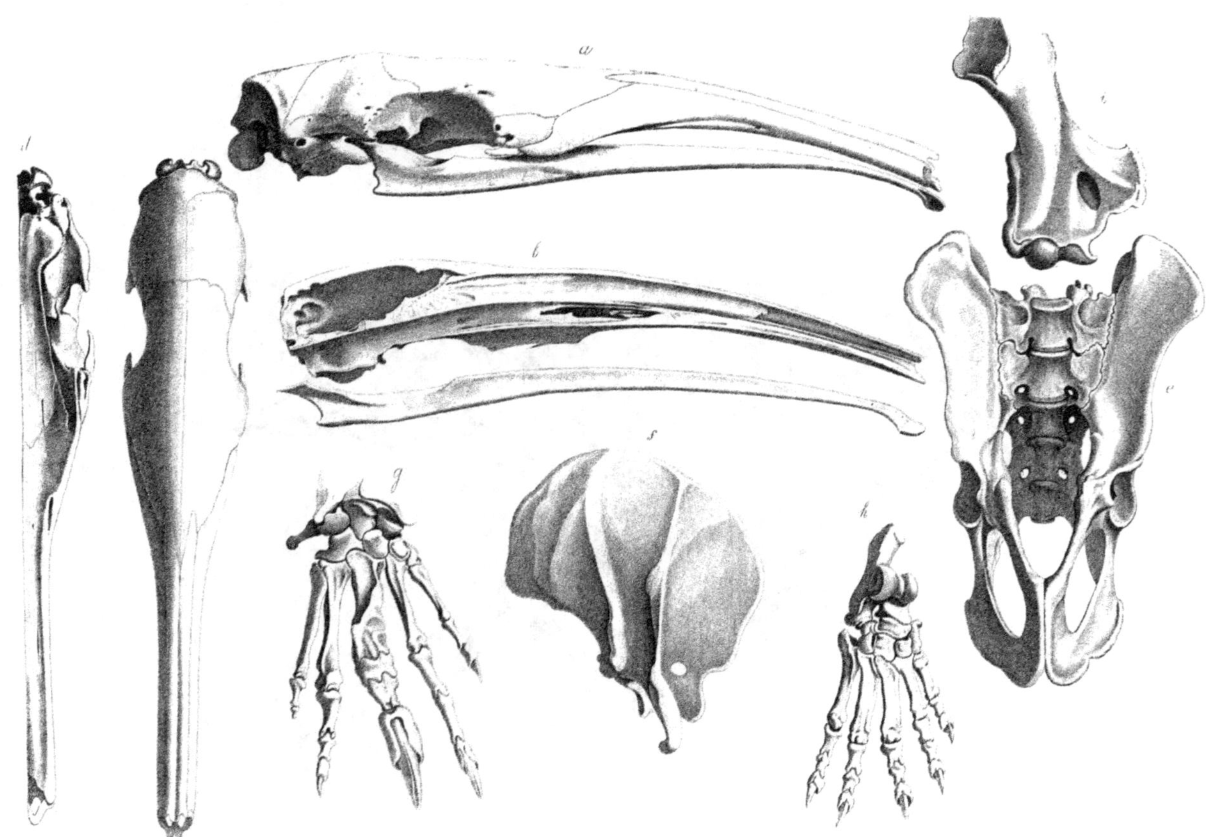

A56

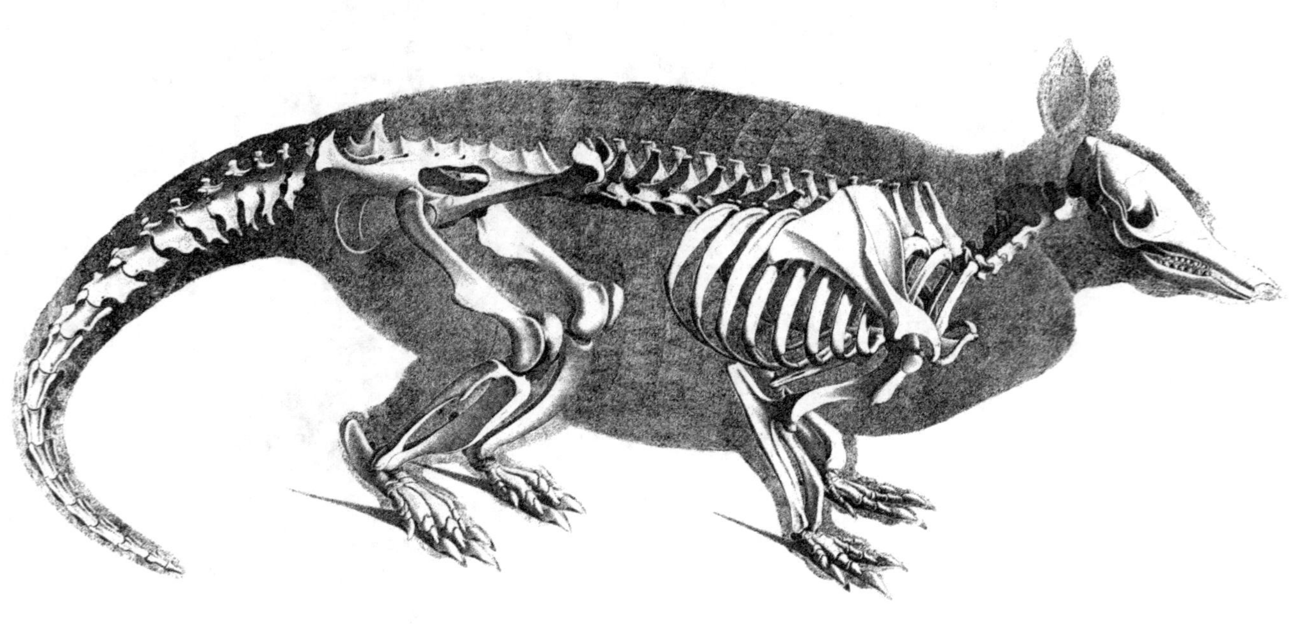

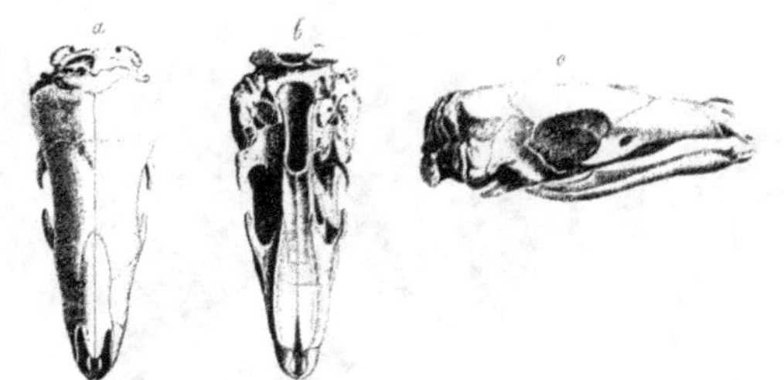

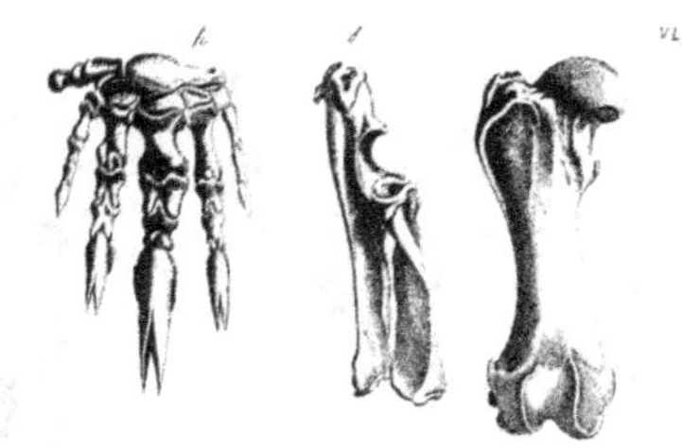

A57

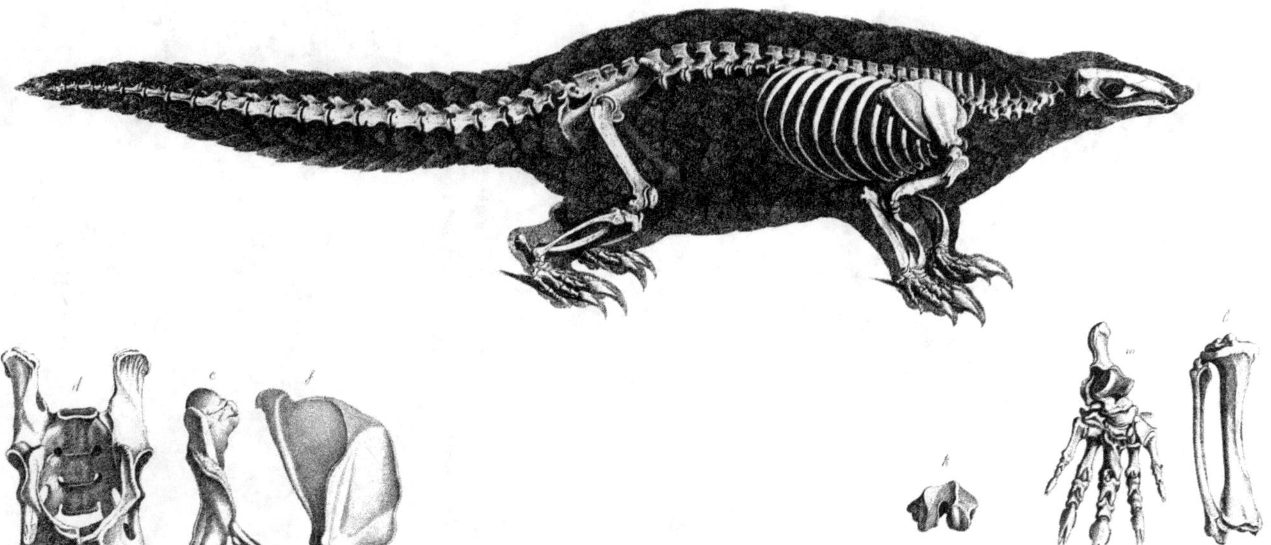

A58

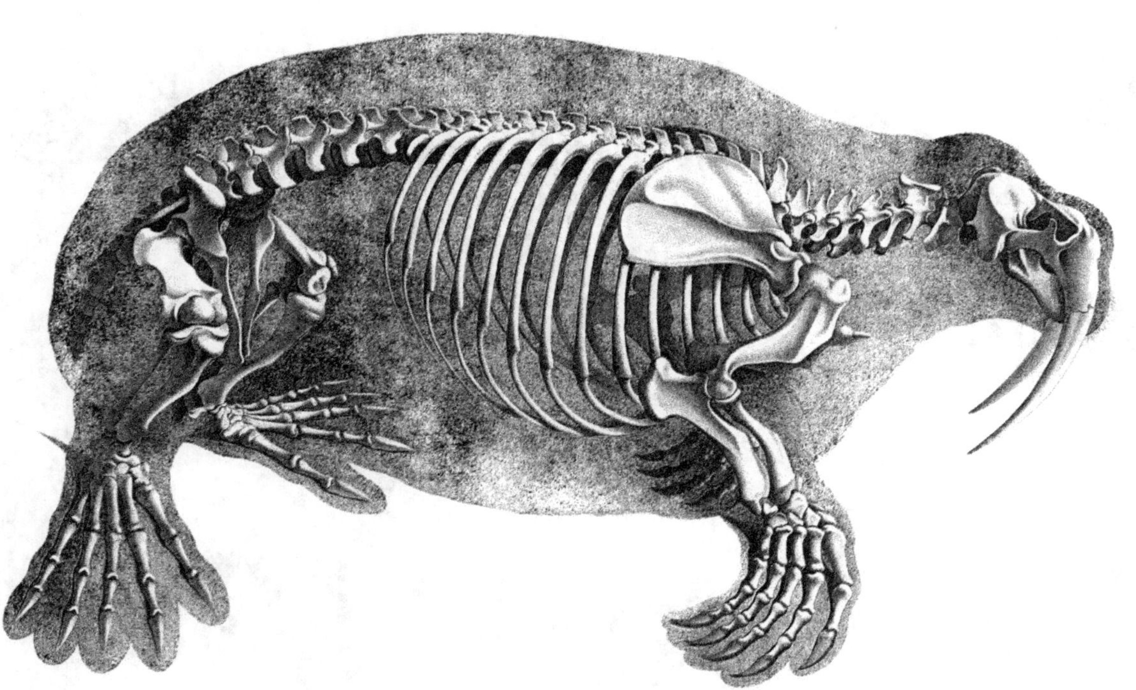

A59

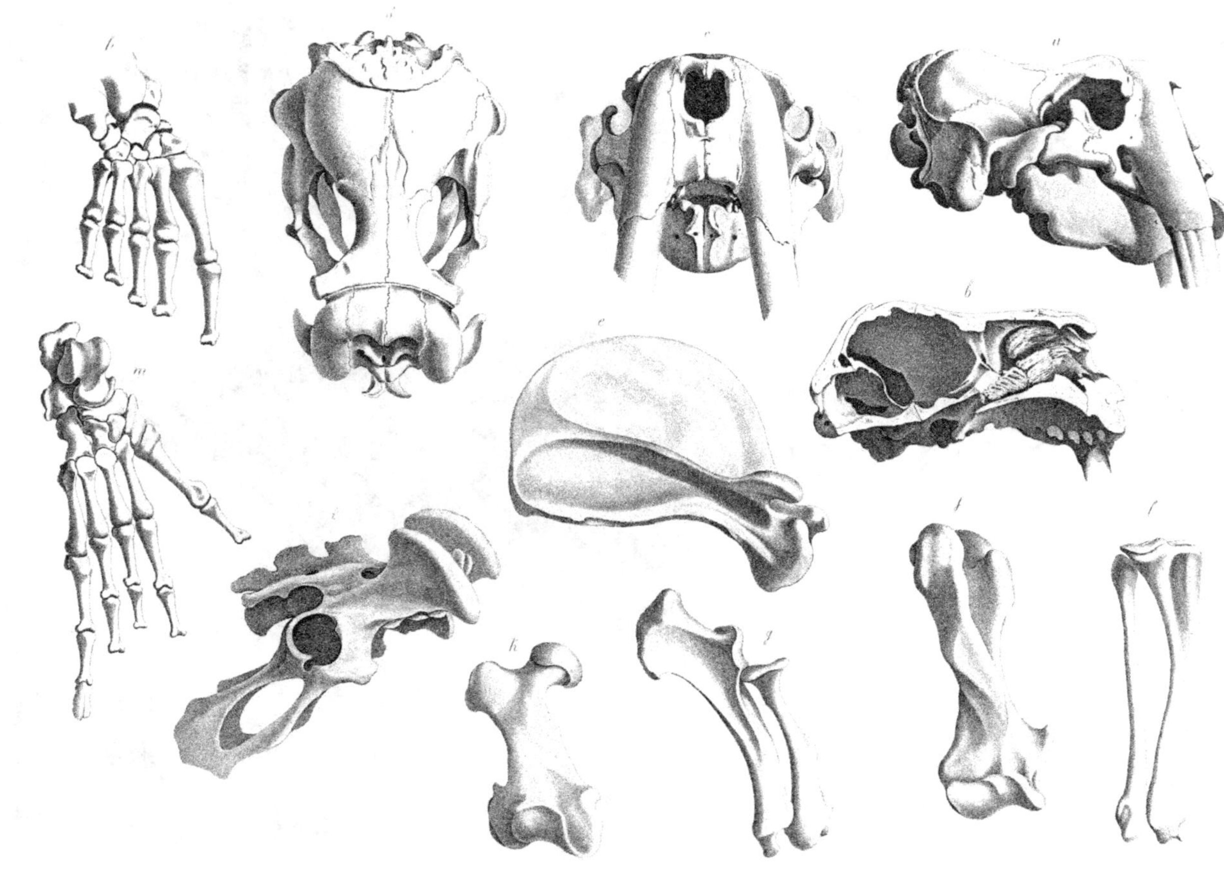

A60

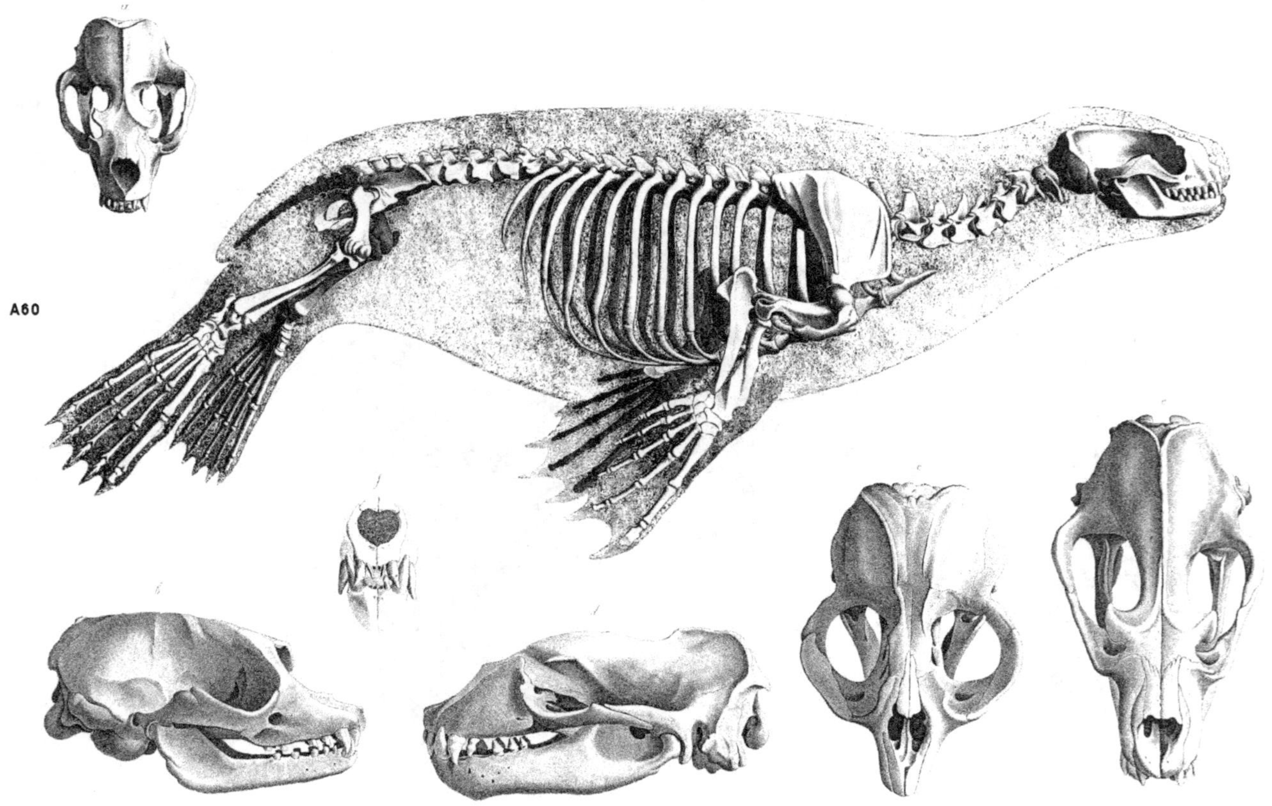

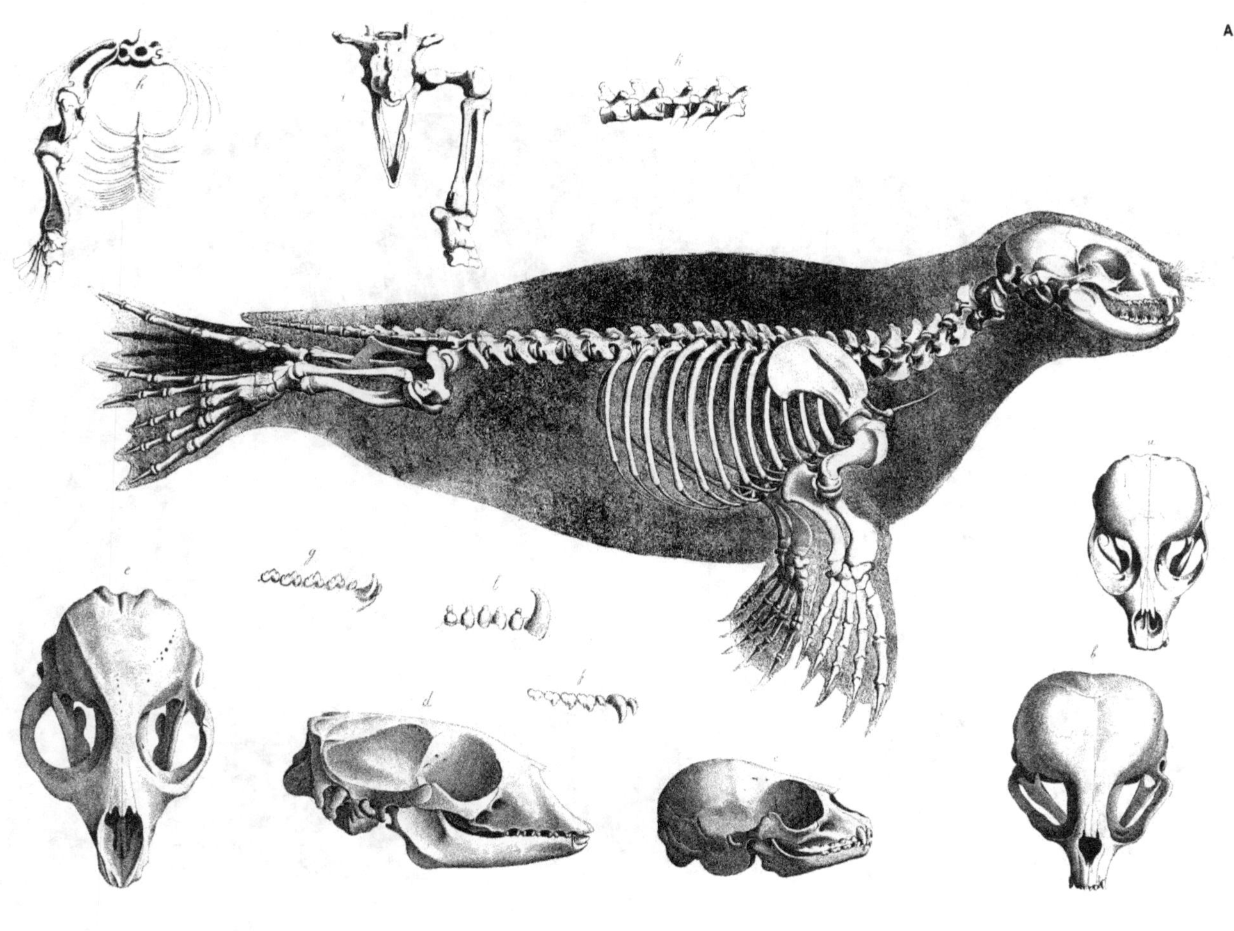

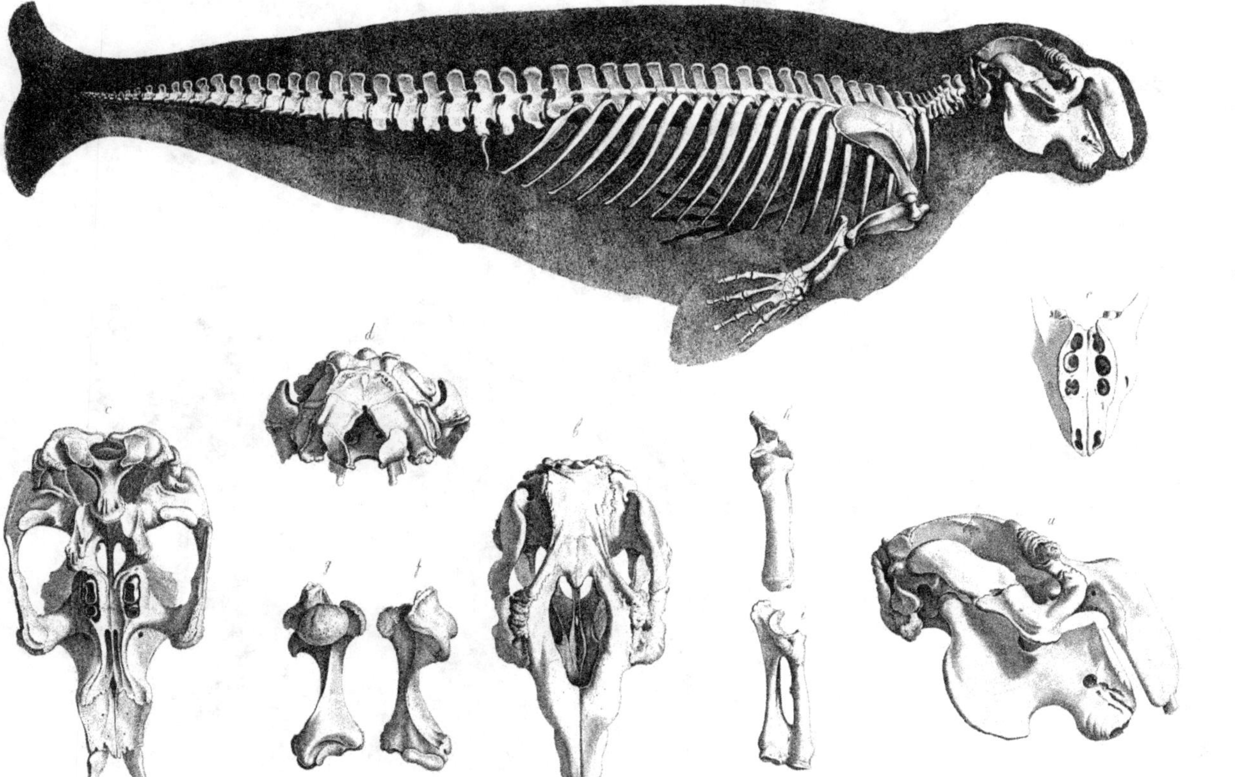

A62

A63

A64

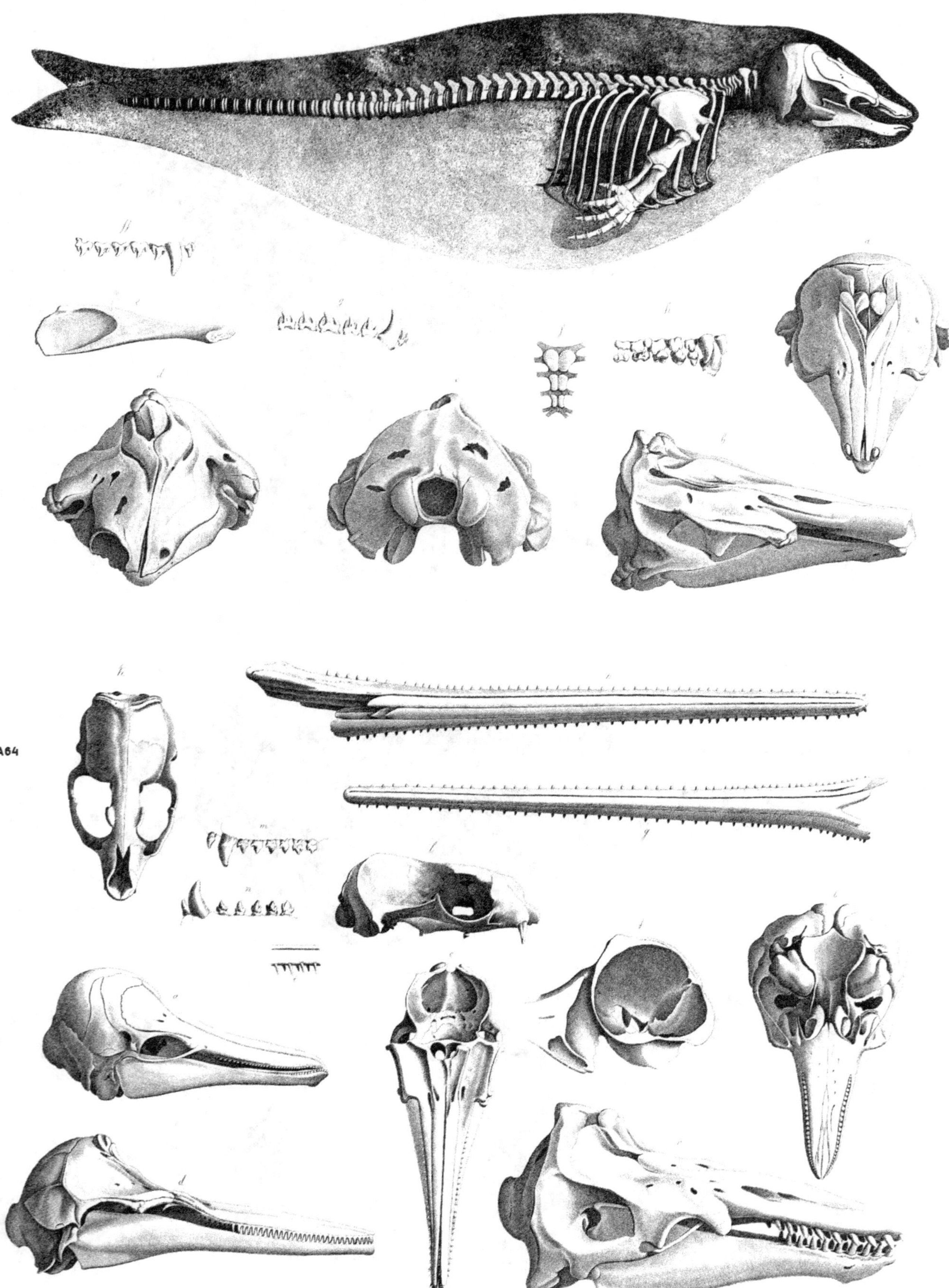

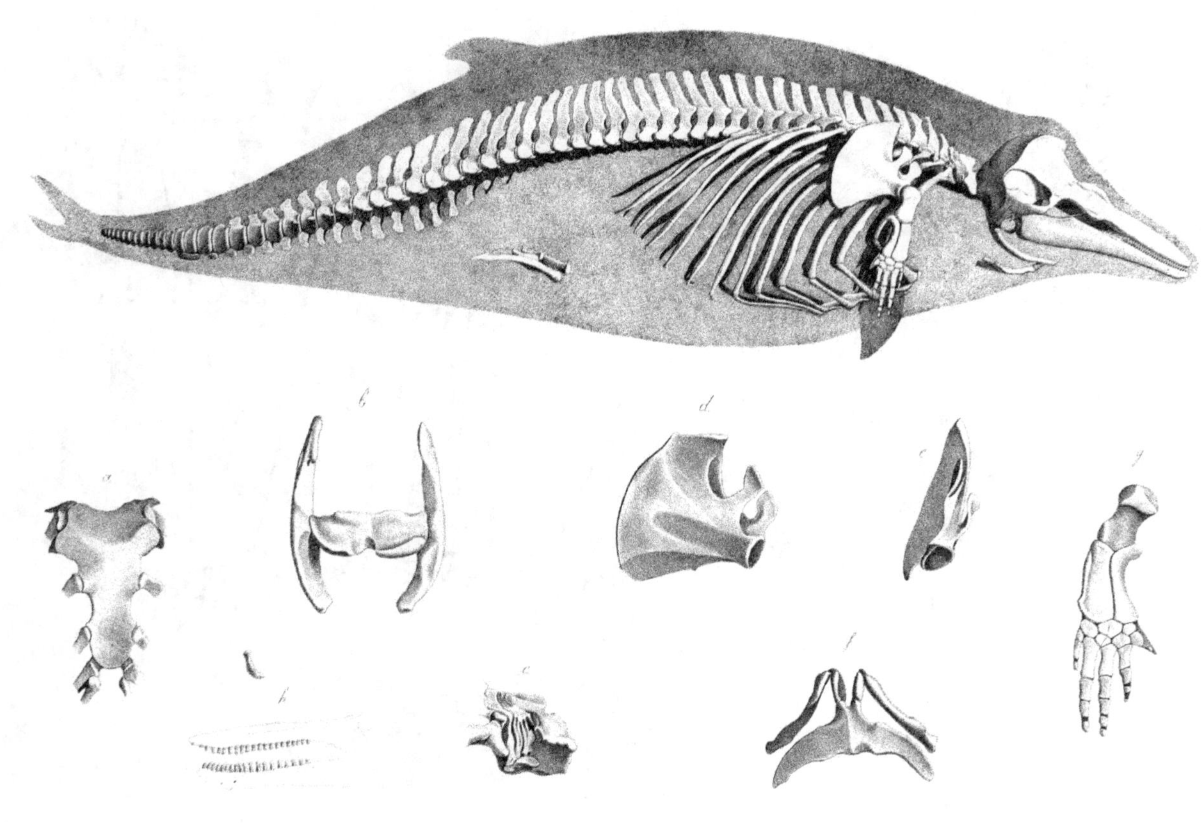

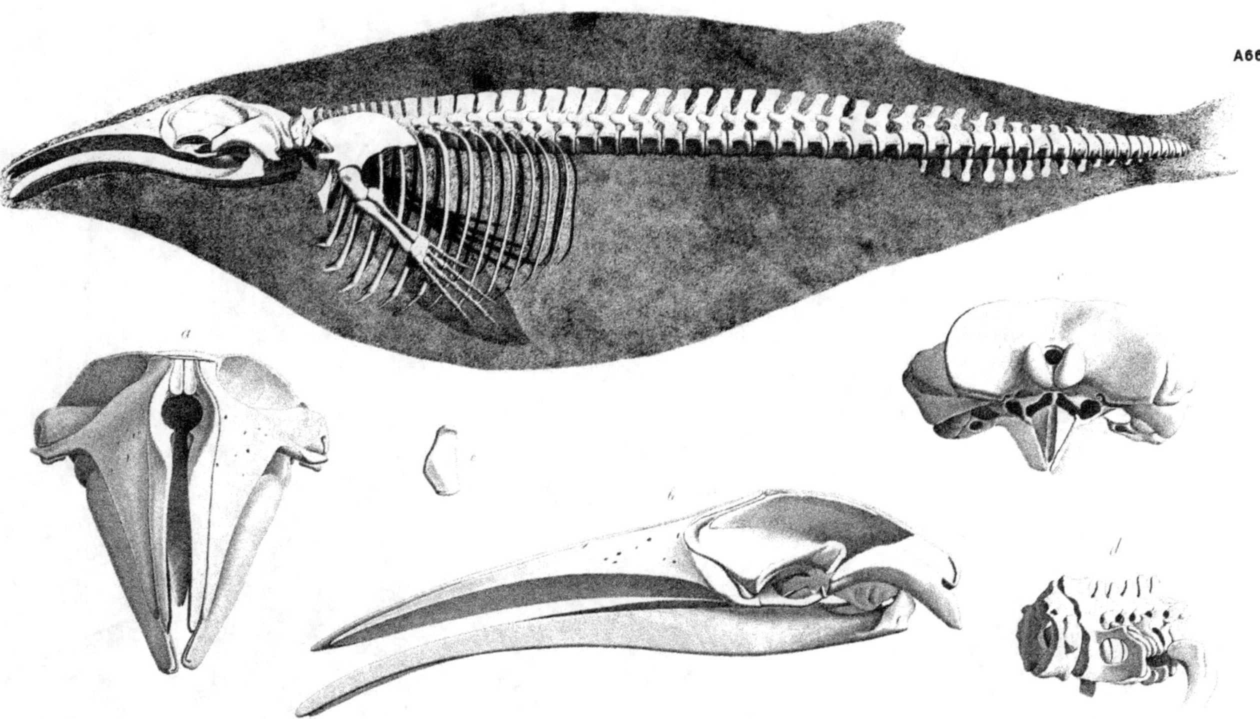

A67

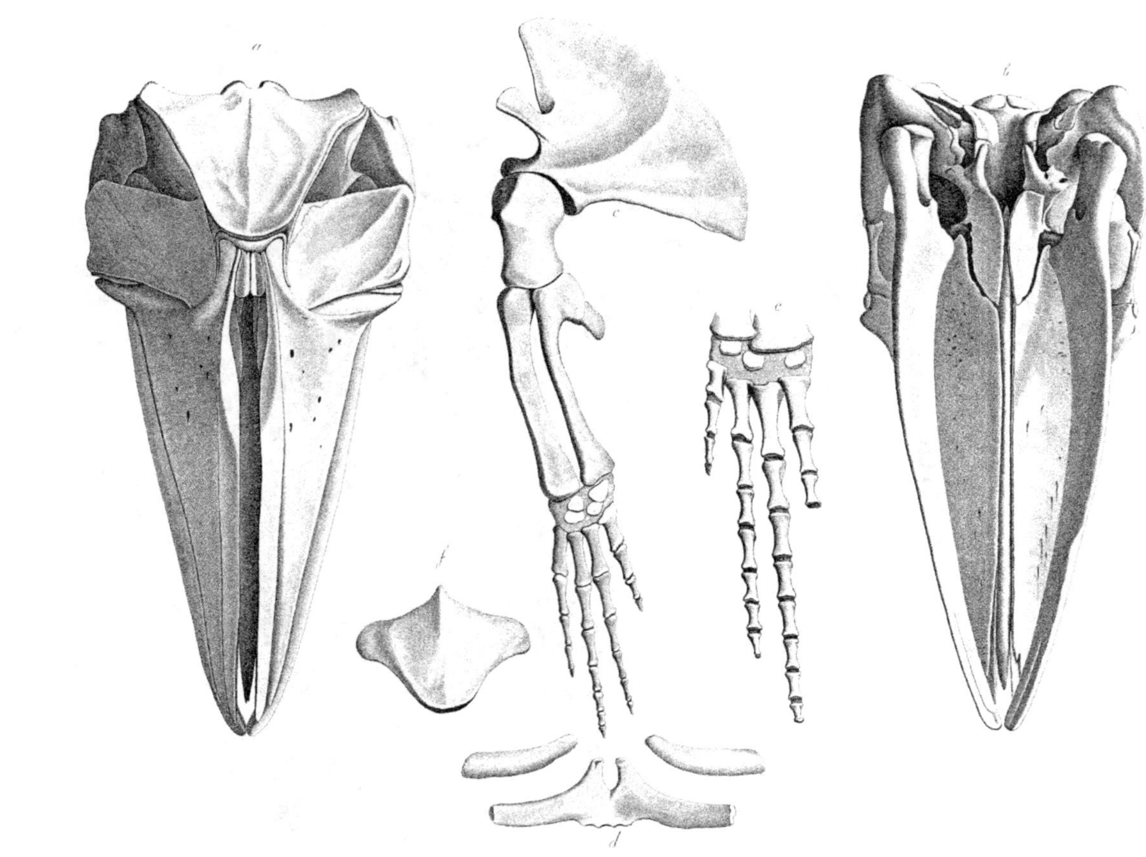

A68

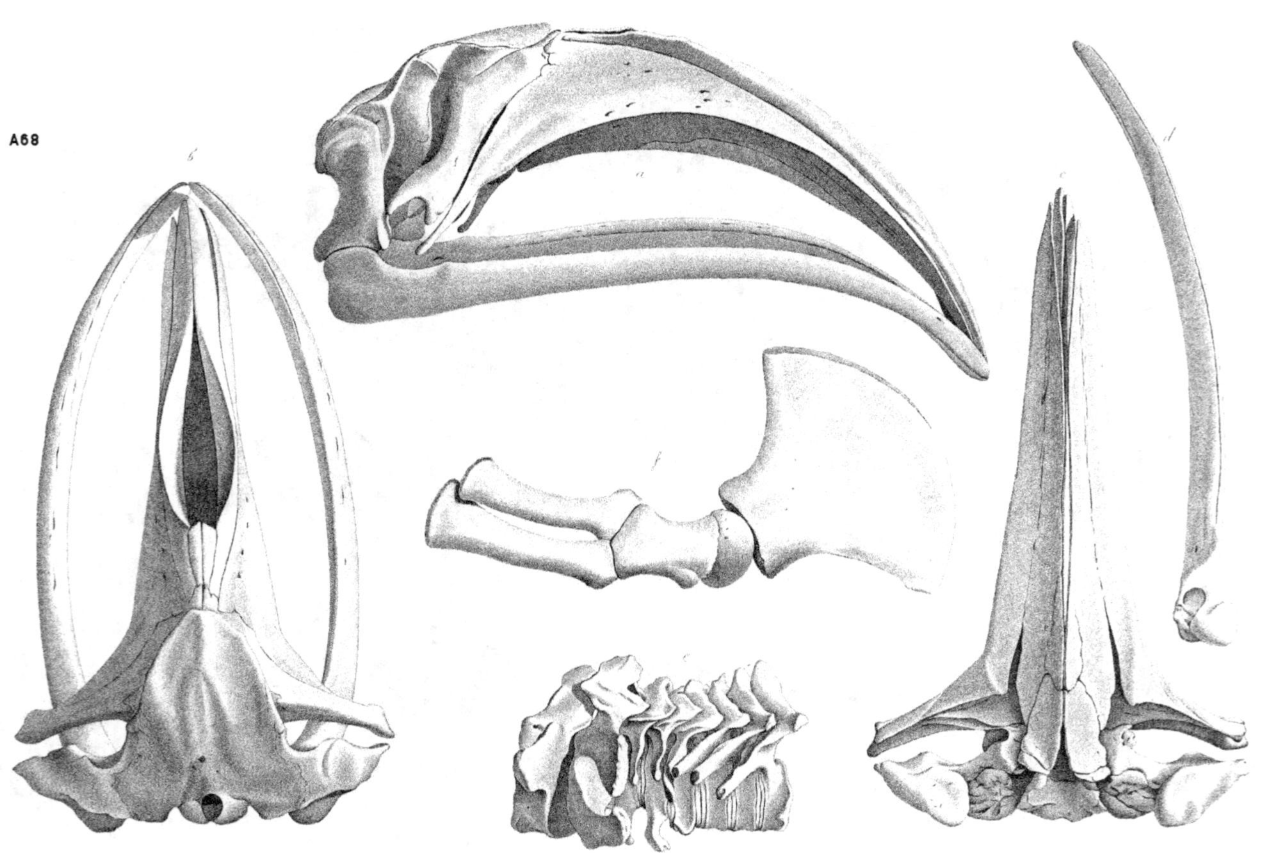

A69

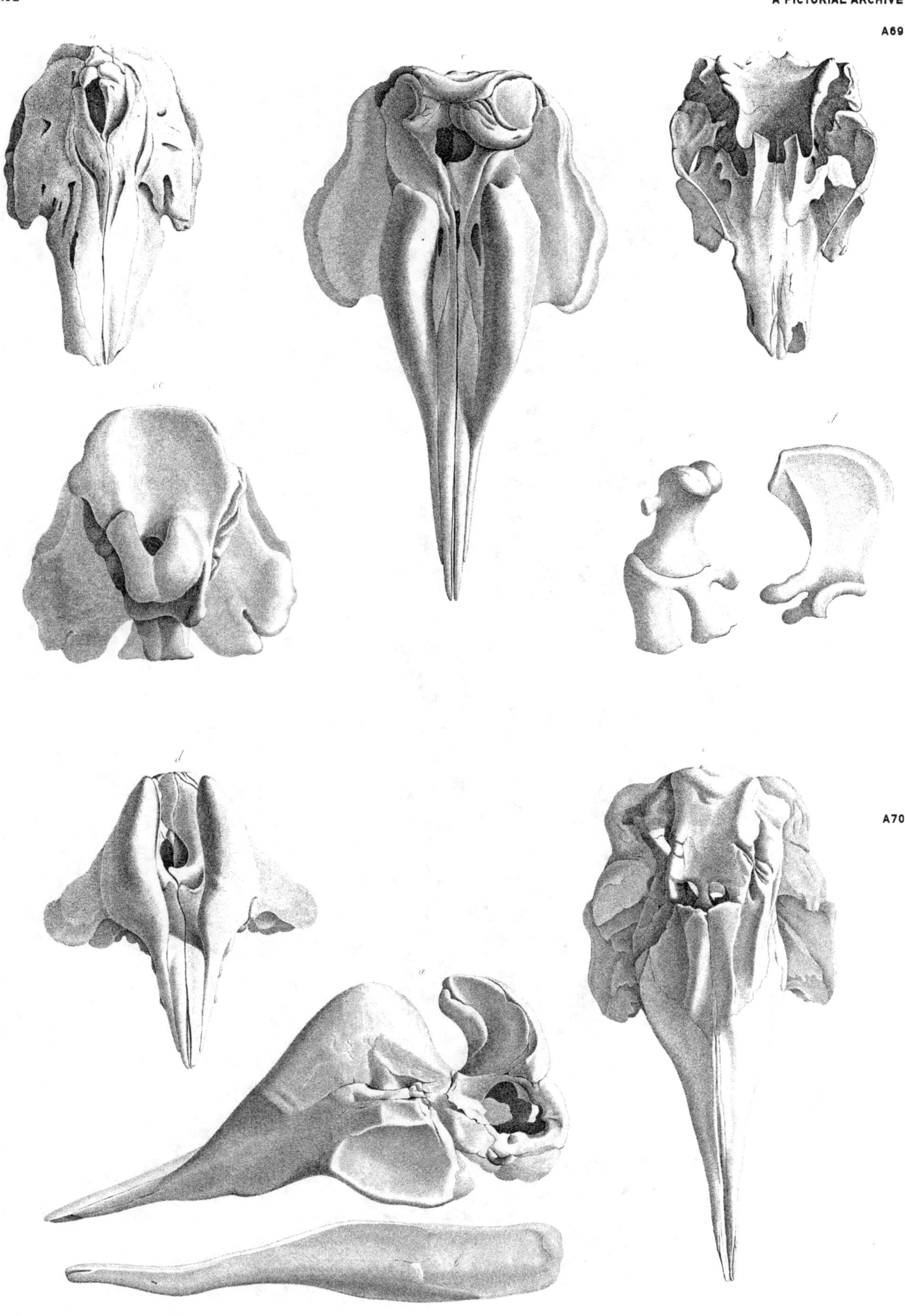

A70

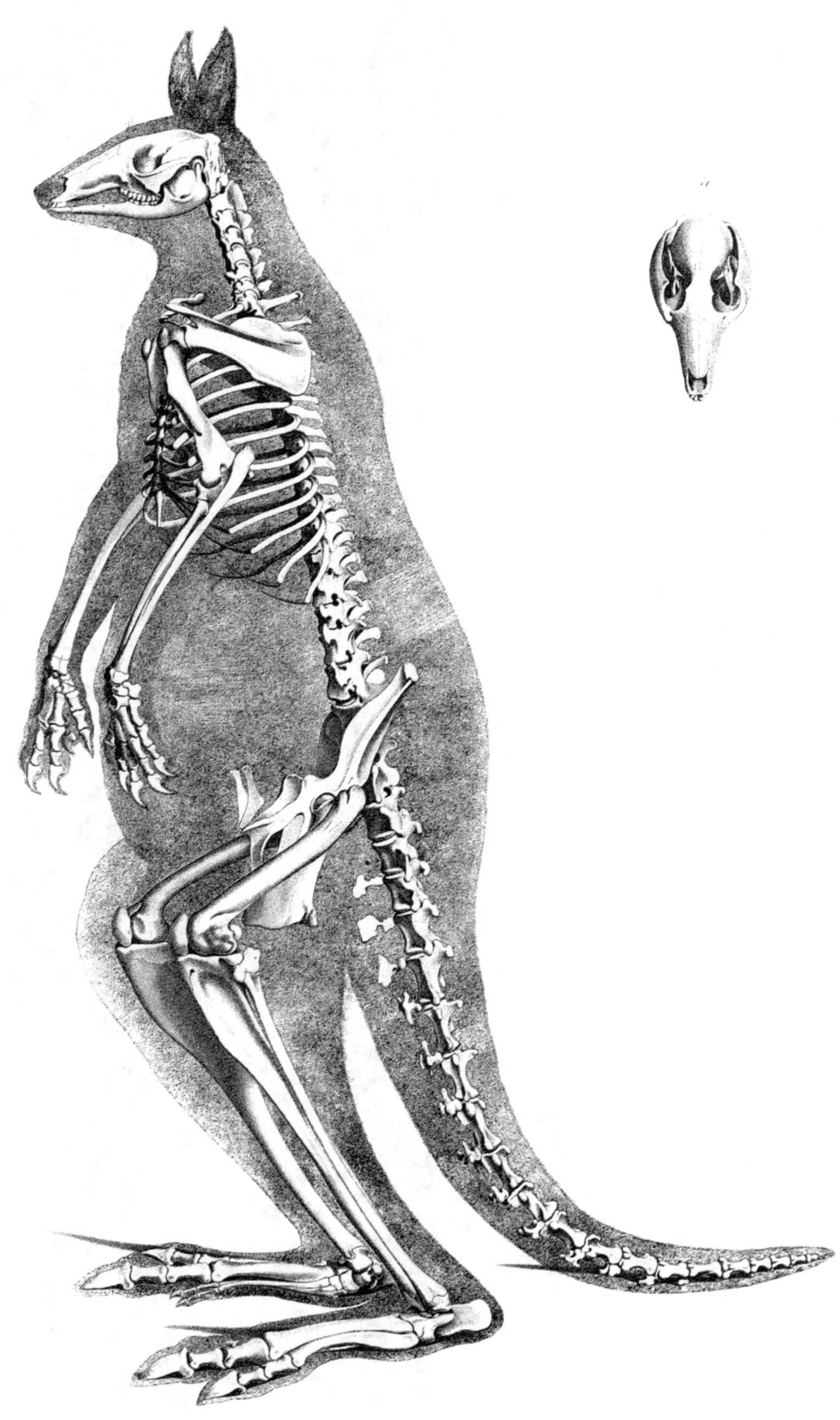

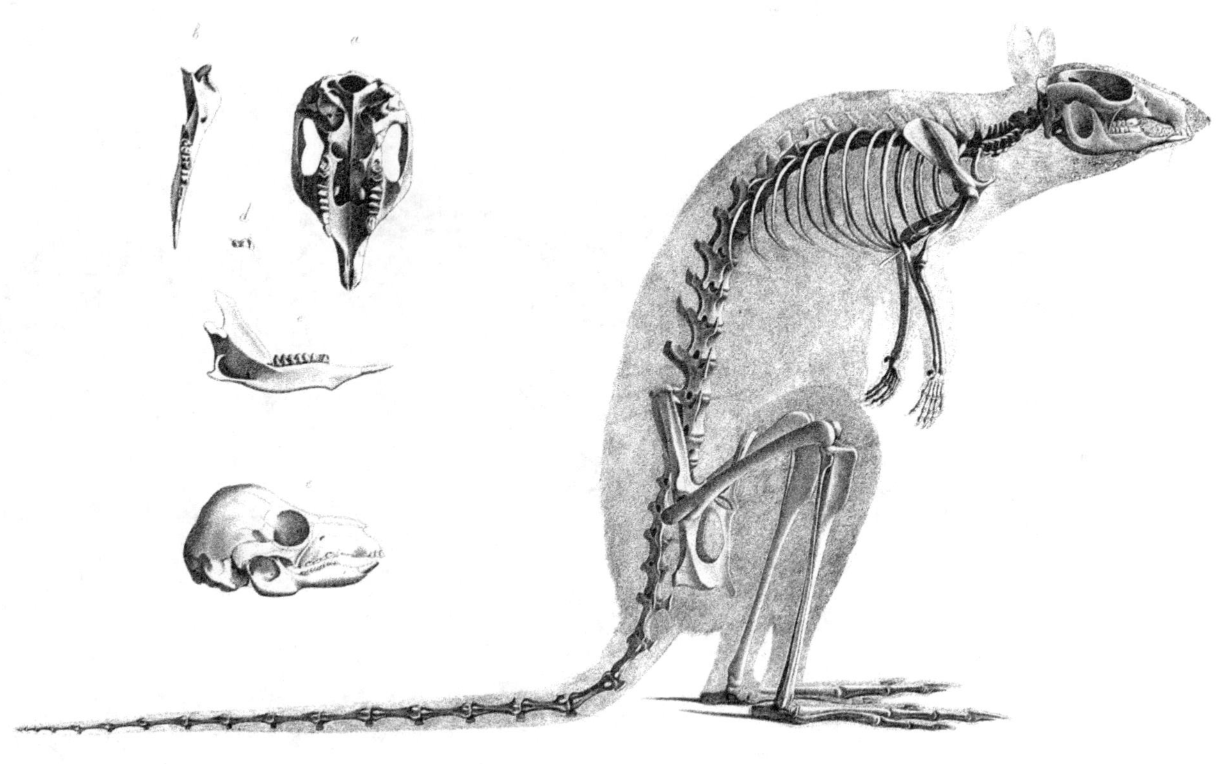

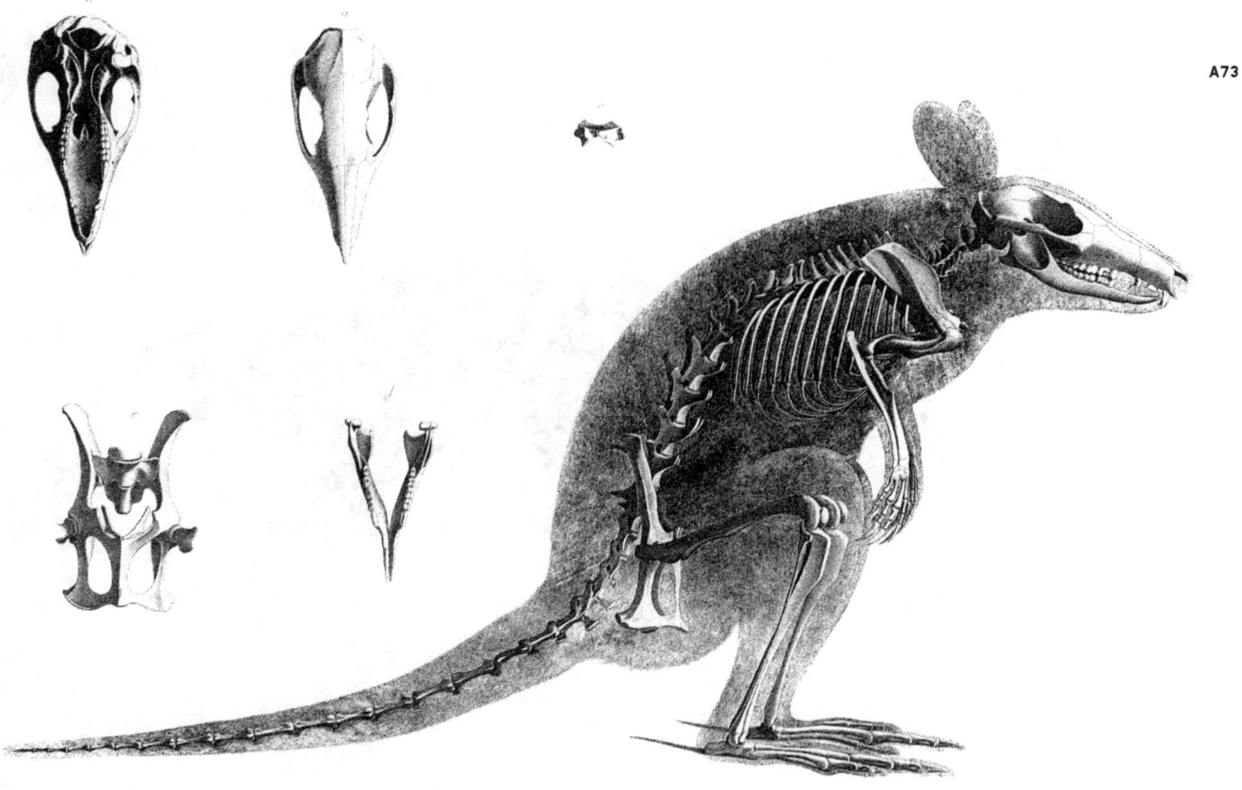

A74

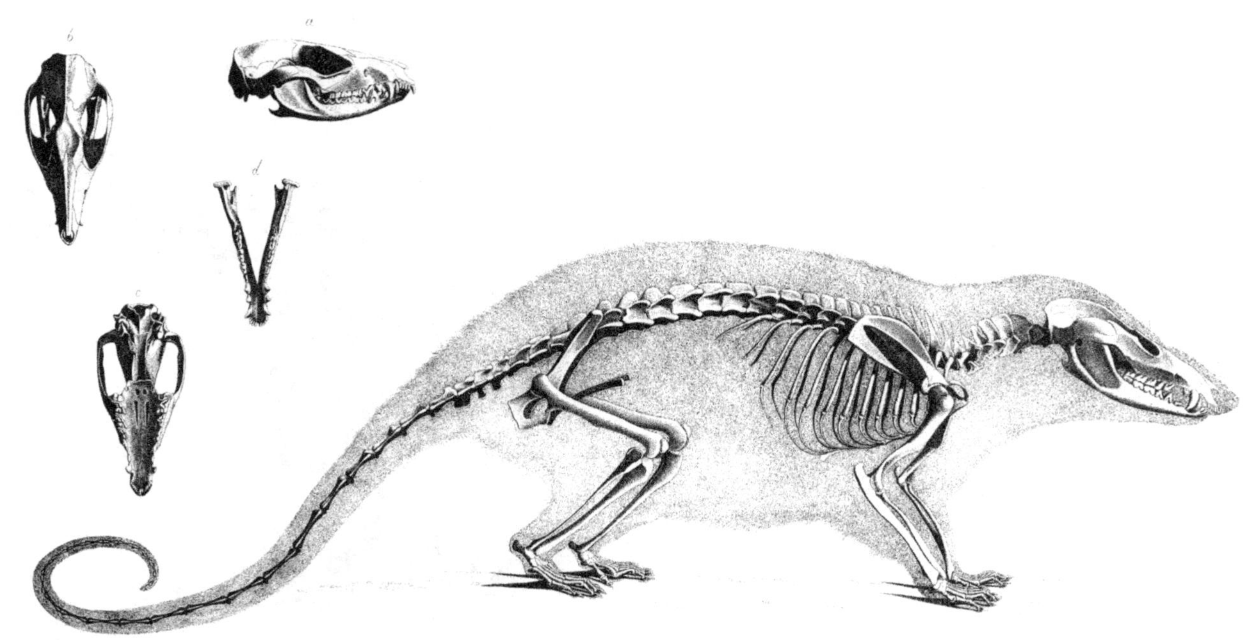

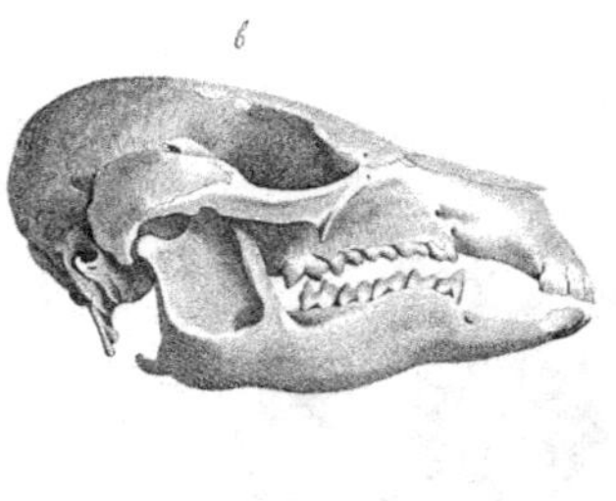

A75

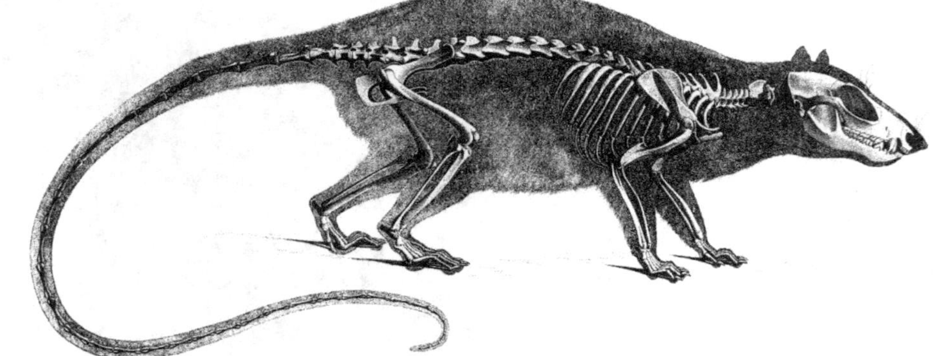

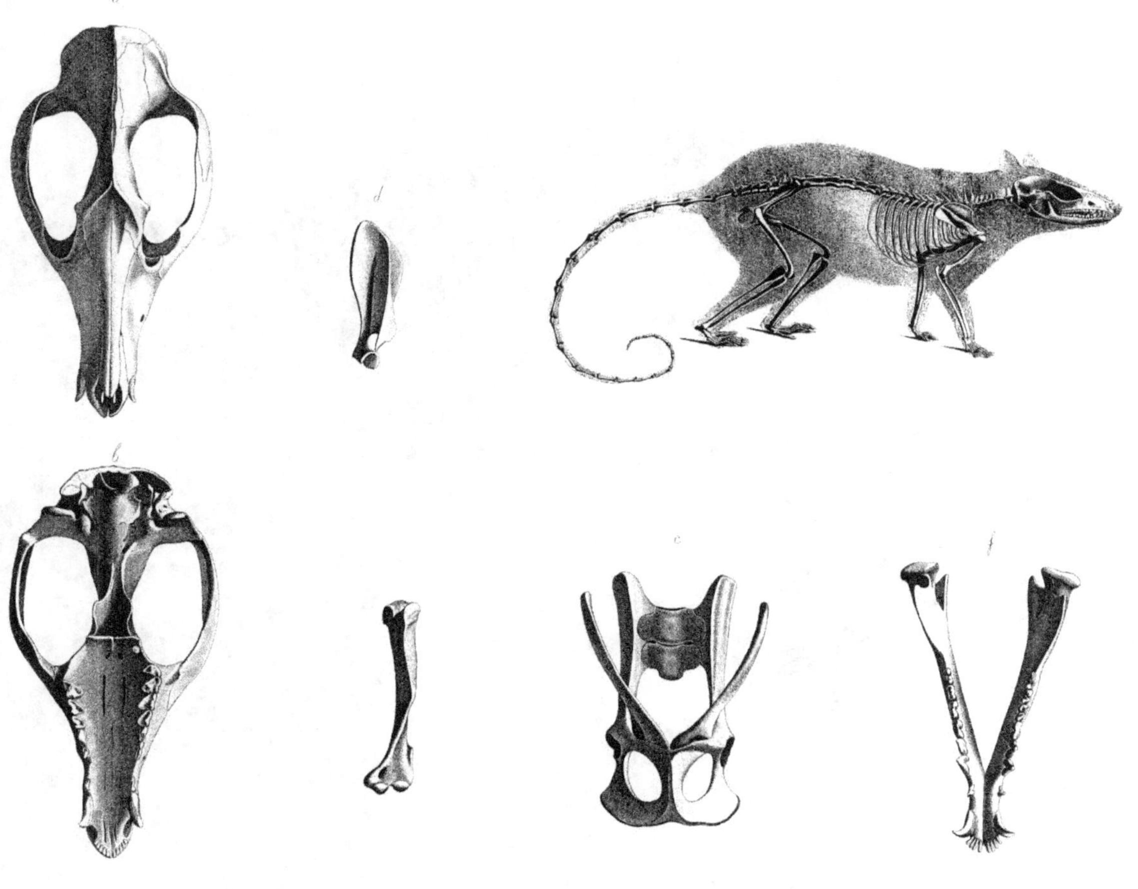

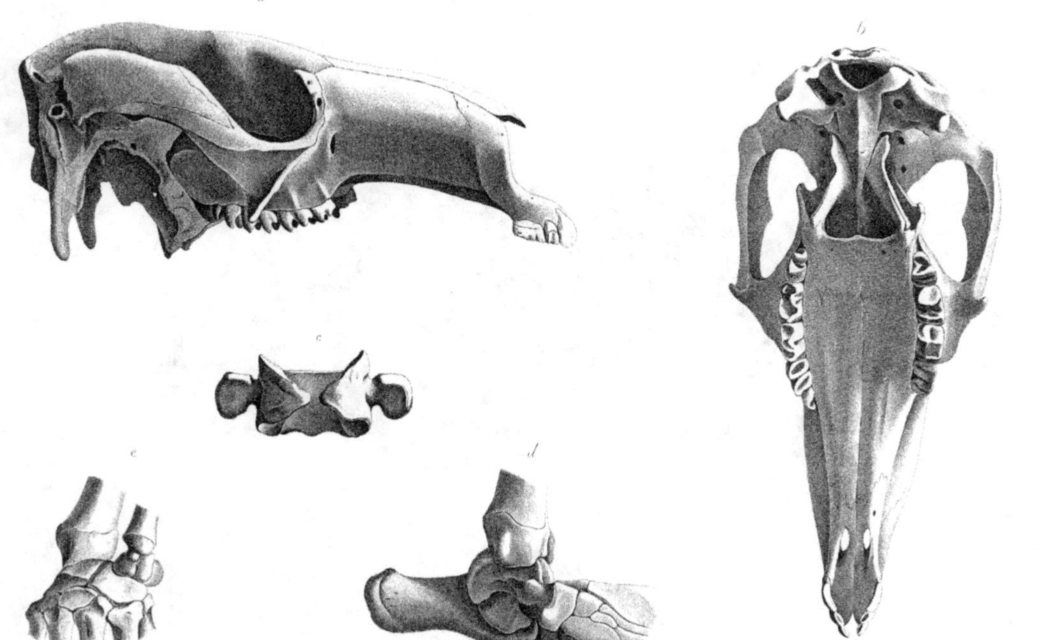

A77

A78

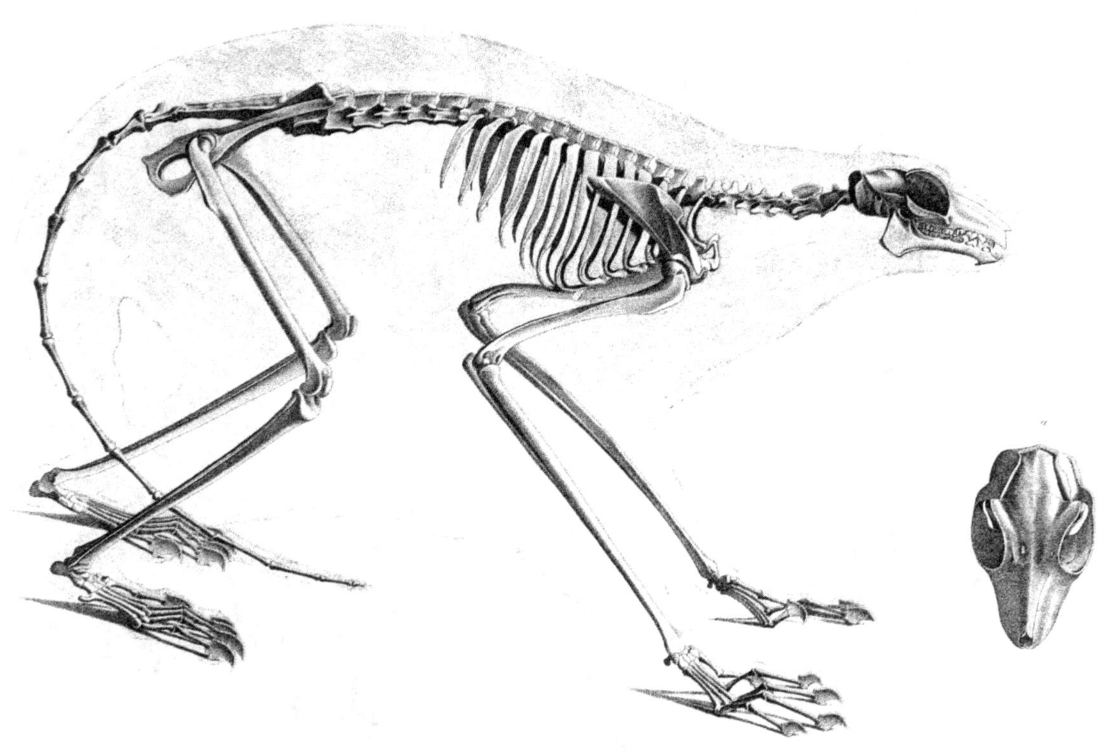

A79

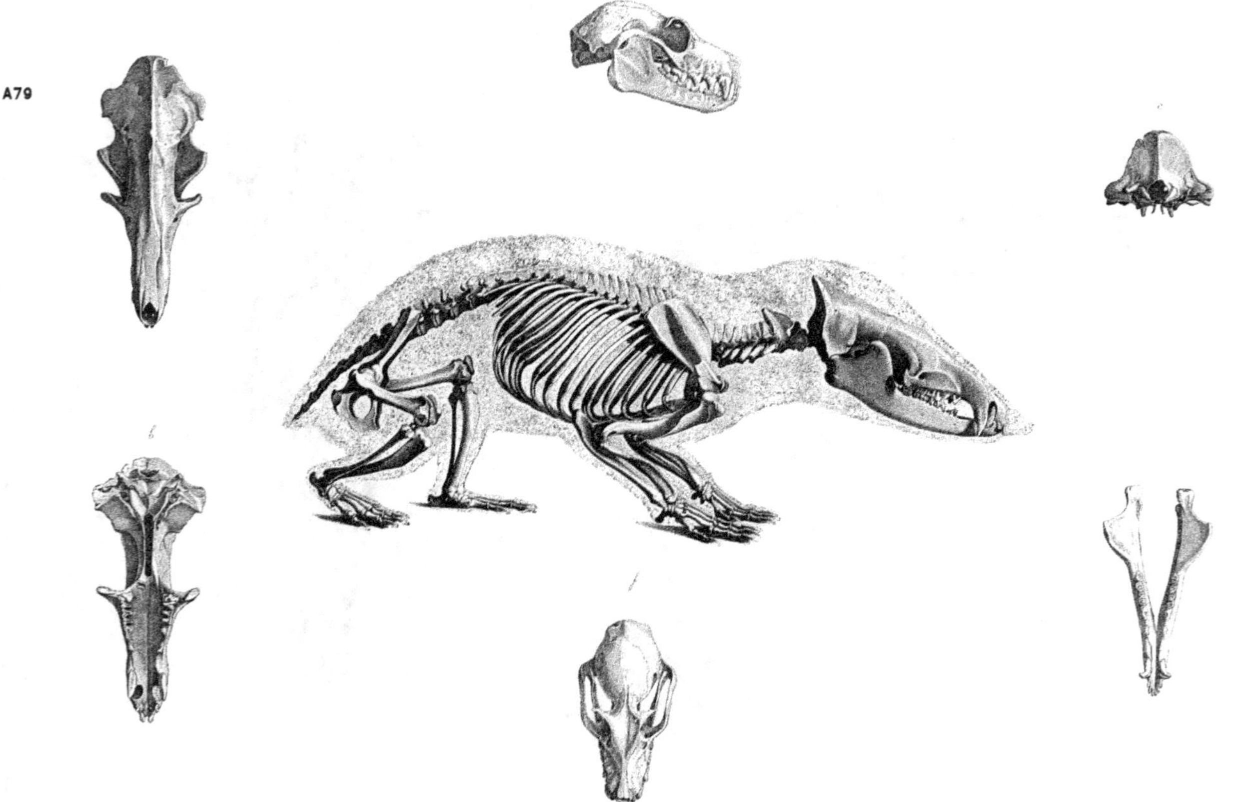

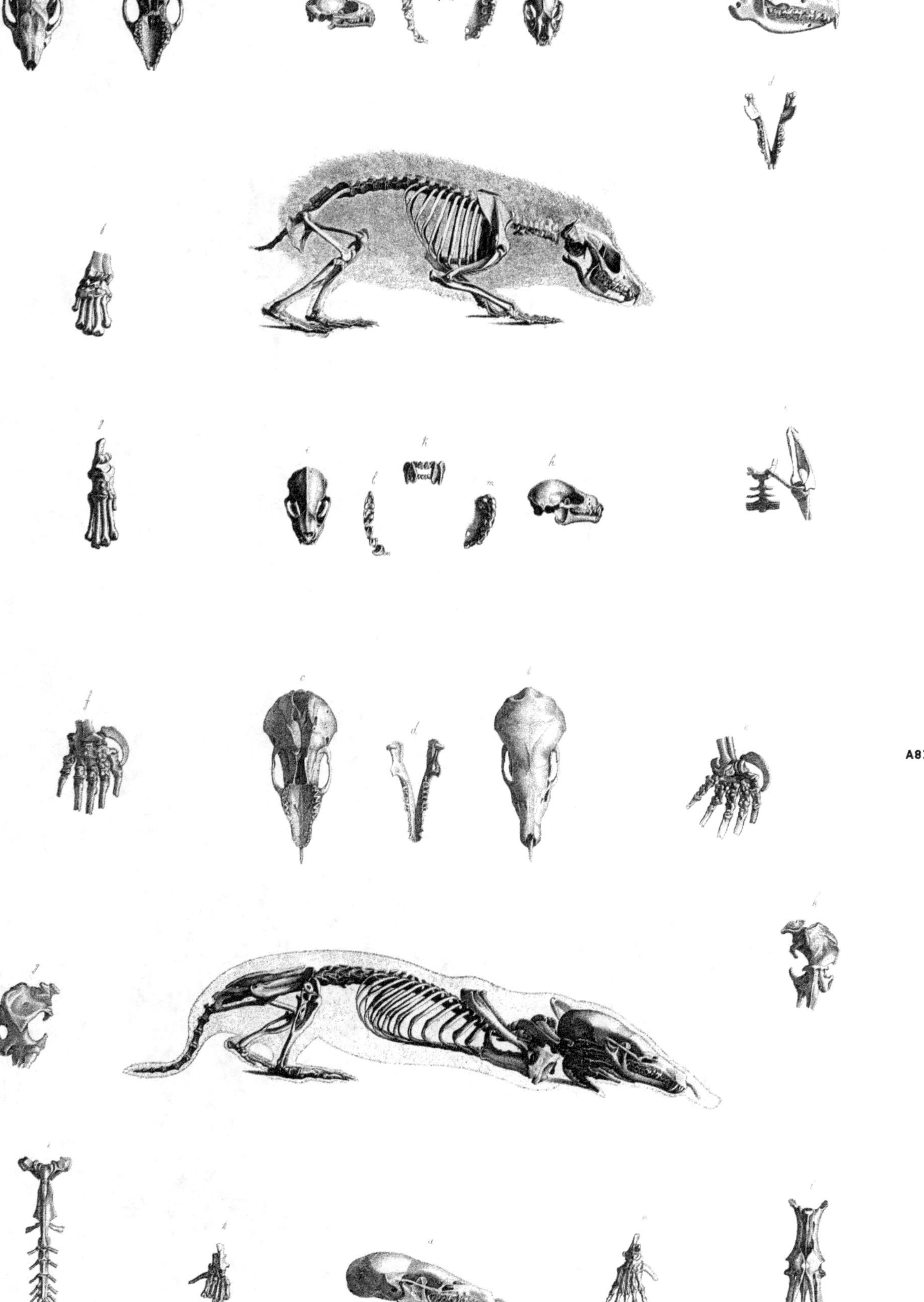

A82

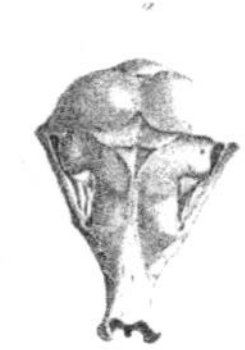
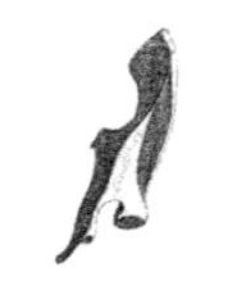
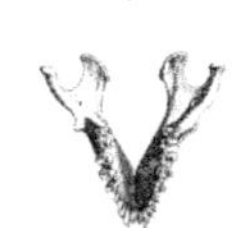
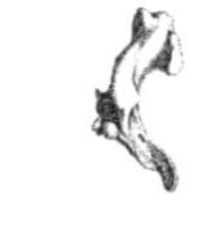
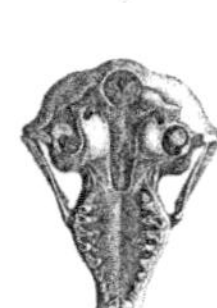

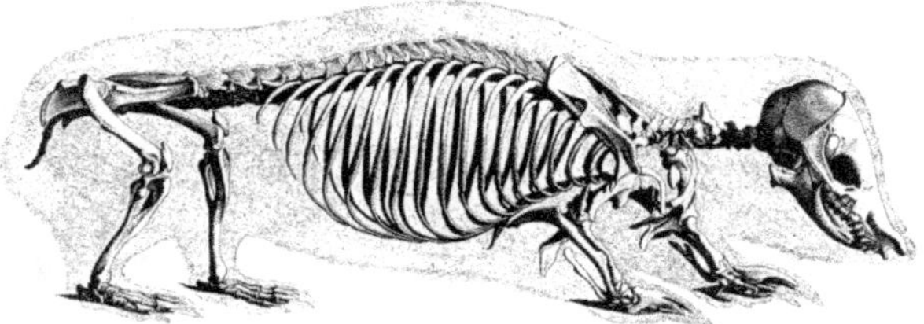

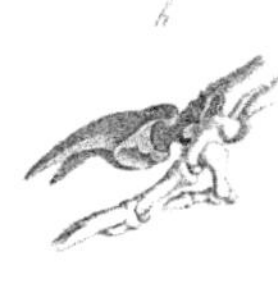
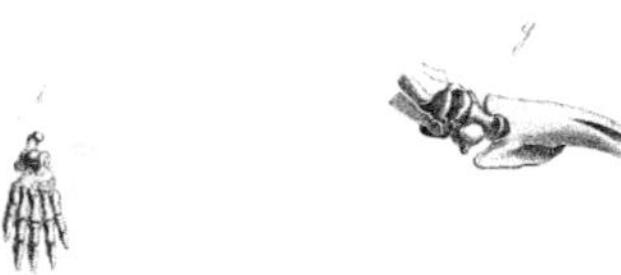
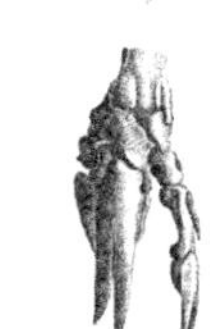

A83

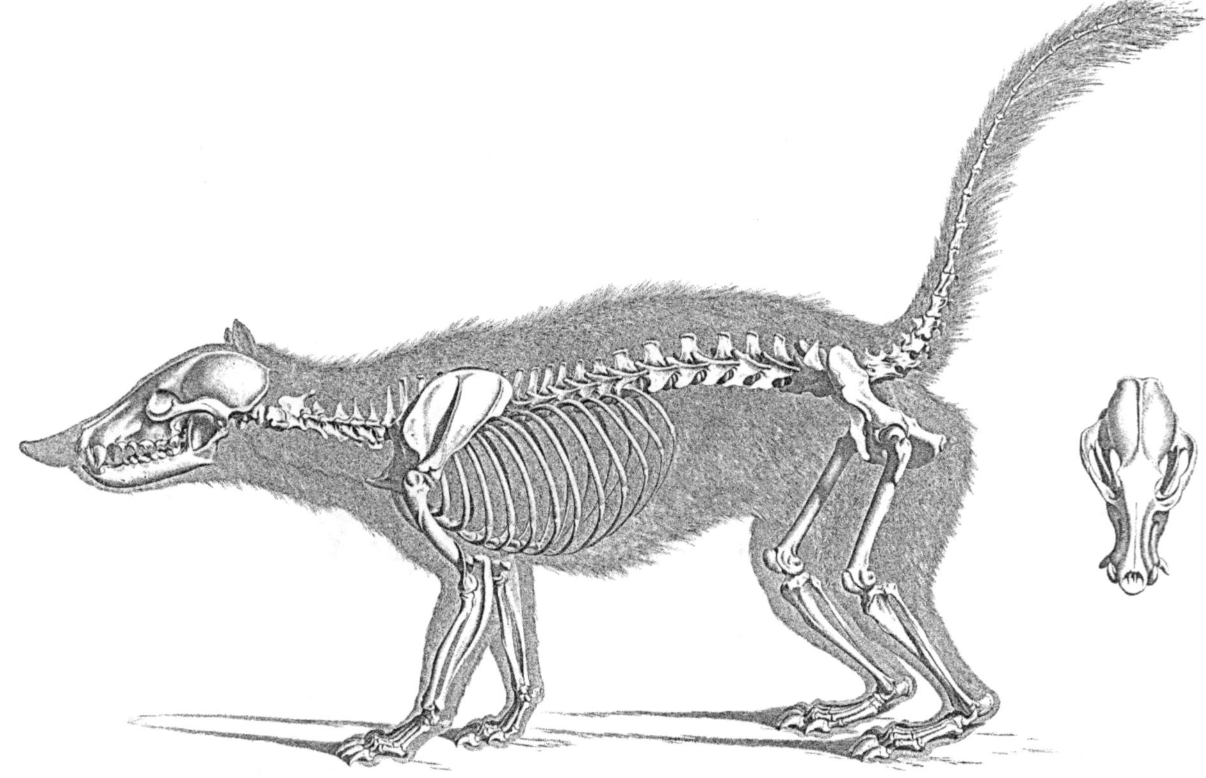

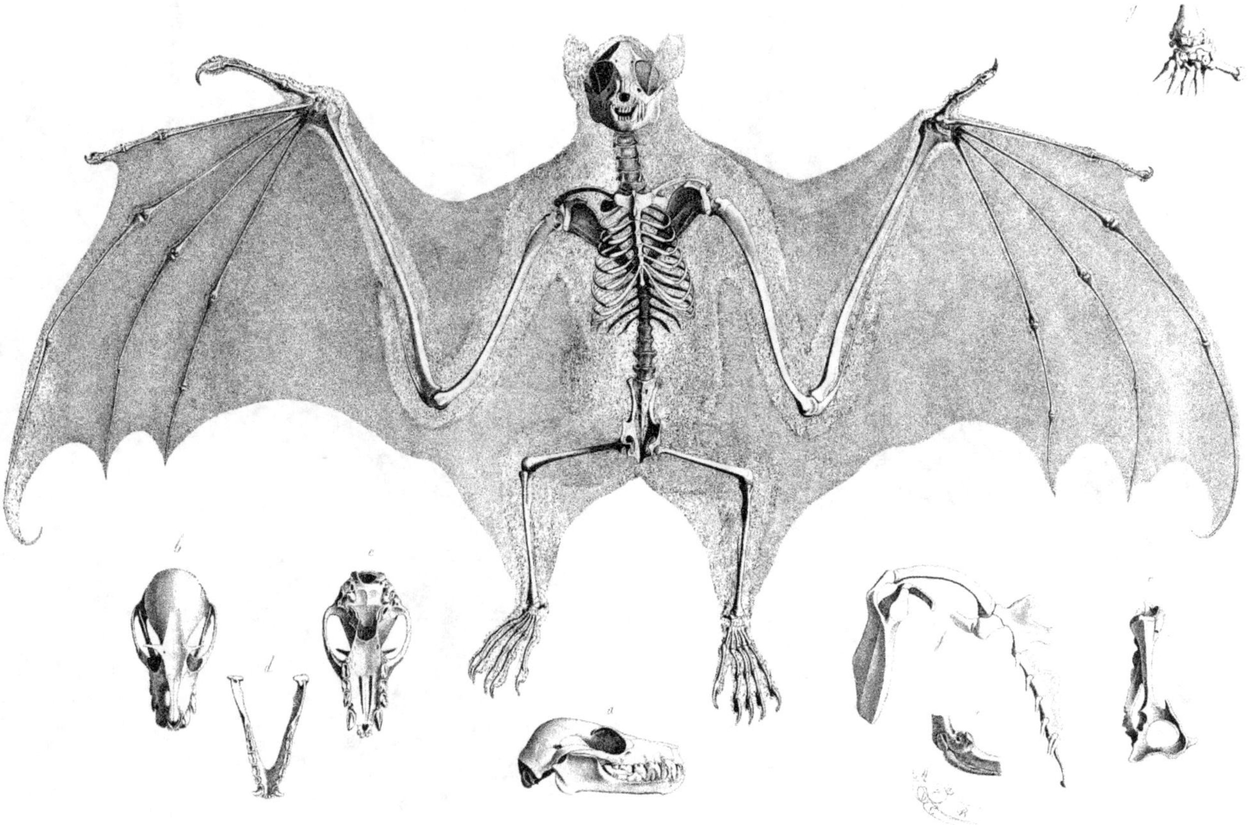

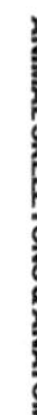

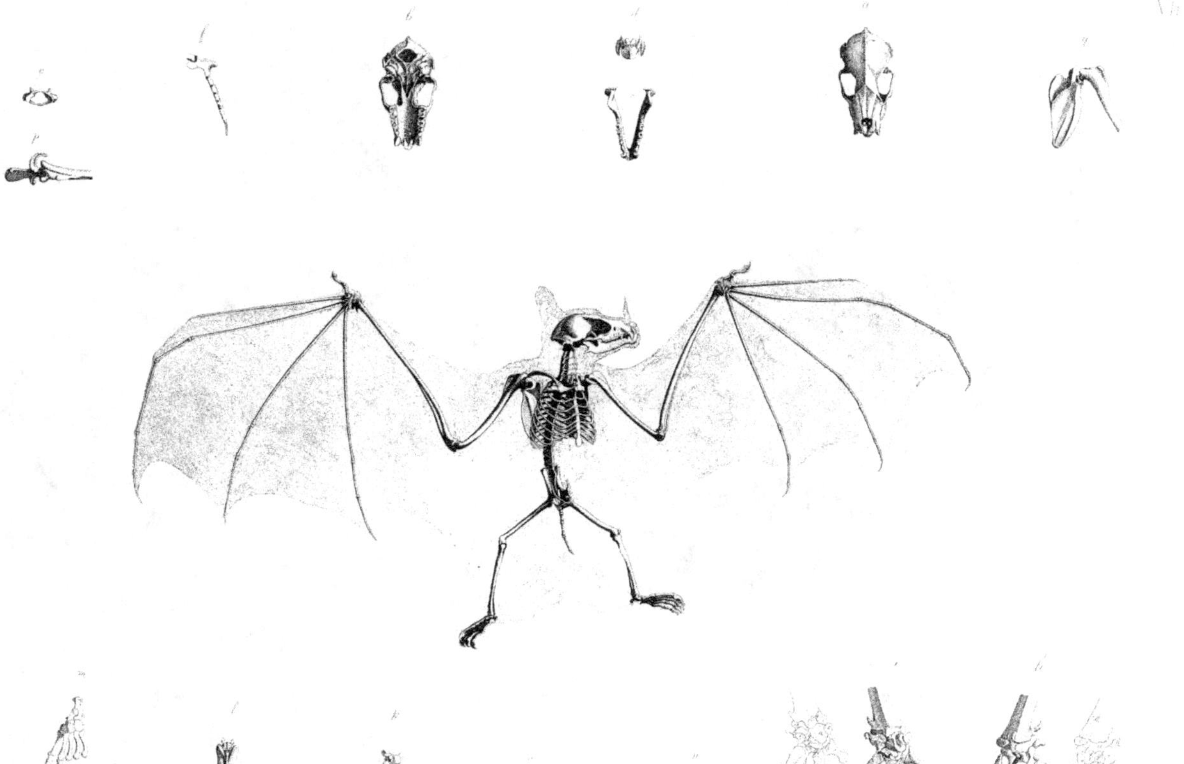

A86

A88

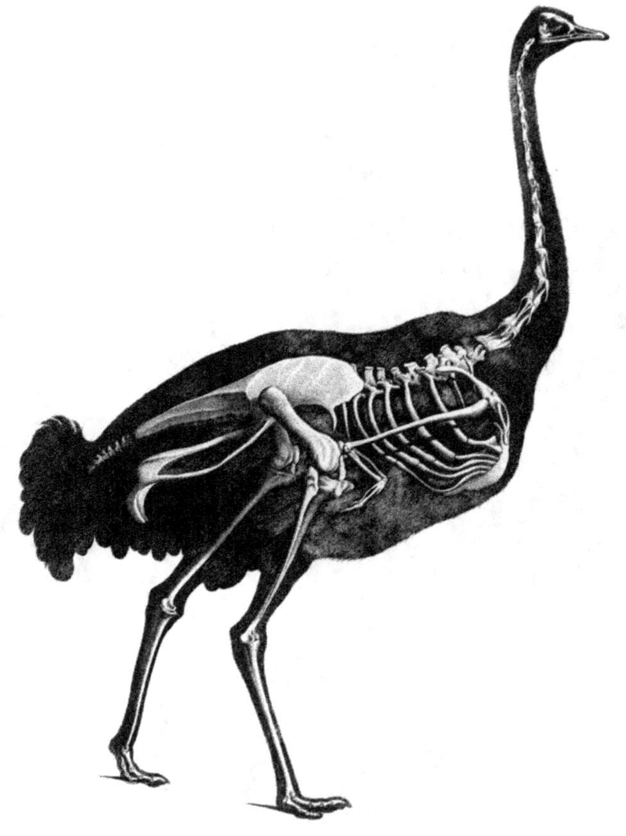

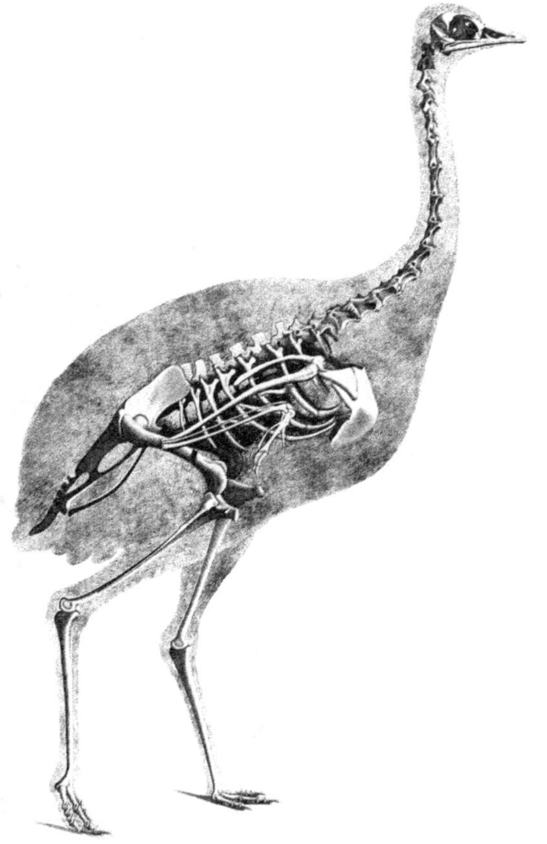

A87

A89

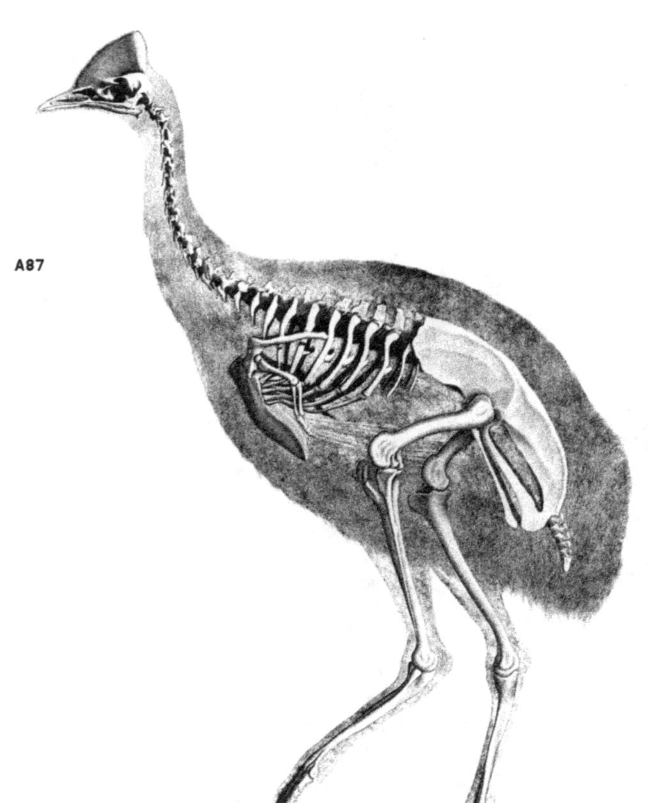

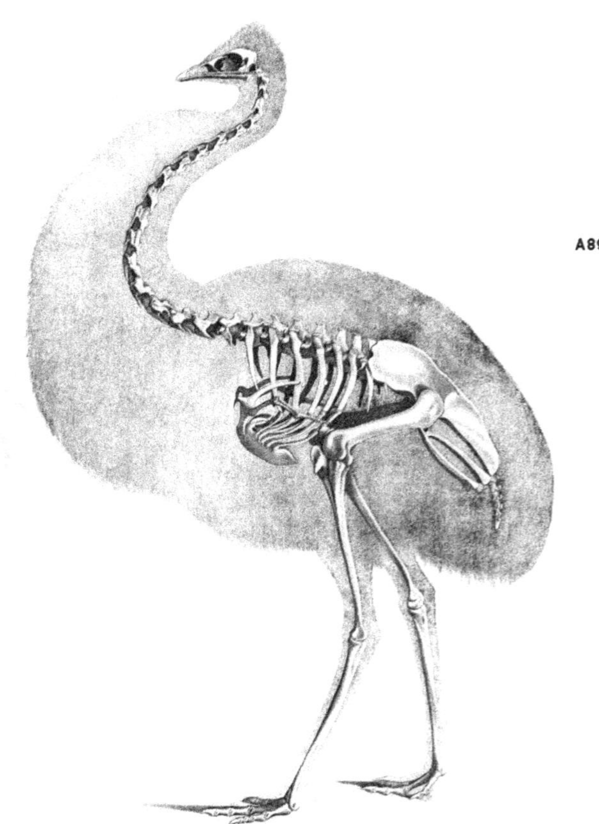

A90

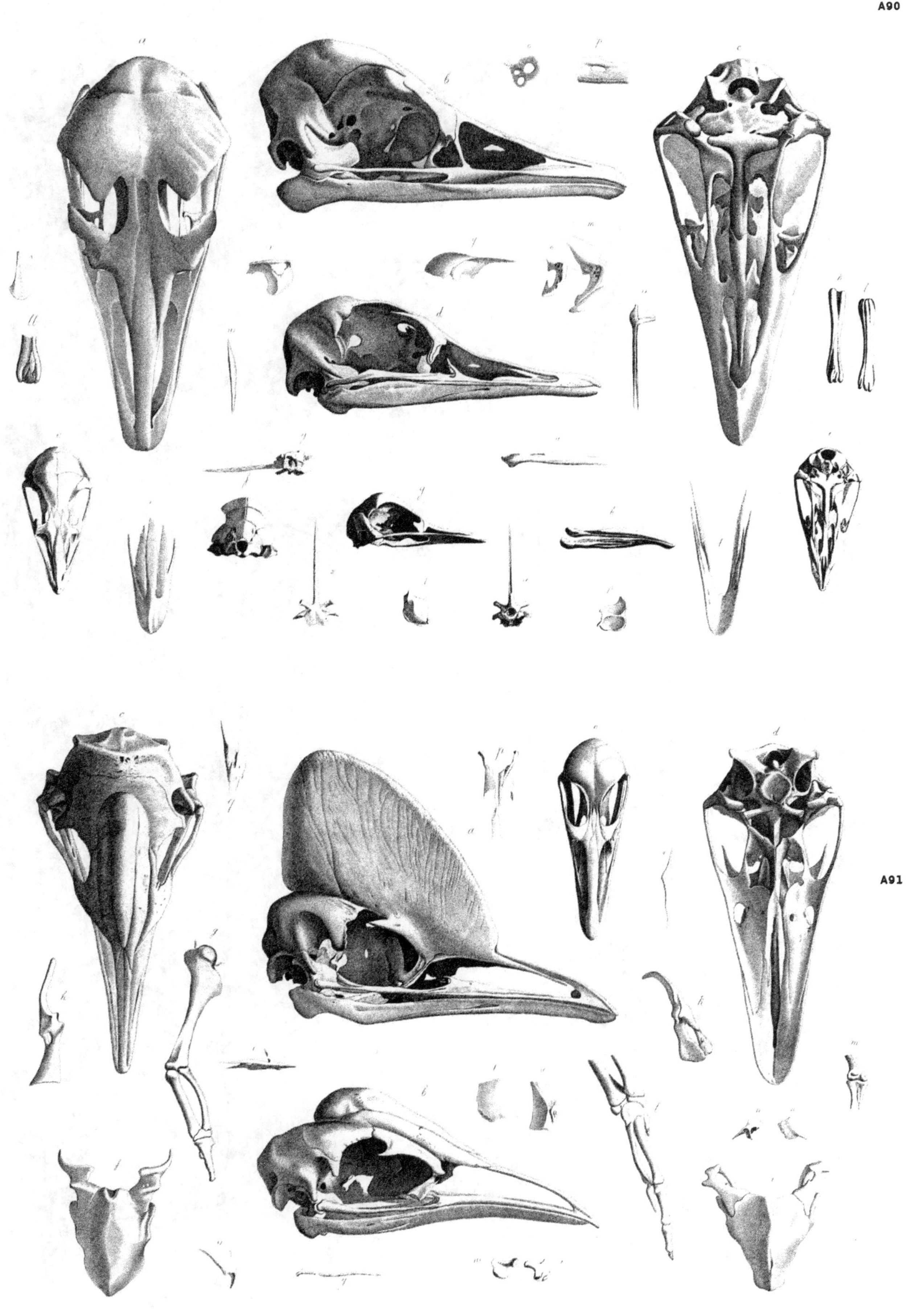

A91

A92

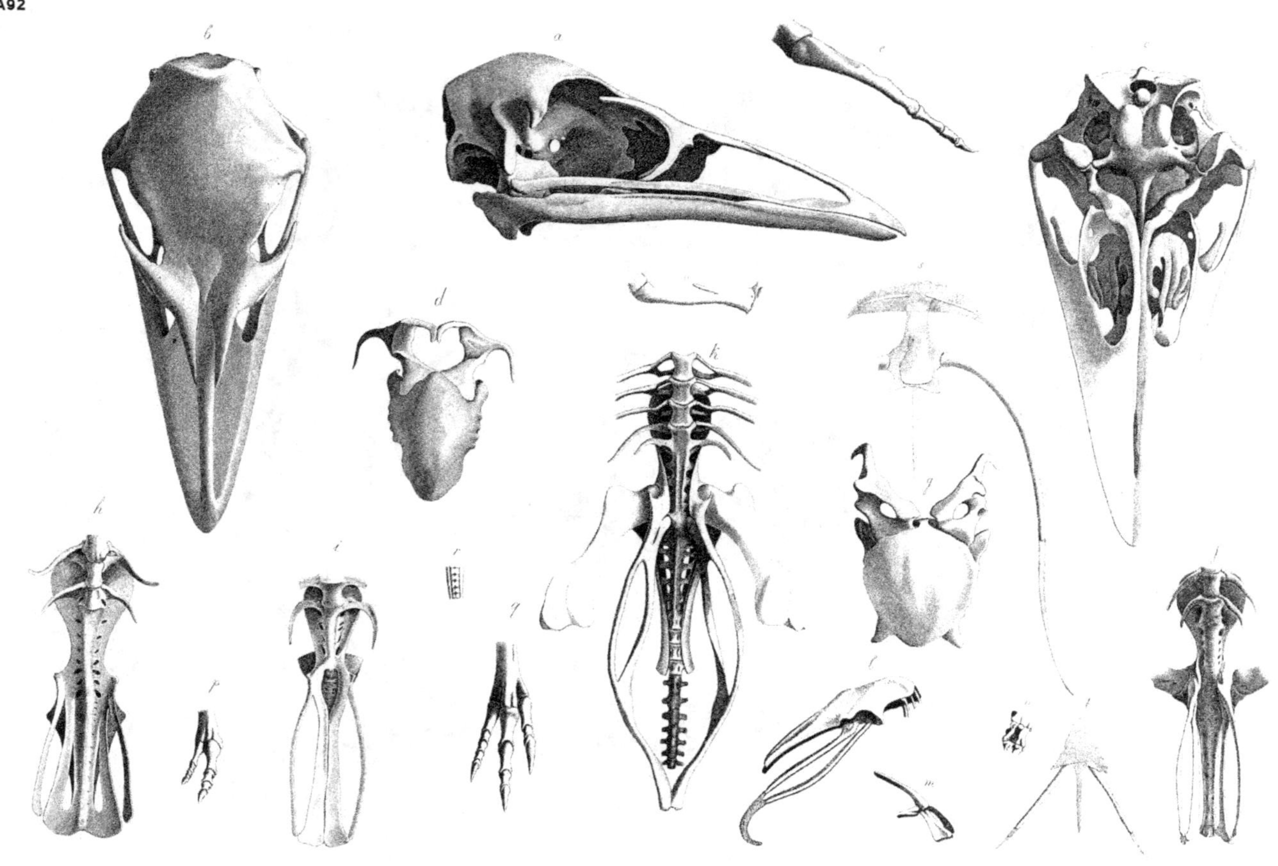

A93 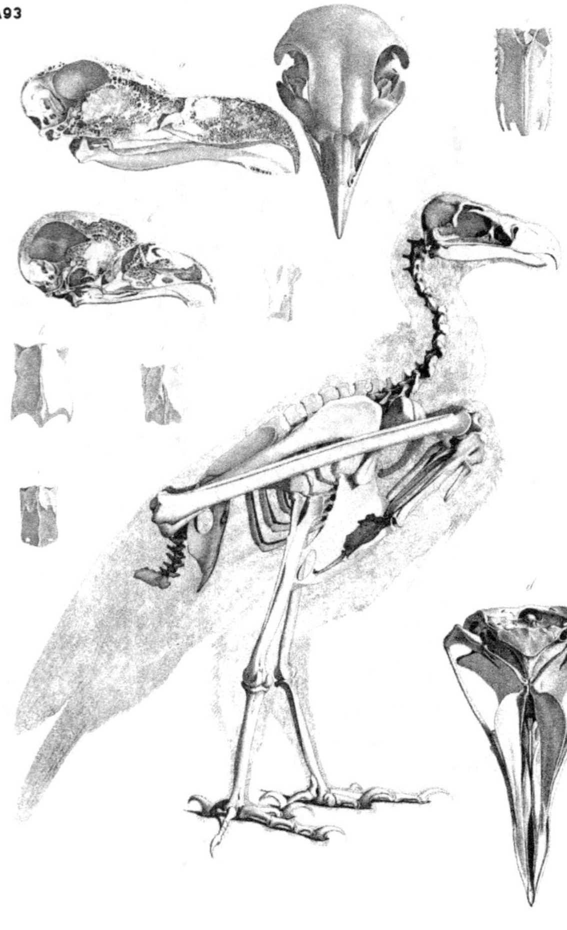   A94

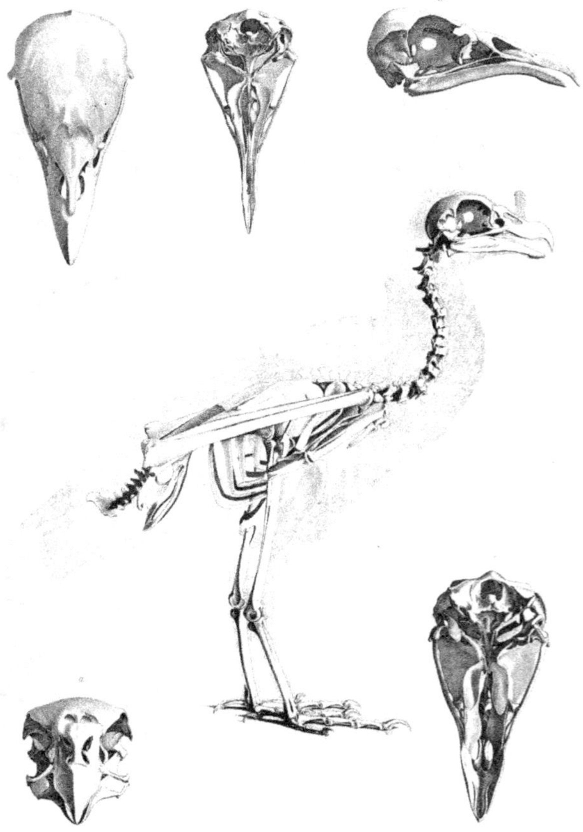

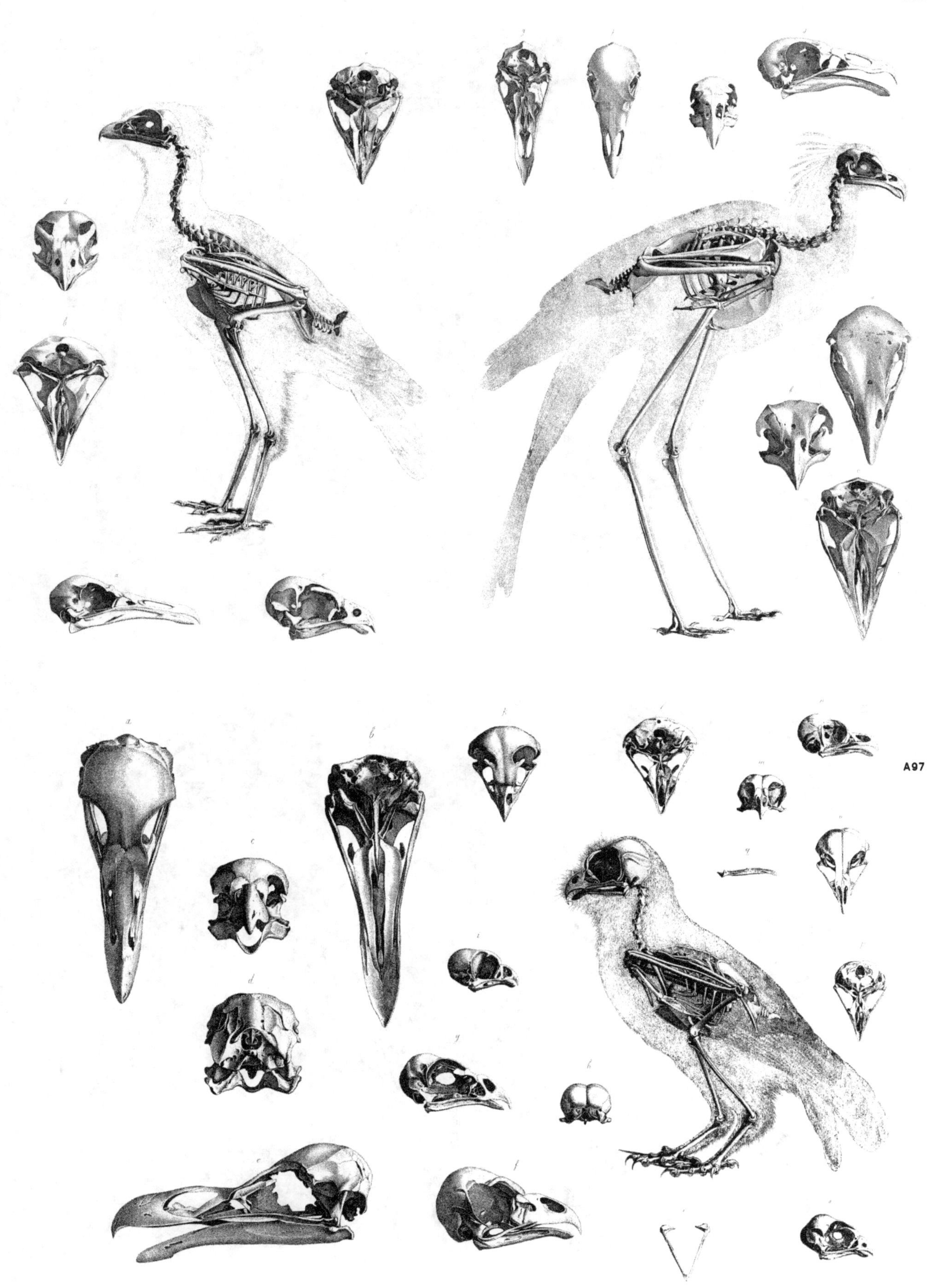

A97

A98

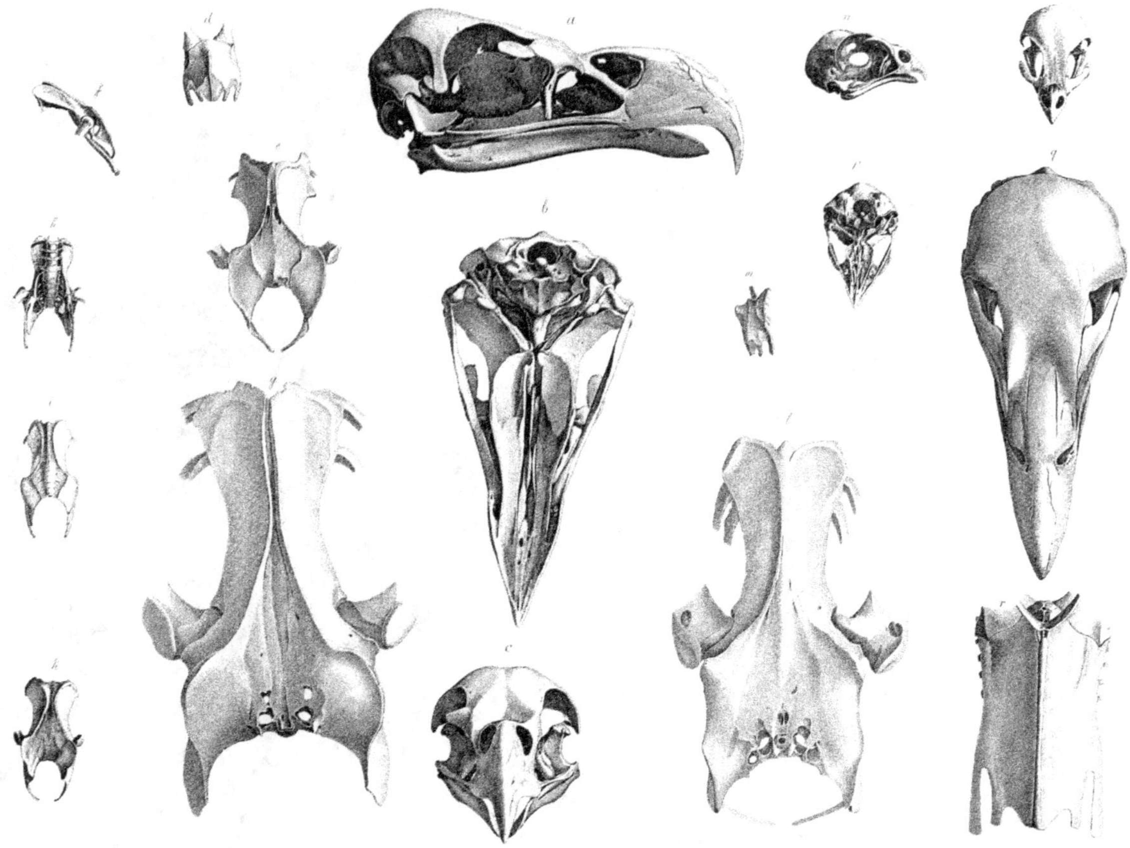

A99

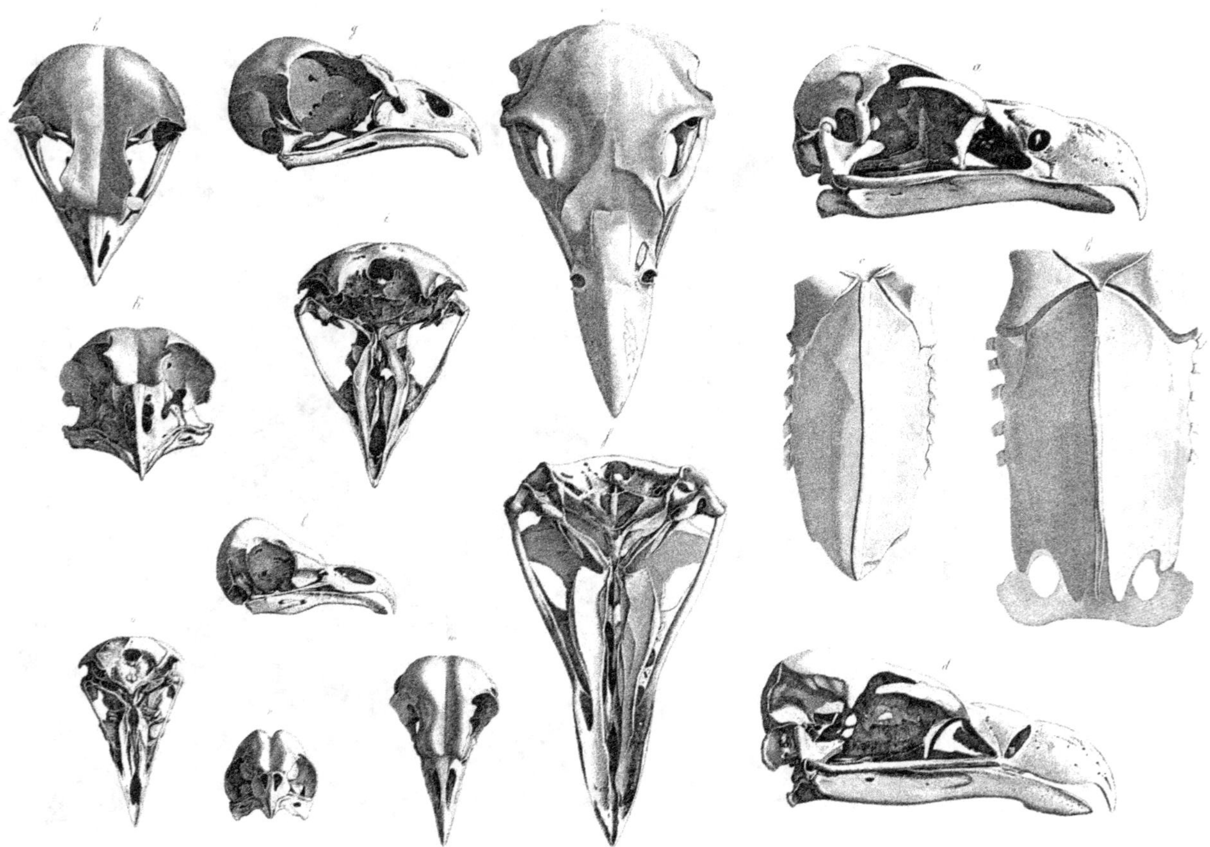

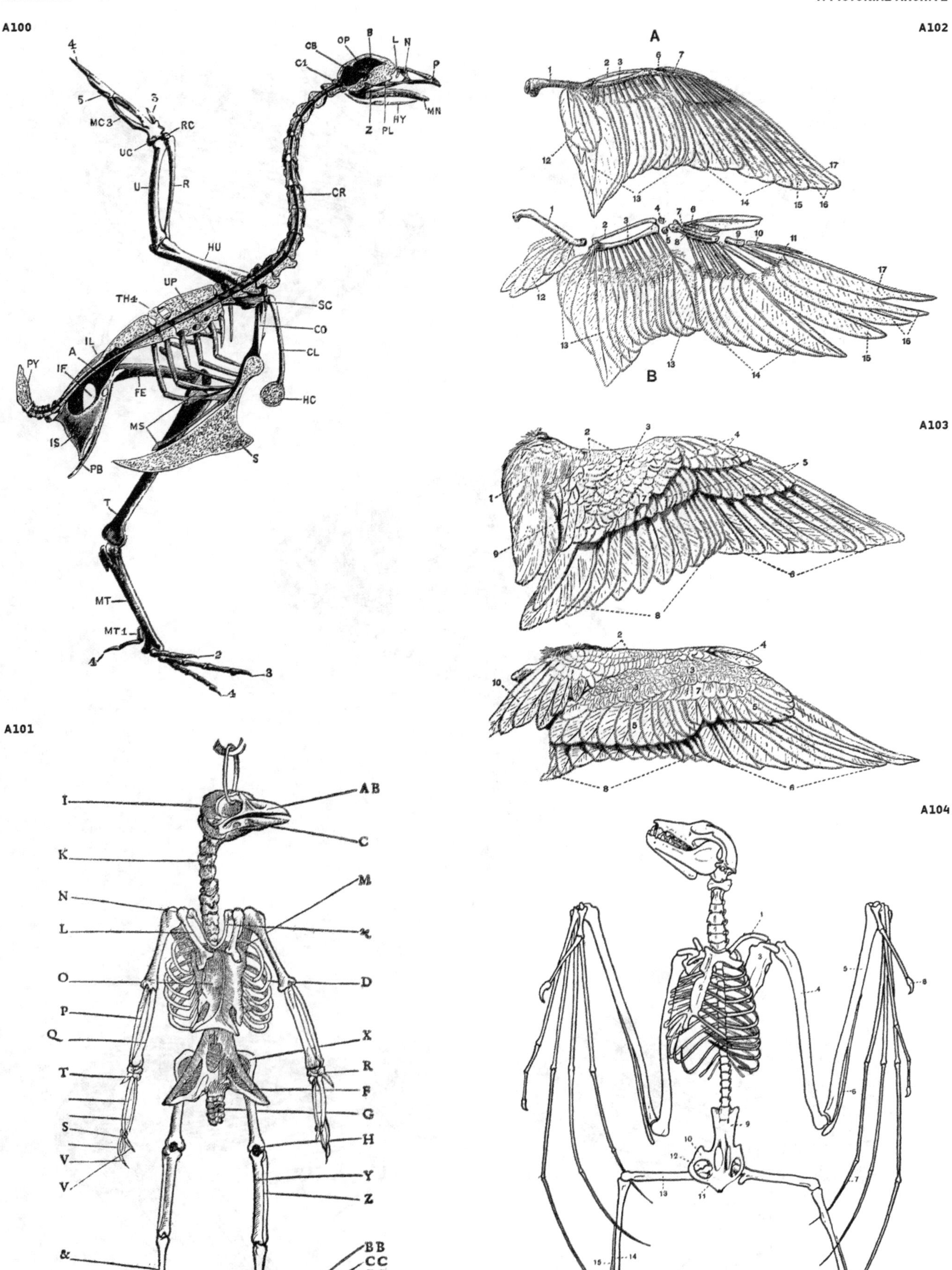
A100
A101
A102
A103
A104
ANIMAL SKELETONS & ANATOMY

A105

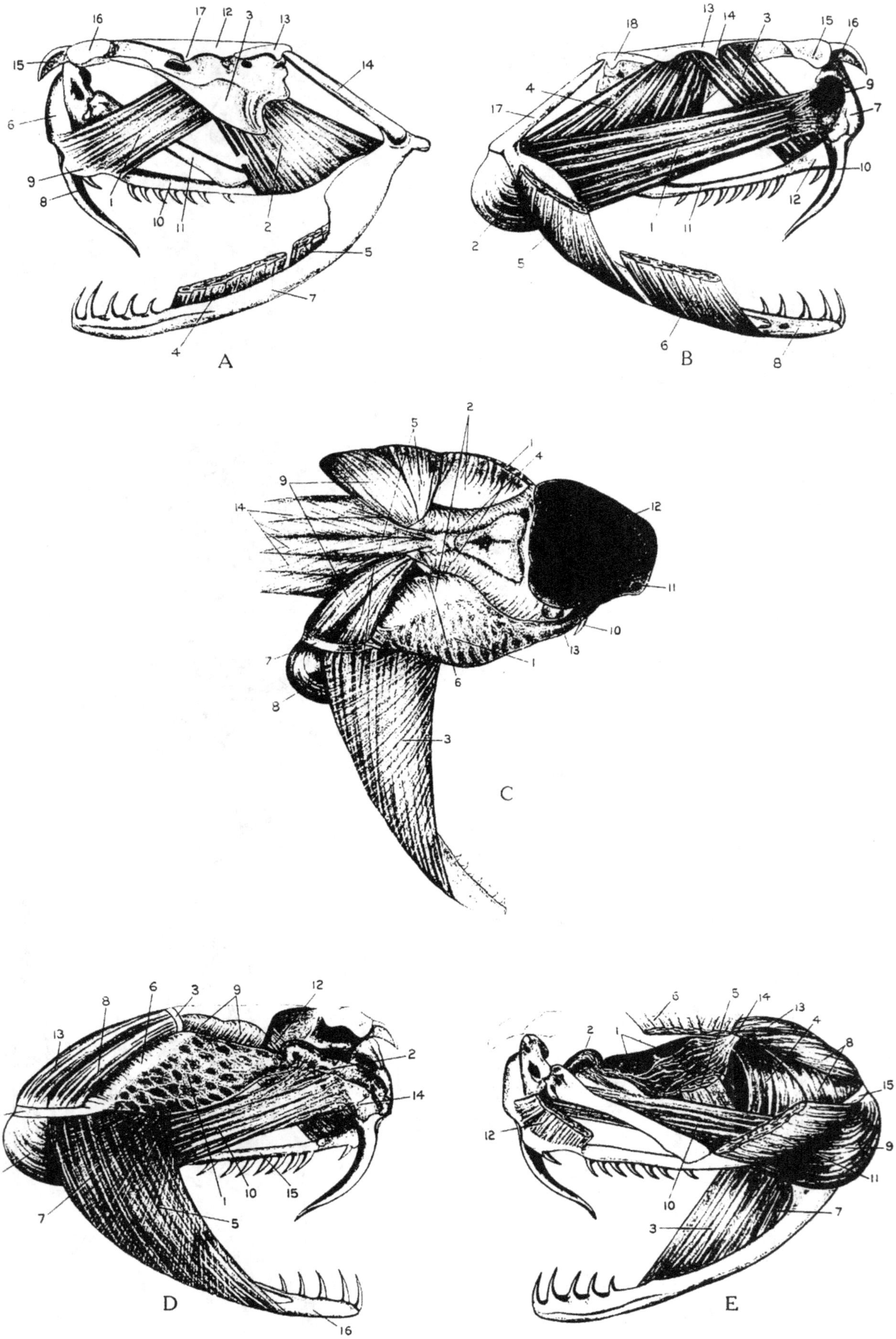

A

B

C

D

E

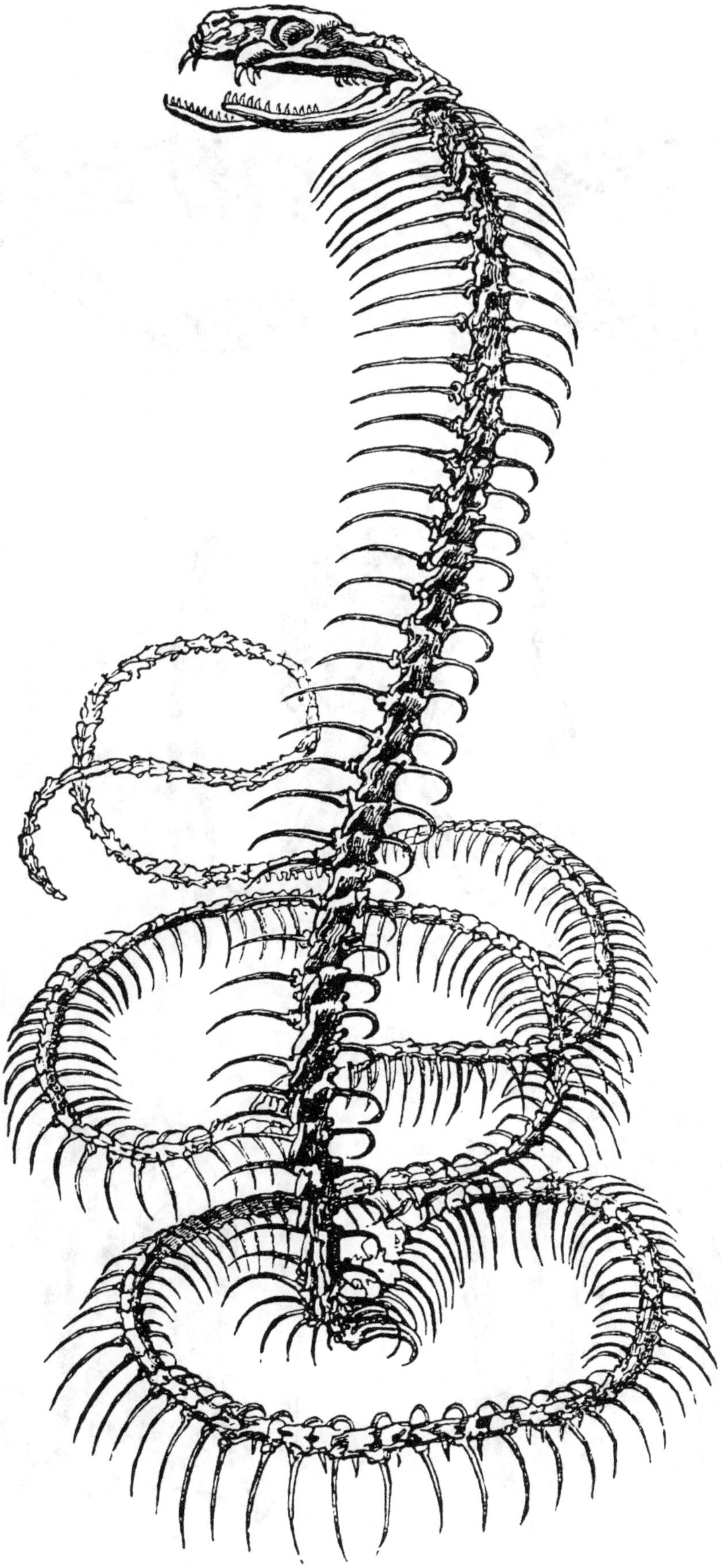

A106

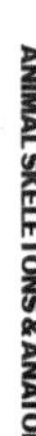

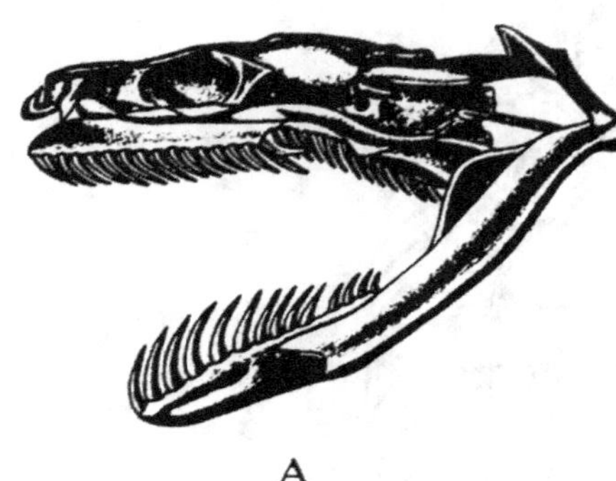

A

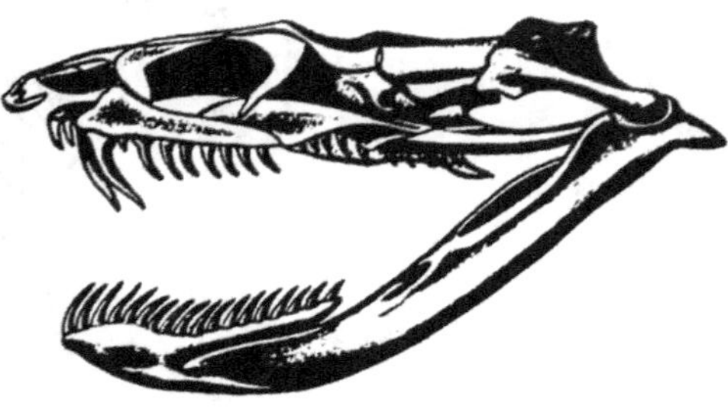

D

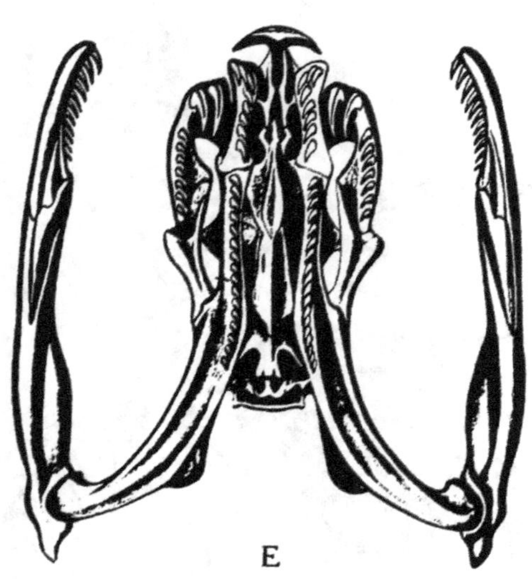

E

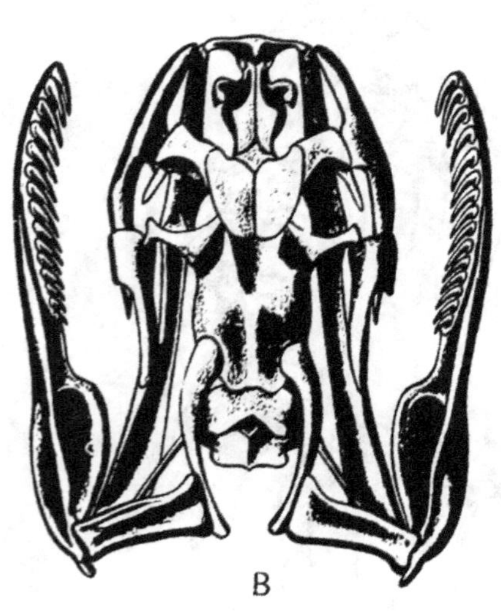

B

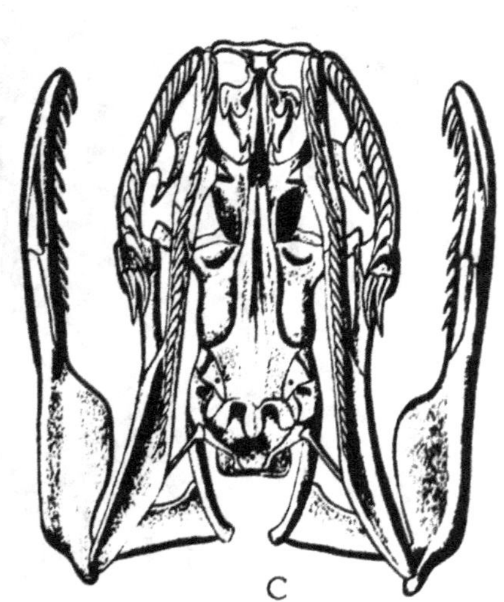

C

A108

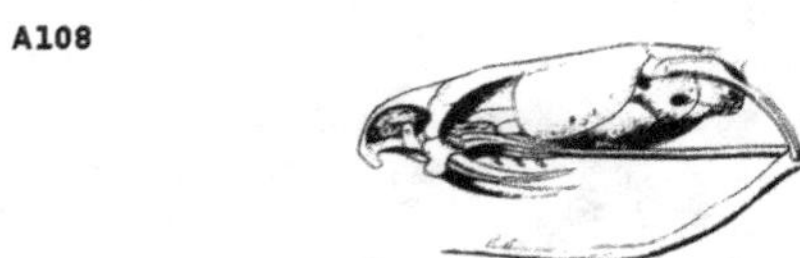

A

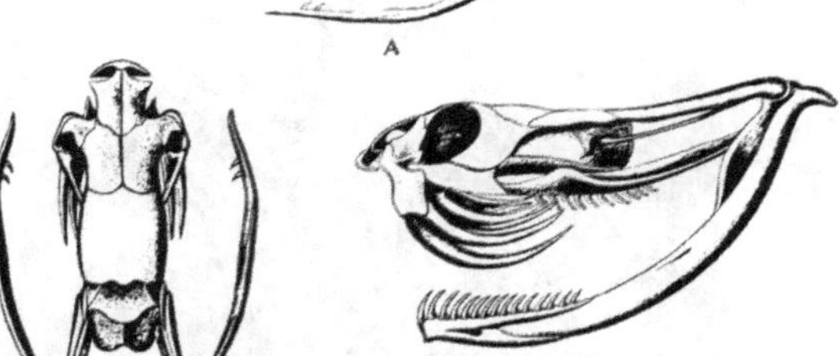

B

D

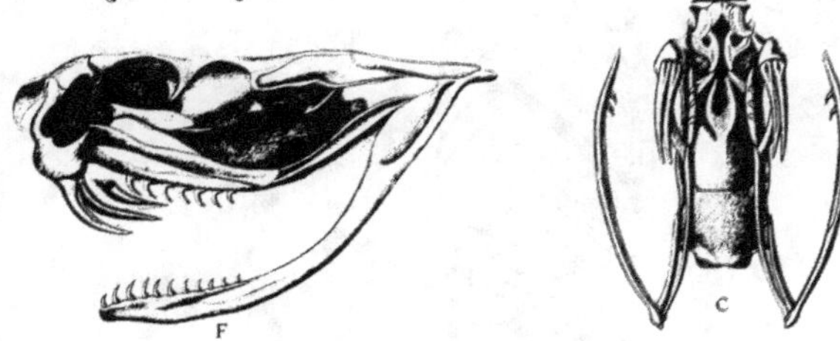

D

F

C

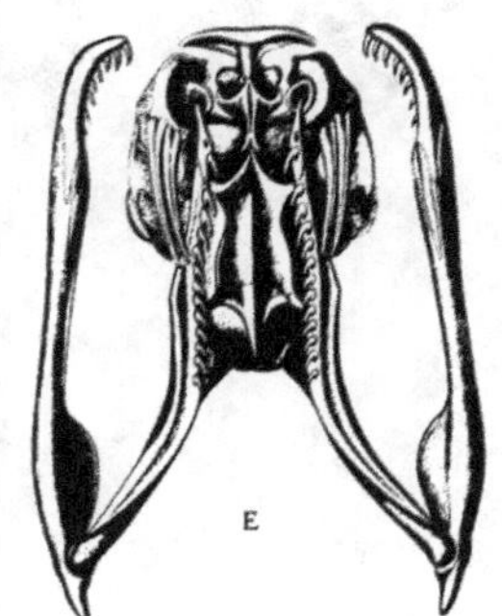

E

A109

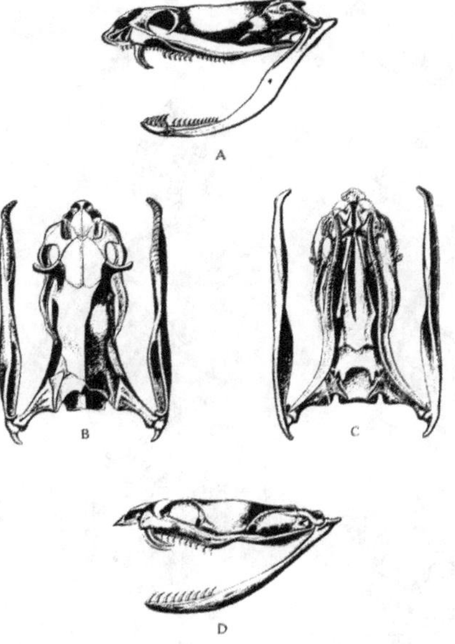

A

B

C

D

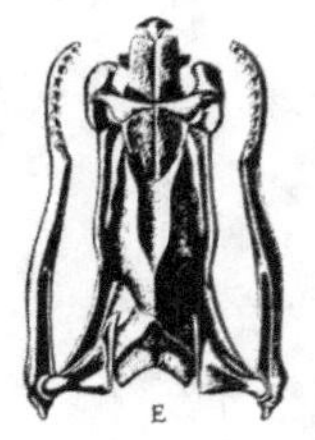

E

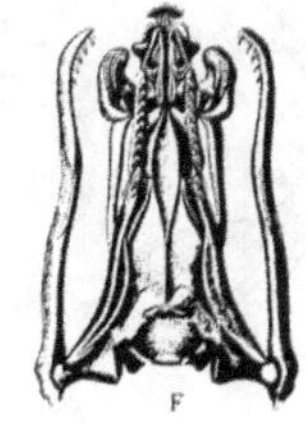

F

A110

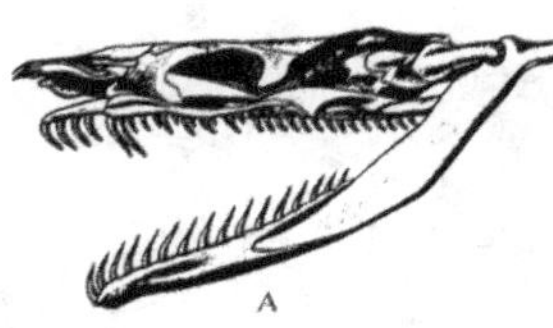

A

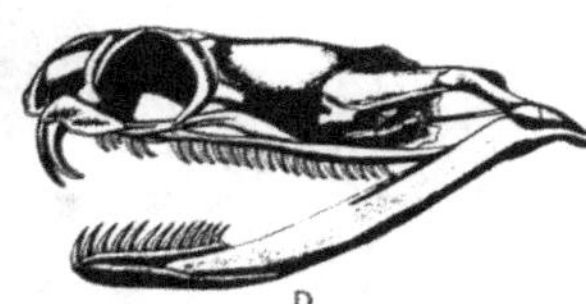

D

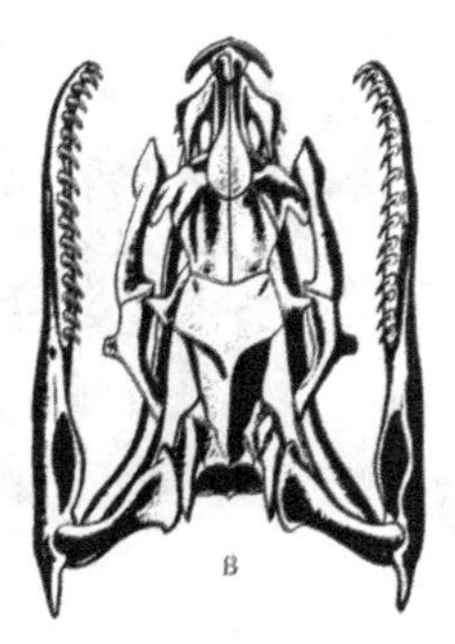

B

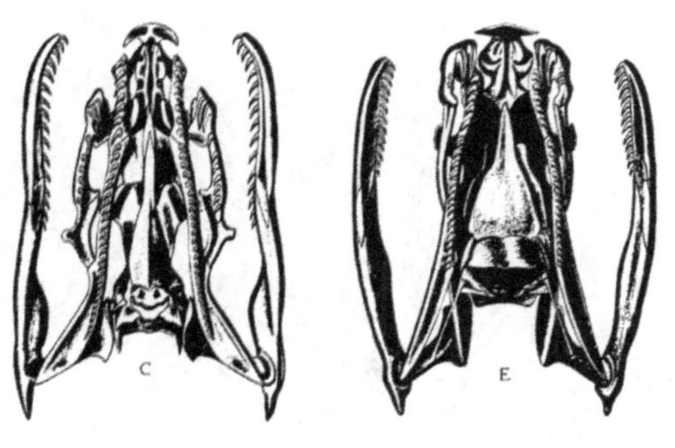

C

E

A111

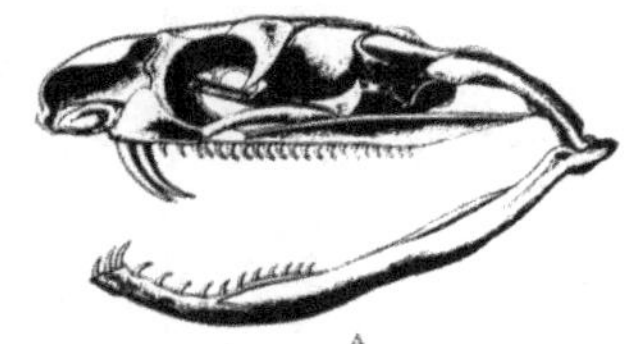

A

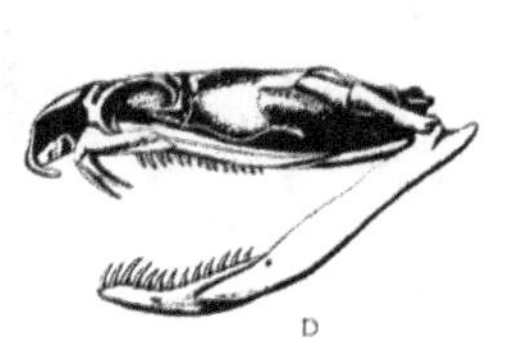

D

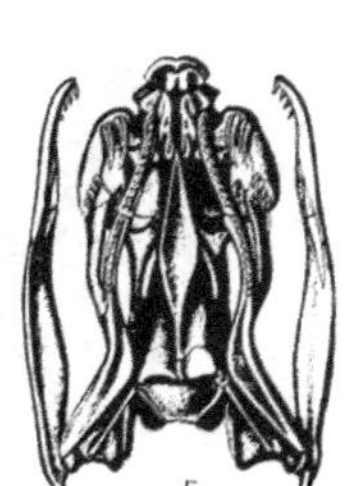

E

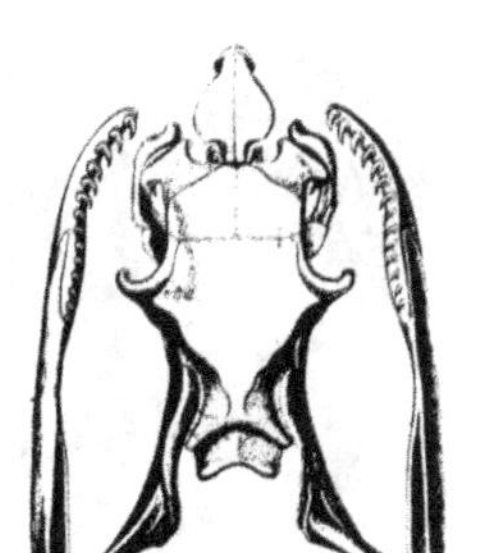

B

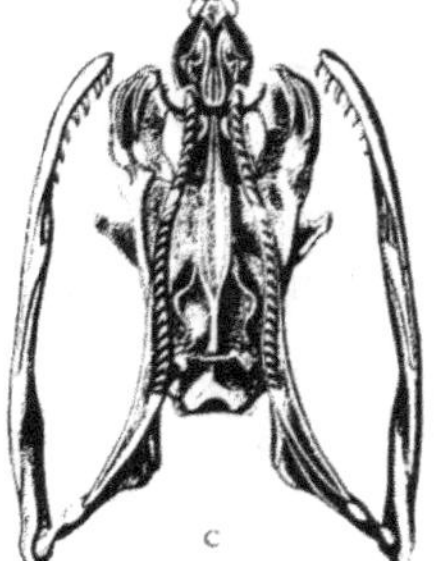

C

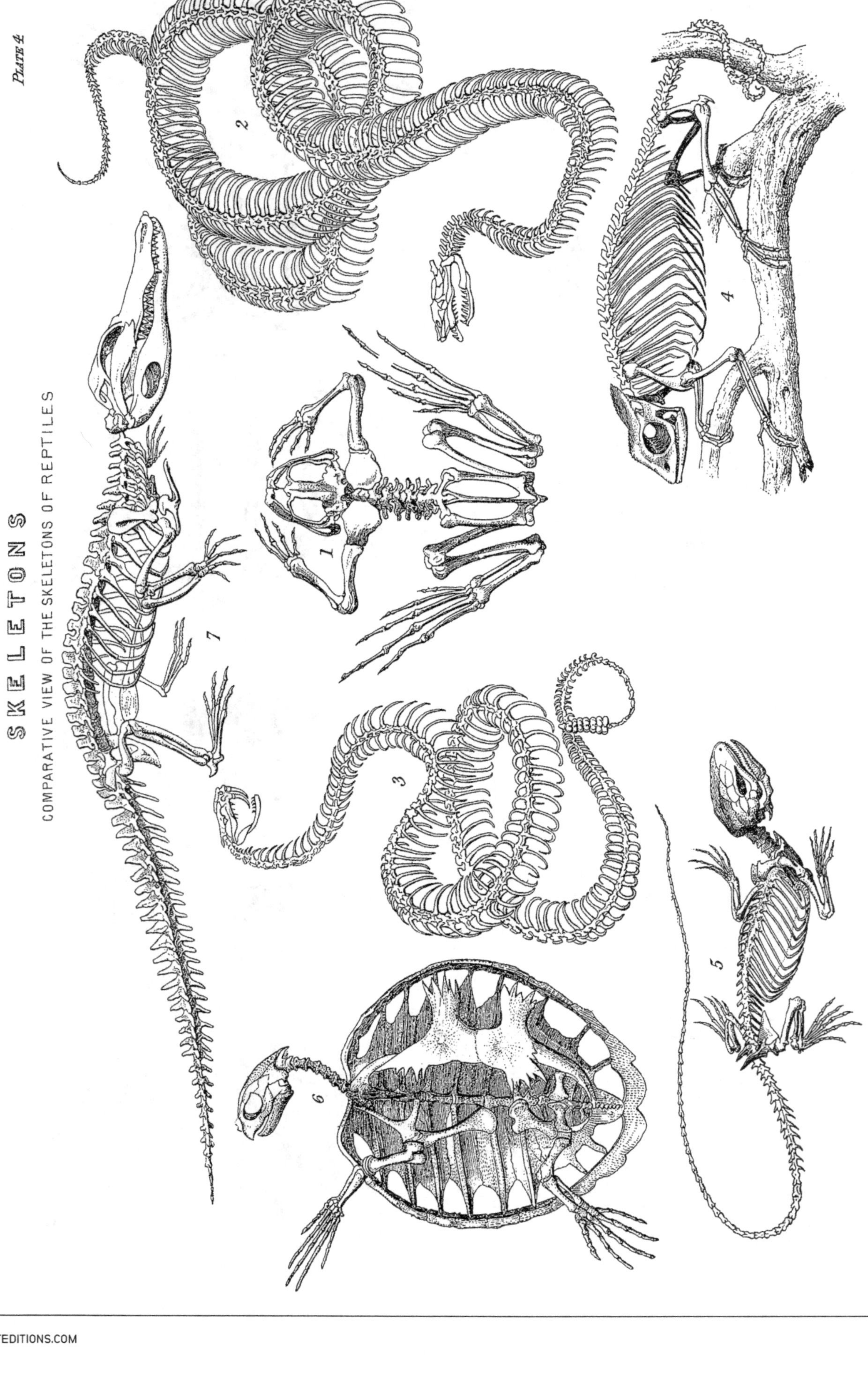

PLATE 4

SKELETONS

COMPARATIVE VIEW OF THE SKELETONS OF REPTILES

SKELETONS

COMPARATIVE VIEW OF THE SKELETONS OF BEASTS

Plate 2.

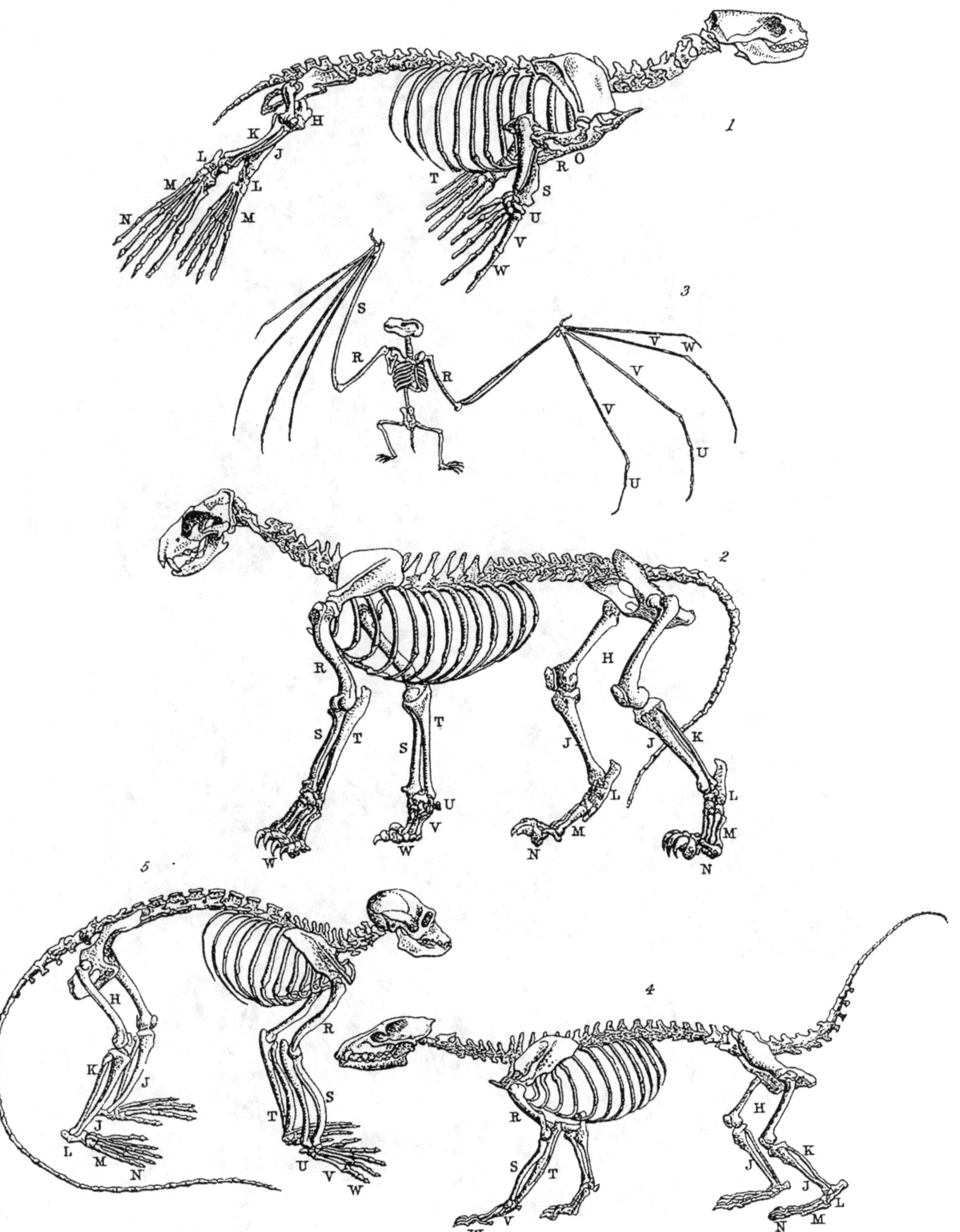

NOTE.—The Roman letters point to the corresponding part in each animal.

A114

Skeleton of a Rabbit, Mole, Armadillo and Cameleon, See
the System of Comparative Anatomy. Section 1.
Rabbit
Mole
Armadillo
Cameleon

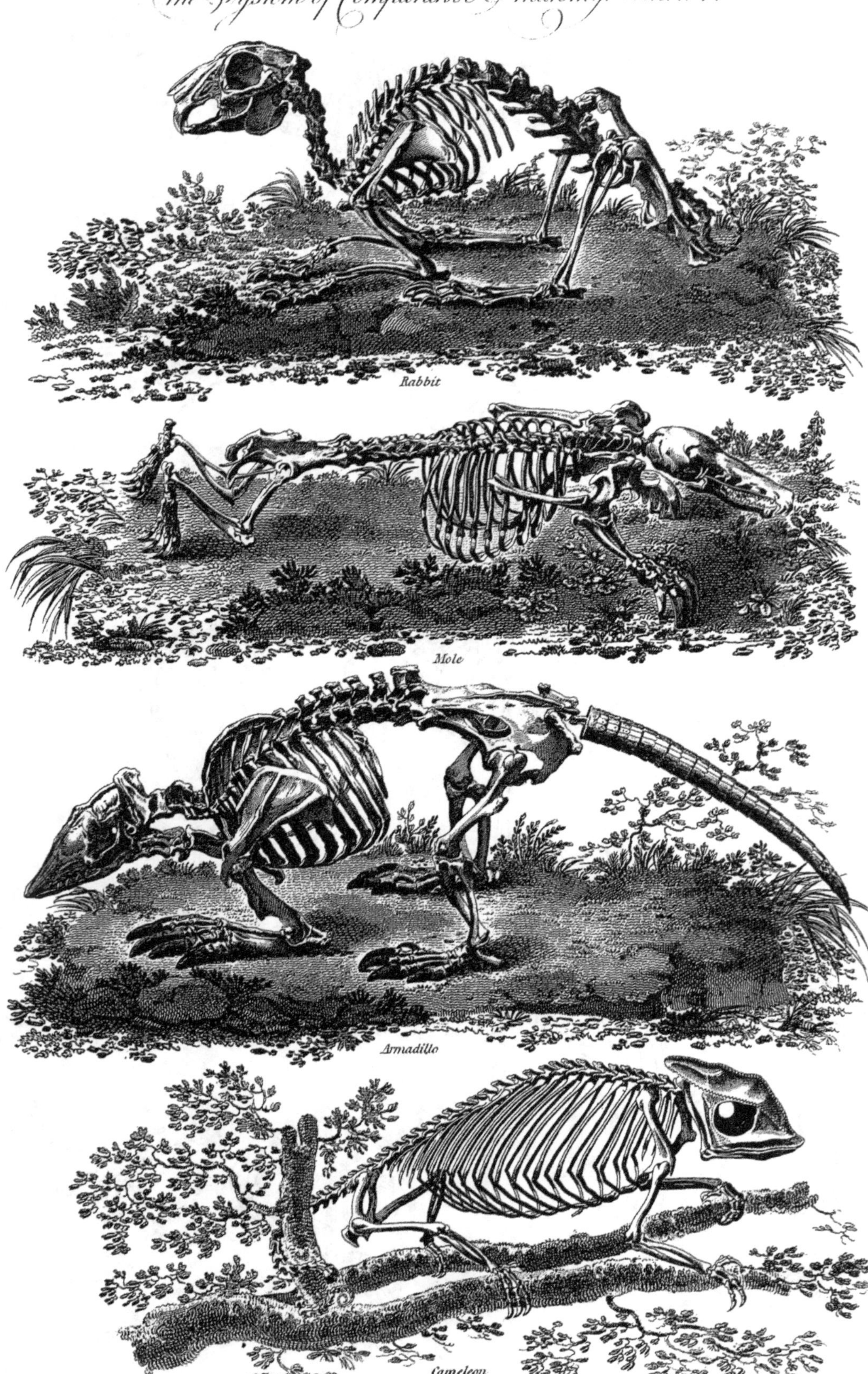

Skeleton of an Hedgehog, Lizard, Bat, Frog, Crocodile and Dog.
See the System of Comparative Anatomy.

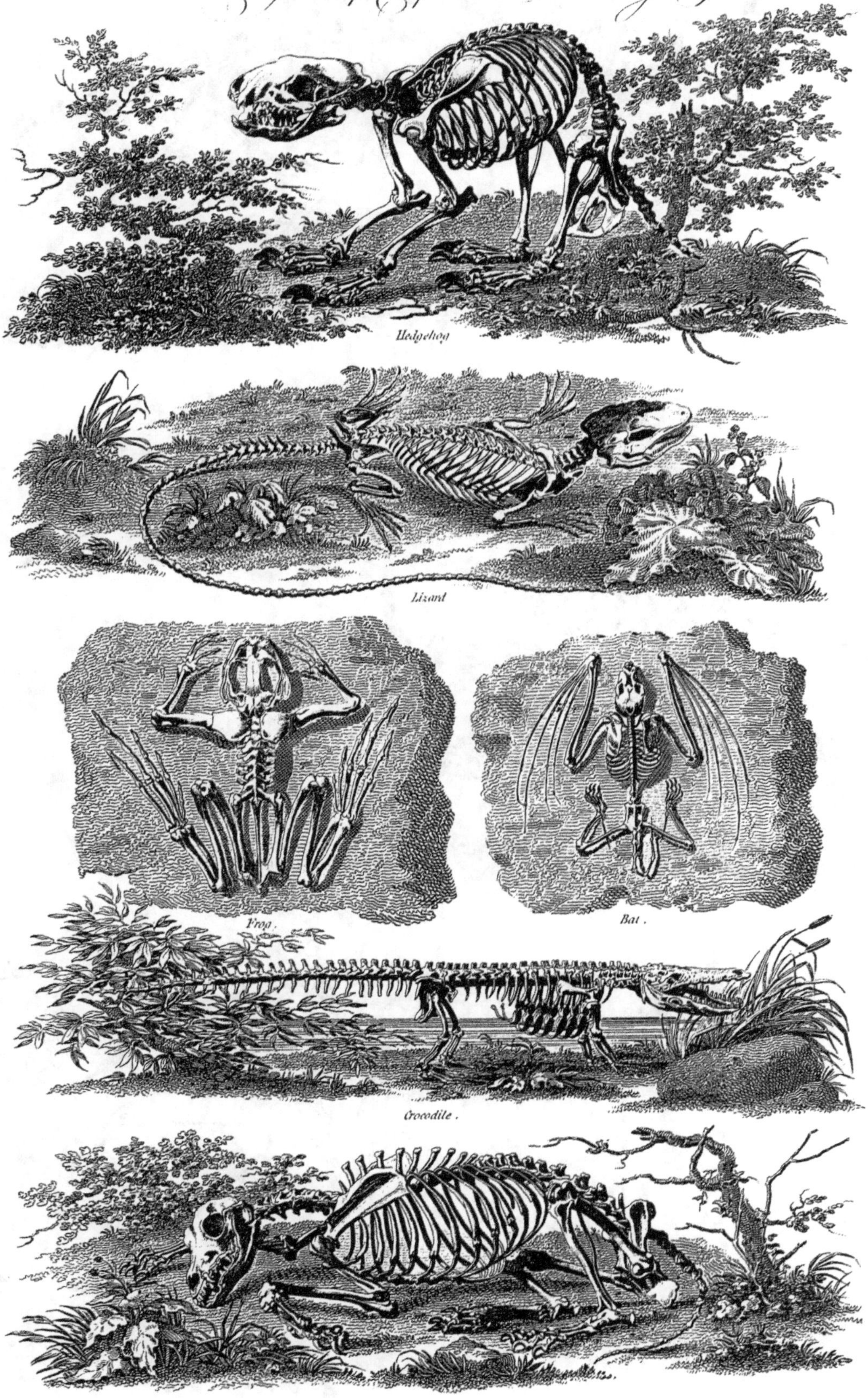

Hedgehog

Lizard

Frog .

Bat .

Crocodile .

Dog .

Engraved for the Royal Encyclopædia, & Published as the Act directs by C. Cooke, Nº 17, Paternoster Row, February 18ᵗʰ 1791.

A116

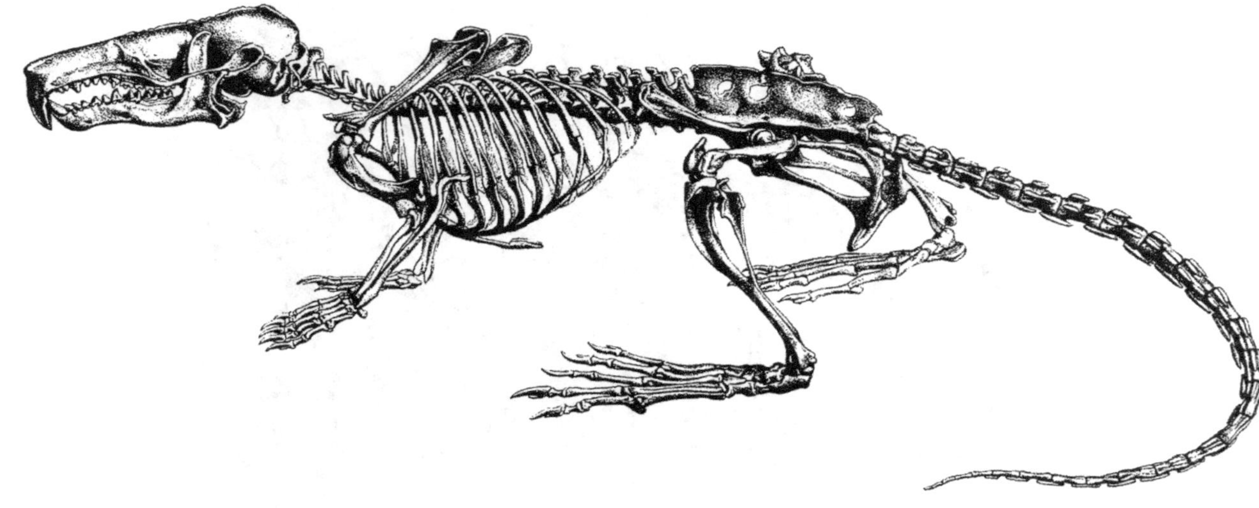

A117

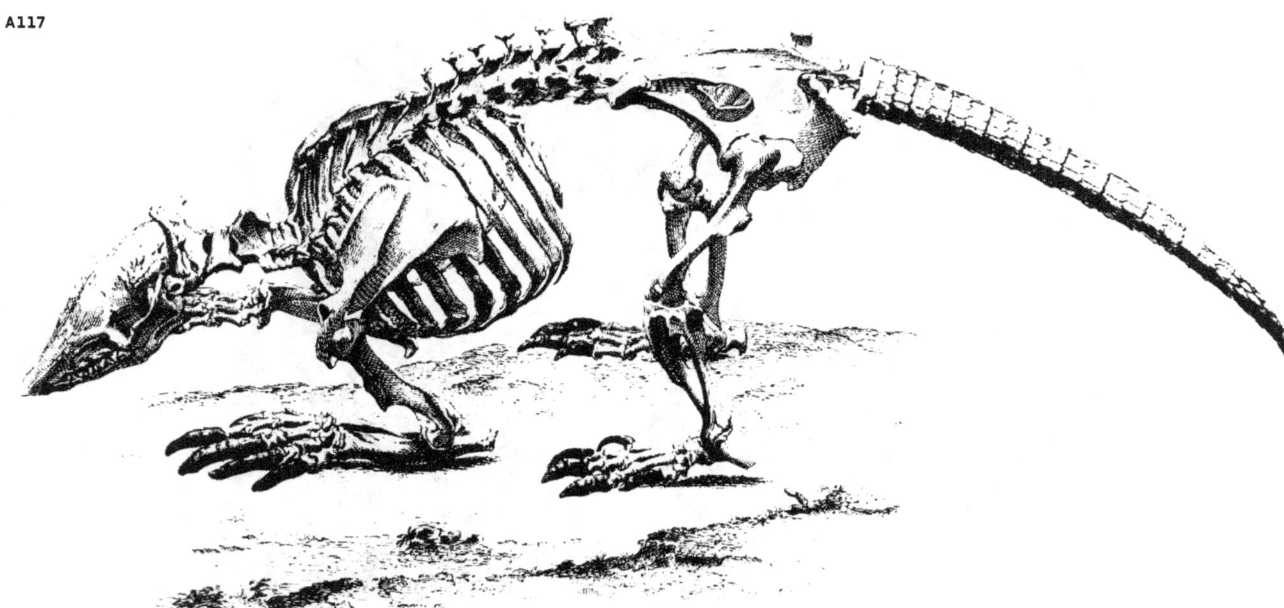

A118

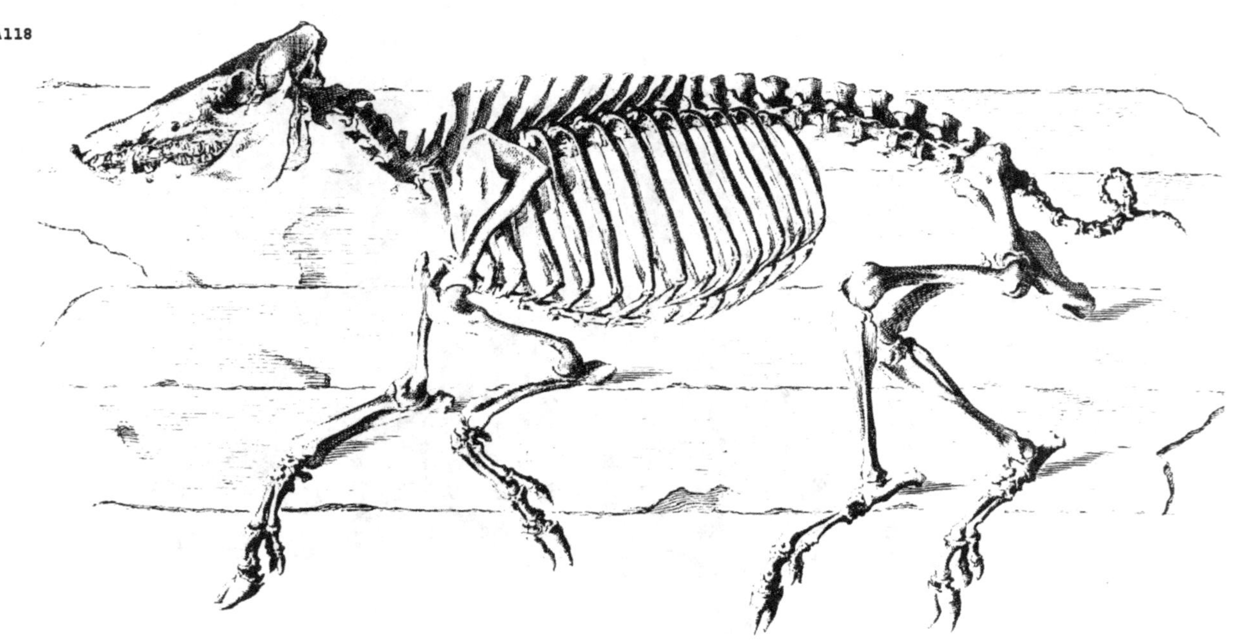

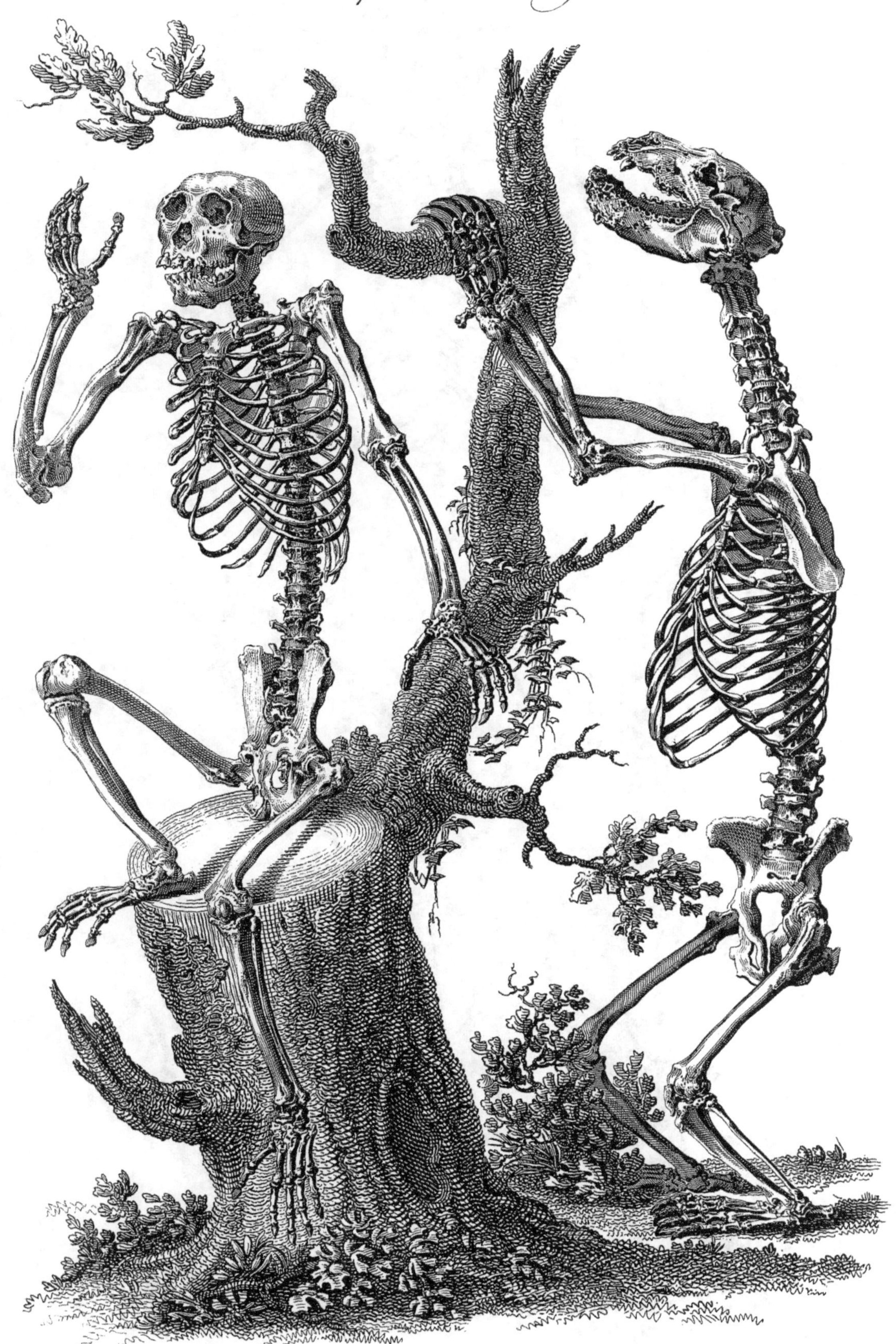

Skeleton of a Bear & Monkey
See Comparative Anatomy.

A120

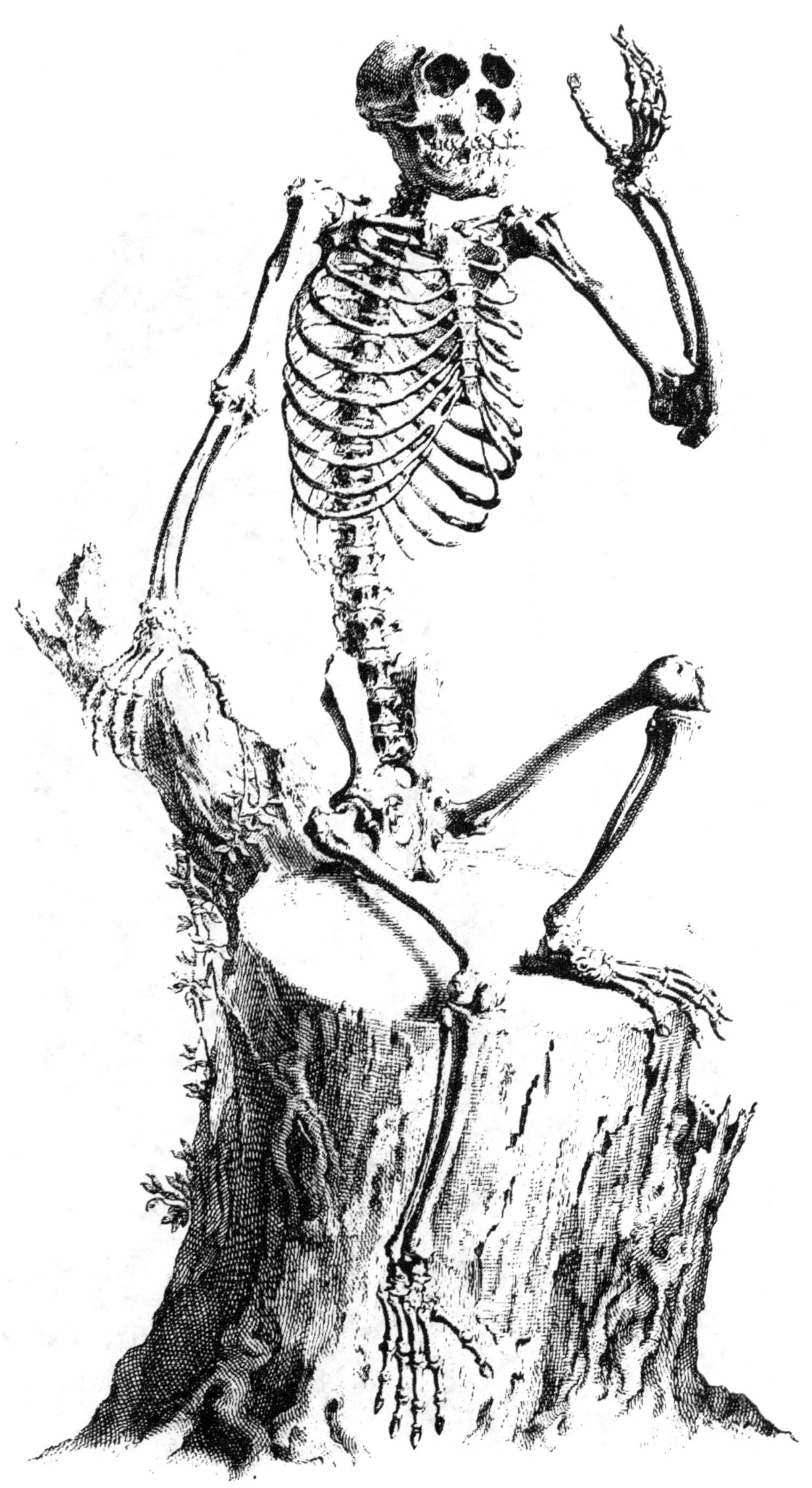

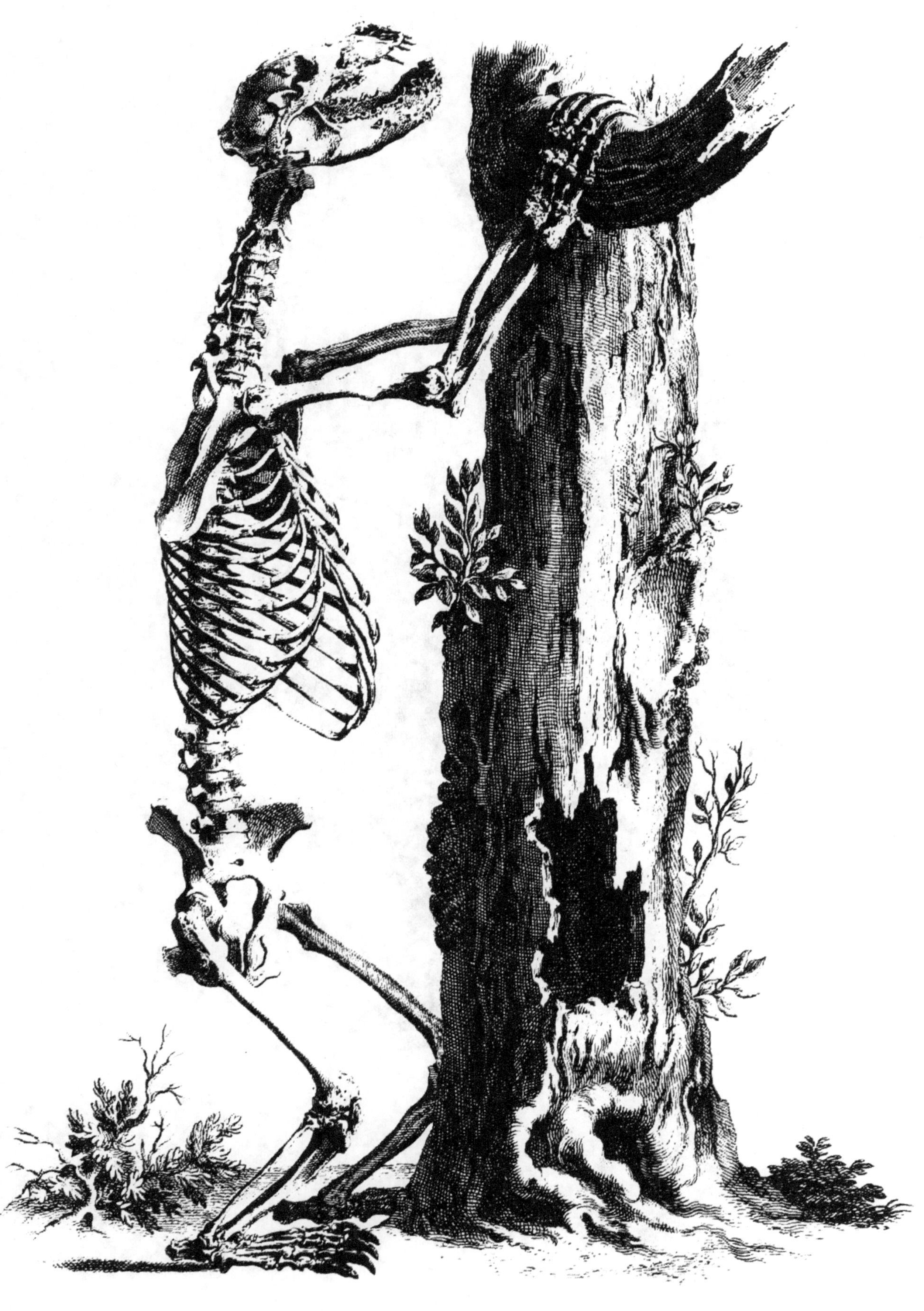

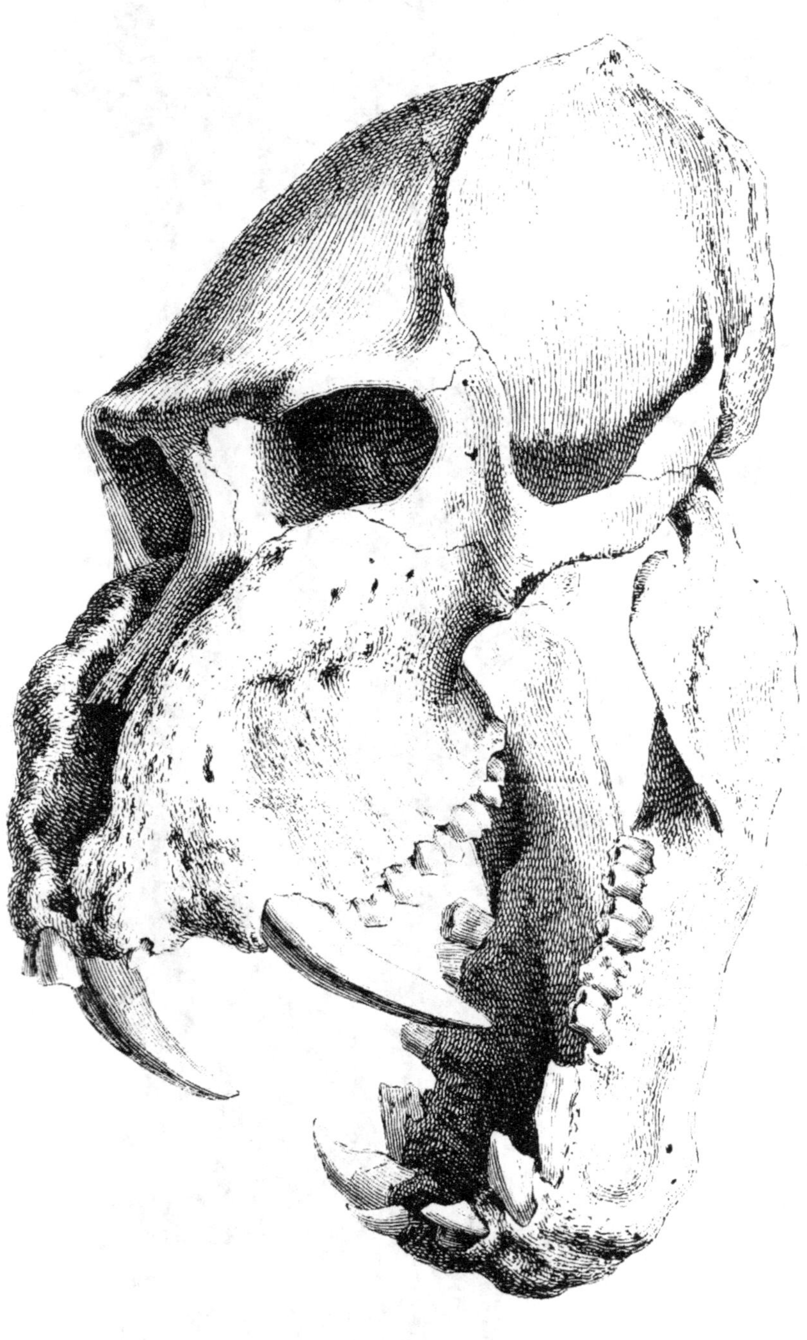

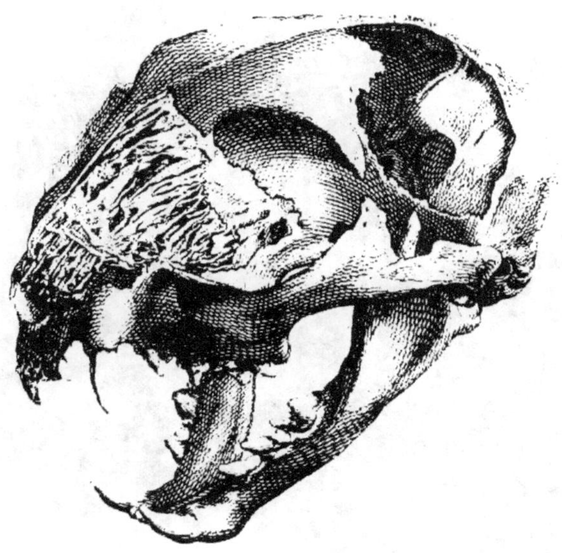

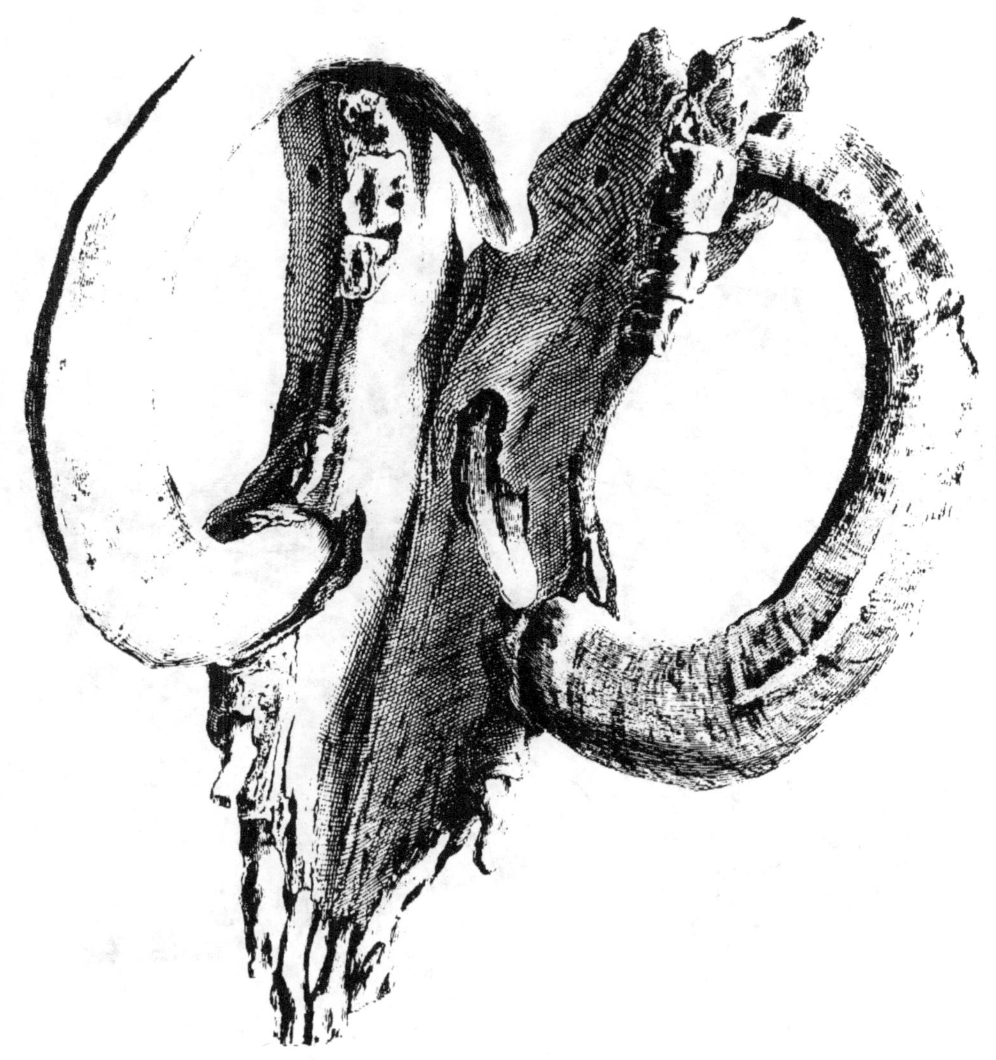

A124

COMPARATIVE ANATOMY.
PL. LXVII.
Skeleton of a Crocodile
Viscera of Female Round Shark.
Drawn from Life by J. Edwards.
London, Published by Geo. Kearsley, Fleet Street, Feb. 1, 1809.

A125

COMPARATIVE ANATOMY.
PL. LXVI.
Porpoise Viscera & Skeleton.
London, Publd. by Geo. Kearsley, Fleet Street, Aug. 1, 1809.

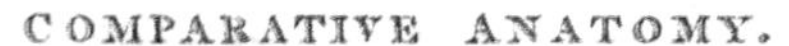

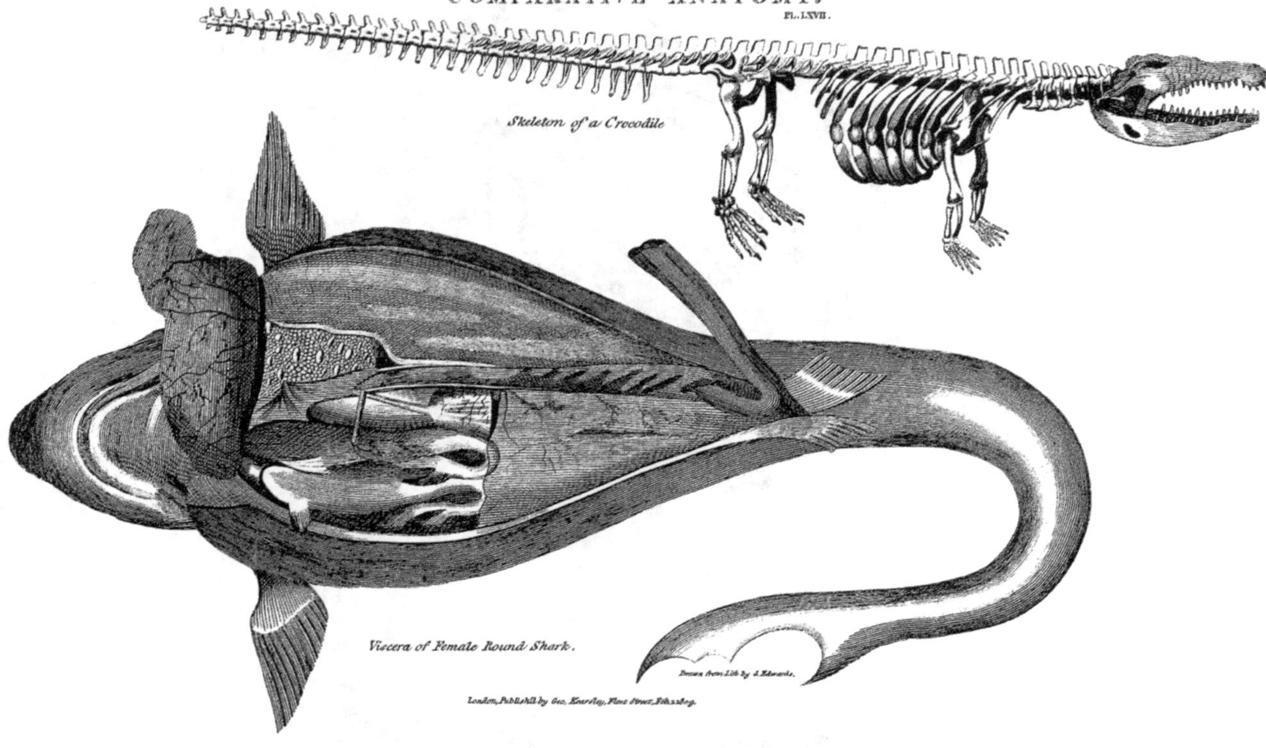

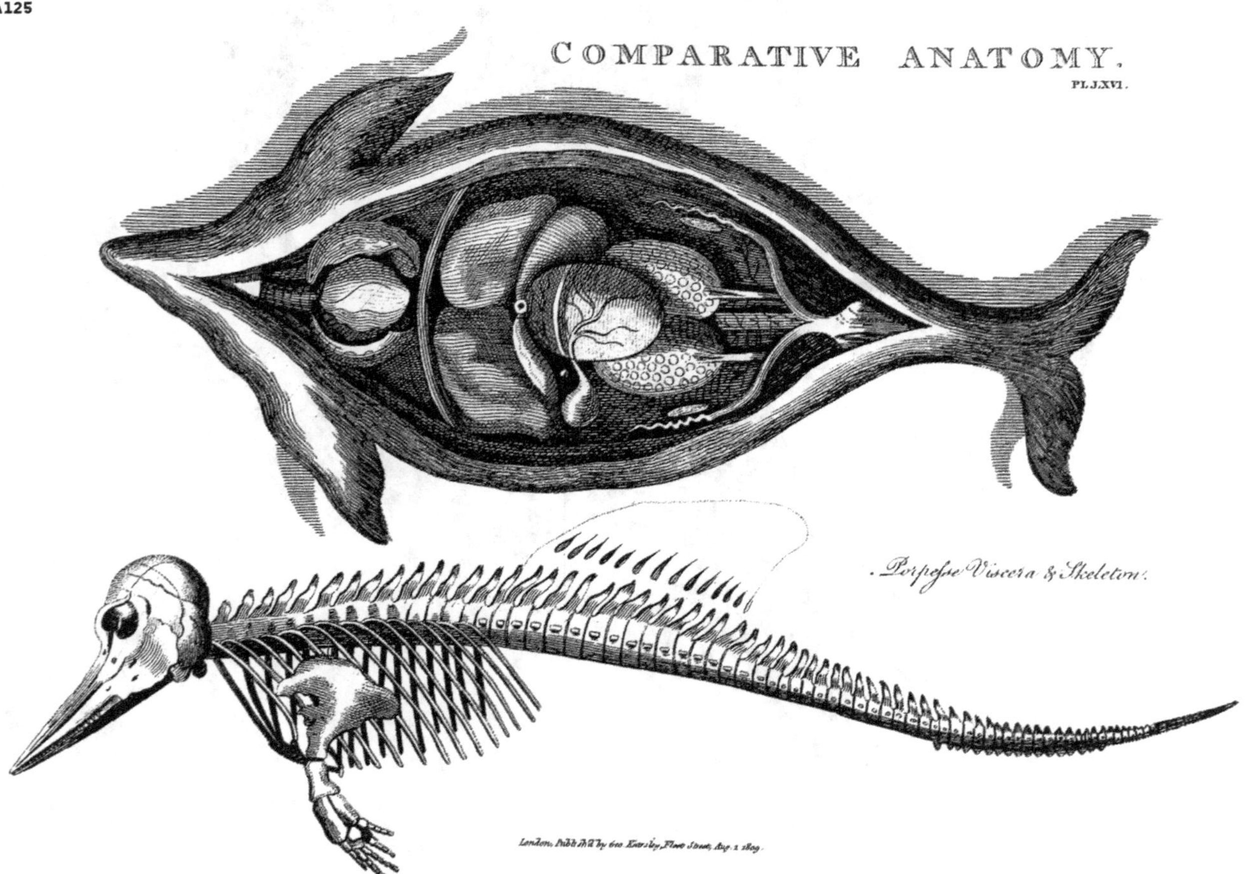

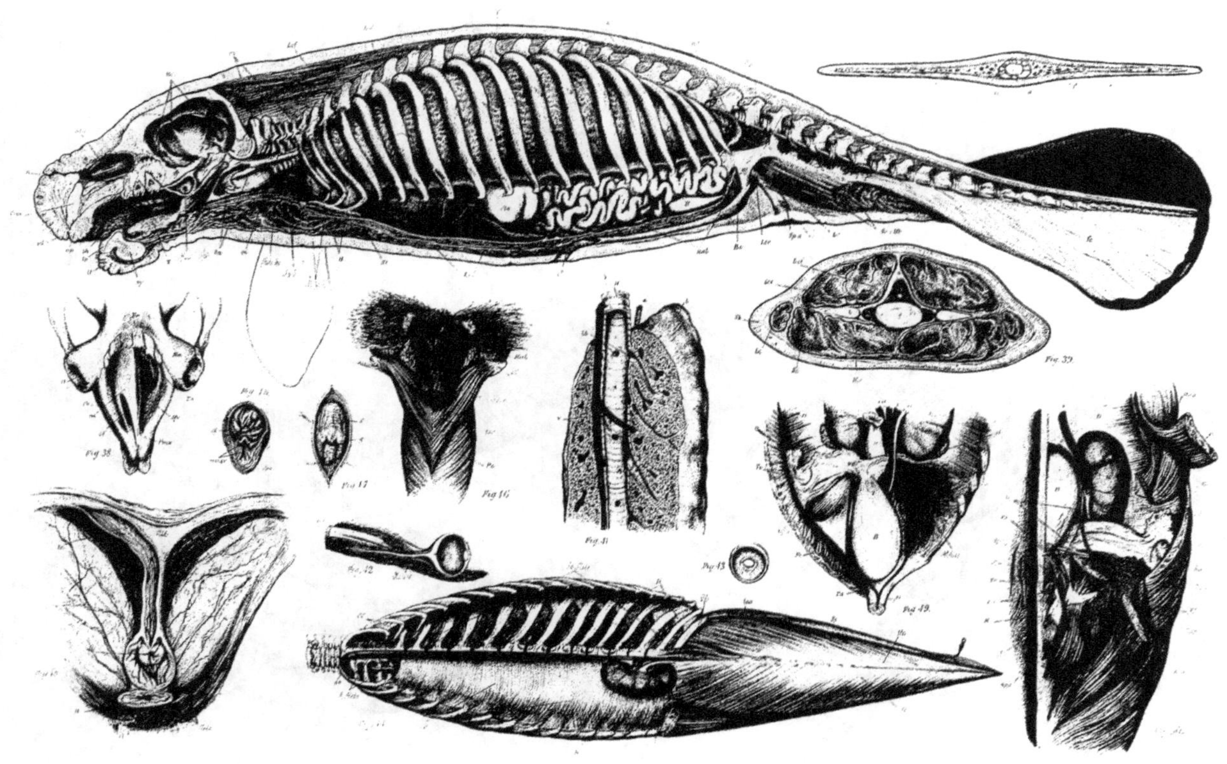

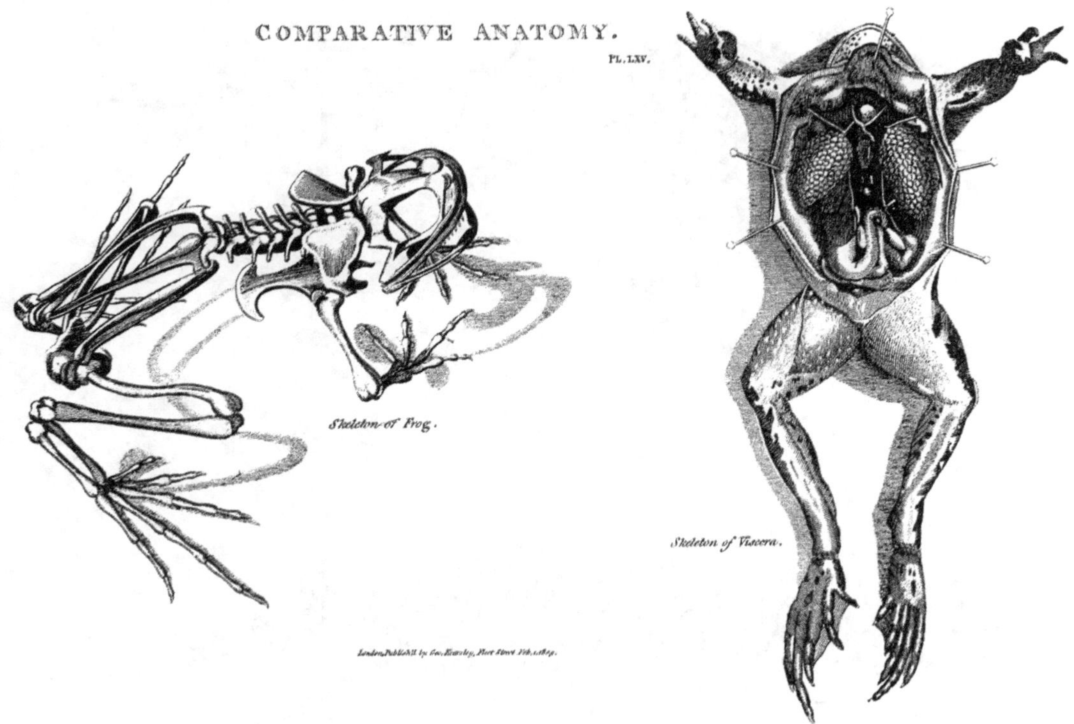
COMPARATIVE ANATOMY.
PL. LXV.
Skeleton of Frog.
Skeleton of Viscera.

A128

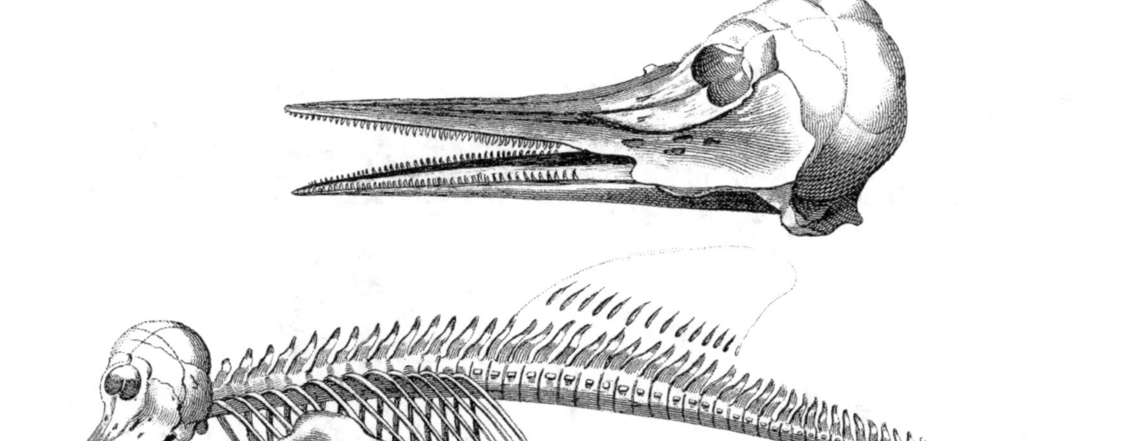

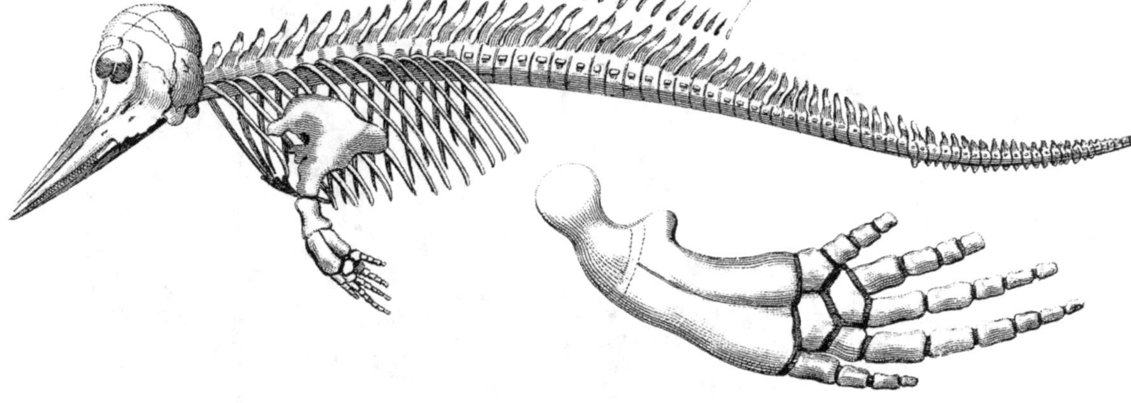

A129

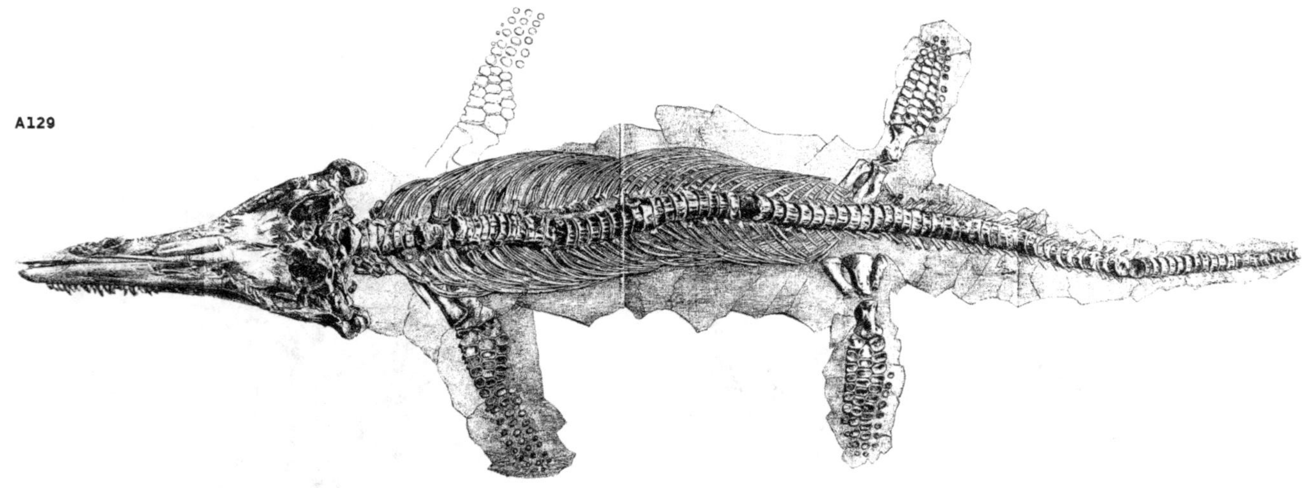

A130

A131

A132

A134

A133

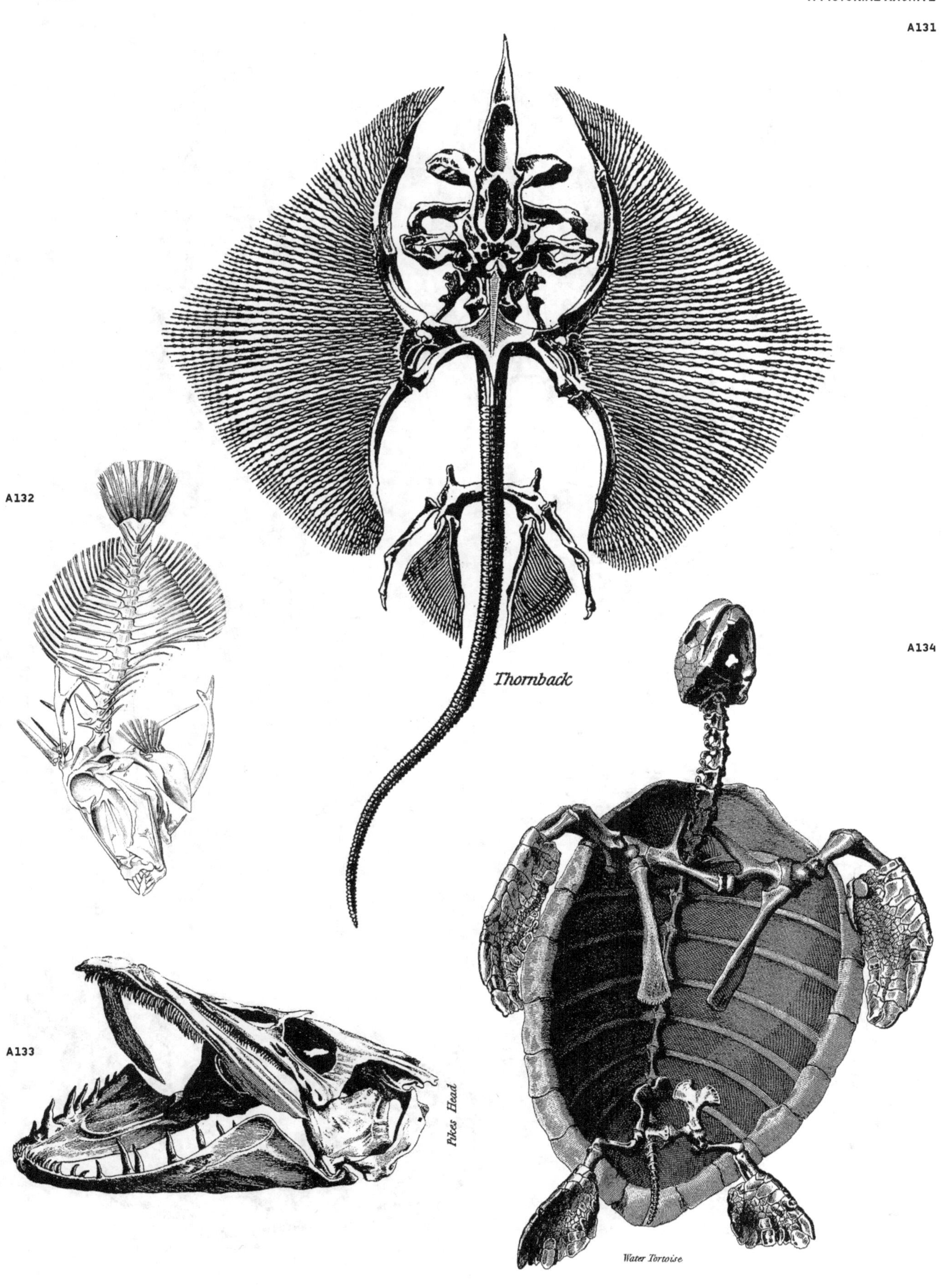

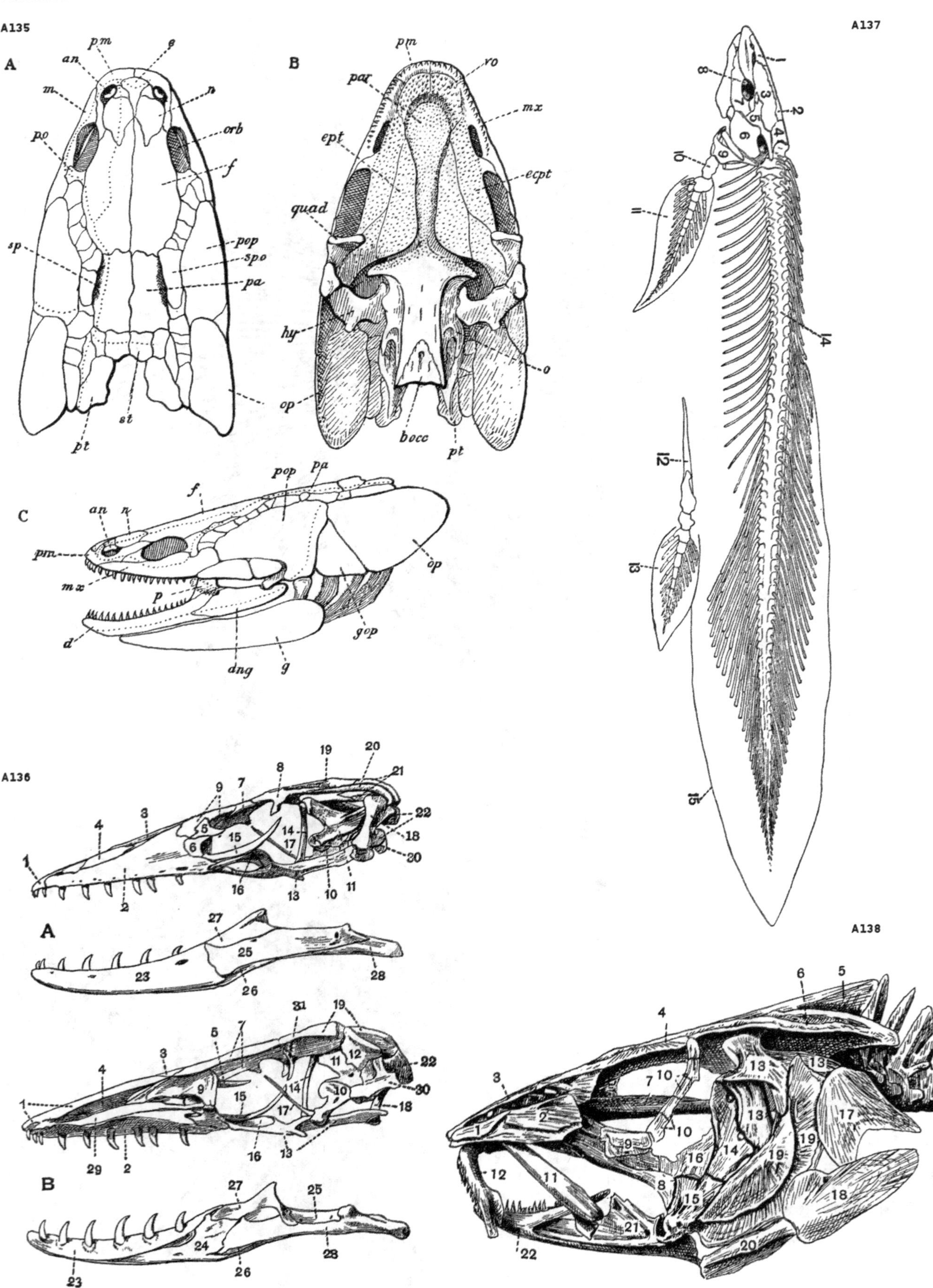
A135
A
pm
an
m
e
n
po
orb
f
sp
pop
spo
pa
st
pt
B
pm
par
ro
ept
mx
quad
ecpt
hy
o
op
bocc
pt
C
an
n
f
pop
pa
pm
mx
op
d
p
dng
g
gop
A136
A
4
3
1
9
7
8
5
6
15
19
20
21
22
18
20
14
17
16
13
10
11
2
27
25
23
26
28
B
3
4
5
7
31
19
11
12
22
30
18
9
14
15
17
16
13
1
29
2
27
25
24
23
26
28
A137
8
7
3
1
2
5
6
4
10
9
11
14
12
13
15
A138
6
5
4
3
13
7
10
13
18
2
1
9
10
14
17
16
19
12
11
8
15
18
21
22
20

A139

A143

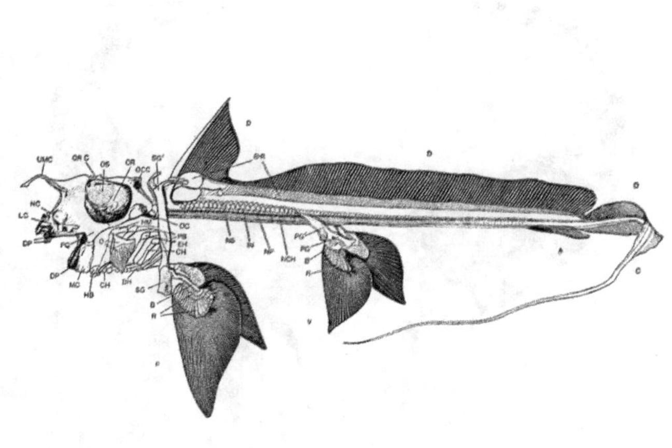

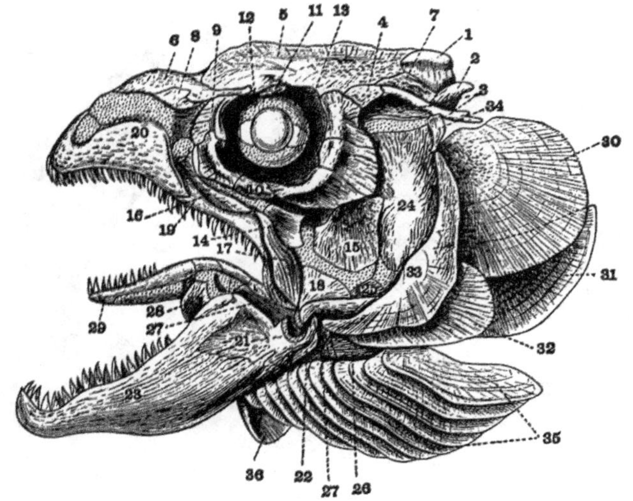

A140

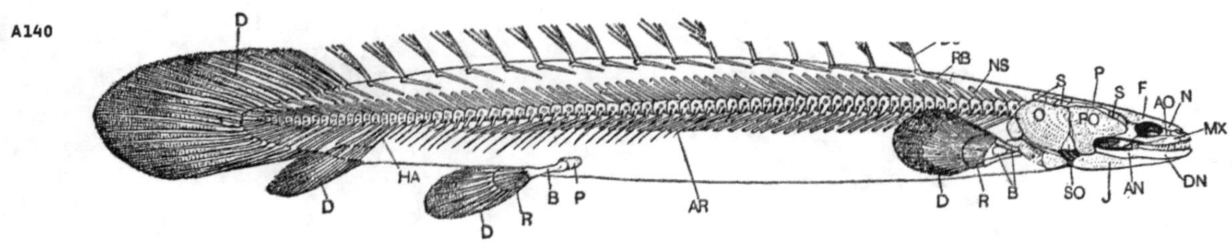

A141

A144

A145

A142

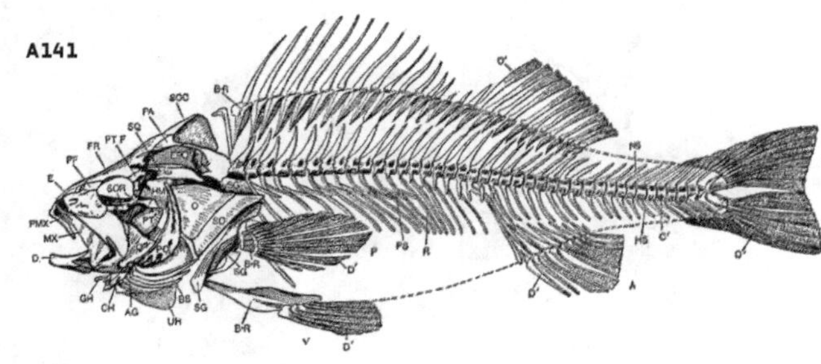

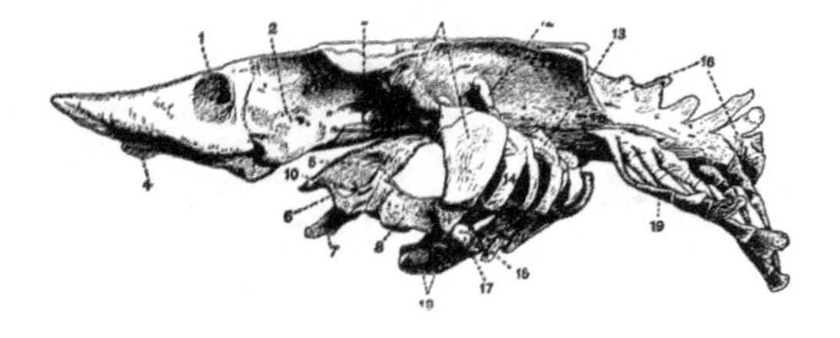

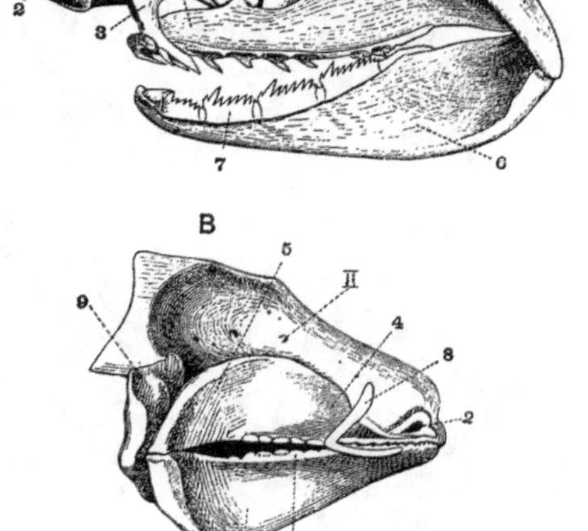

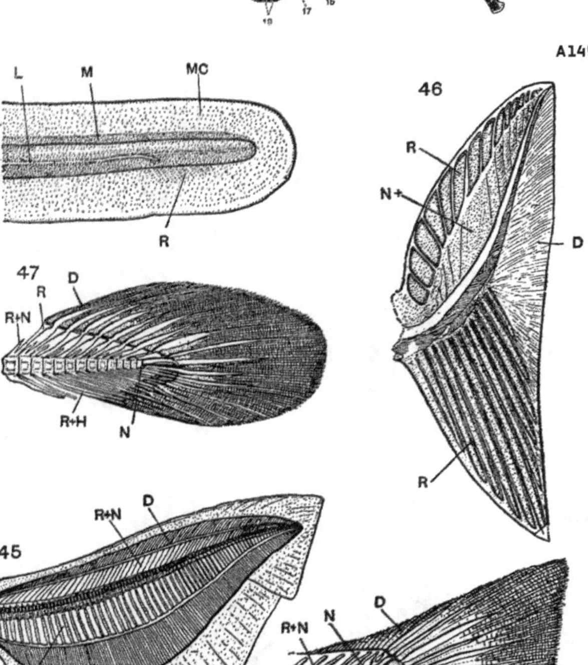

A146

A150

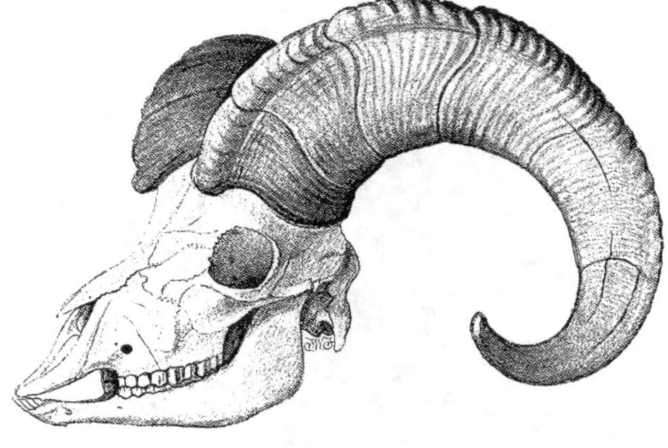

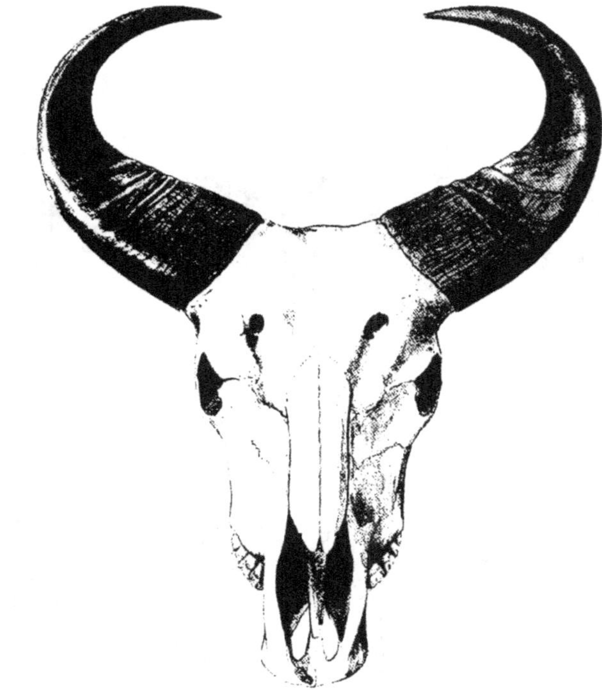

A147

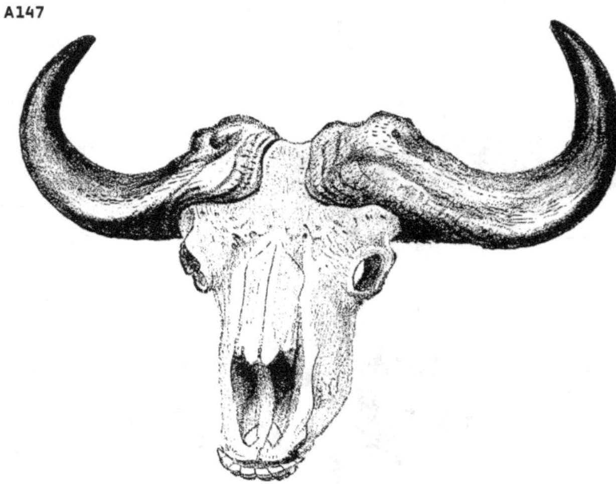

A151

A148

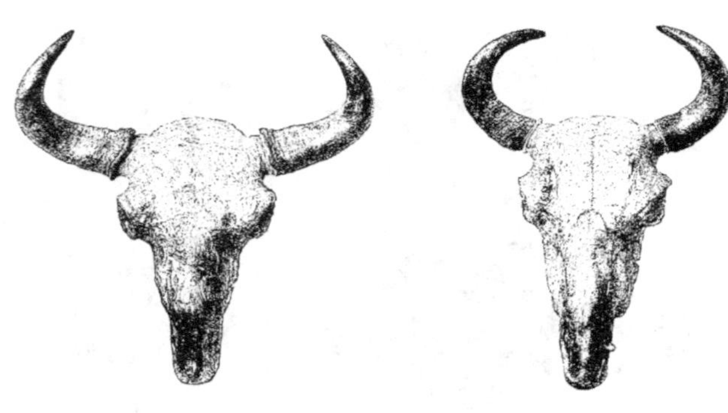

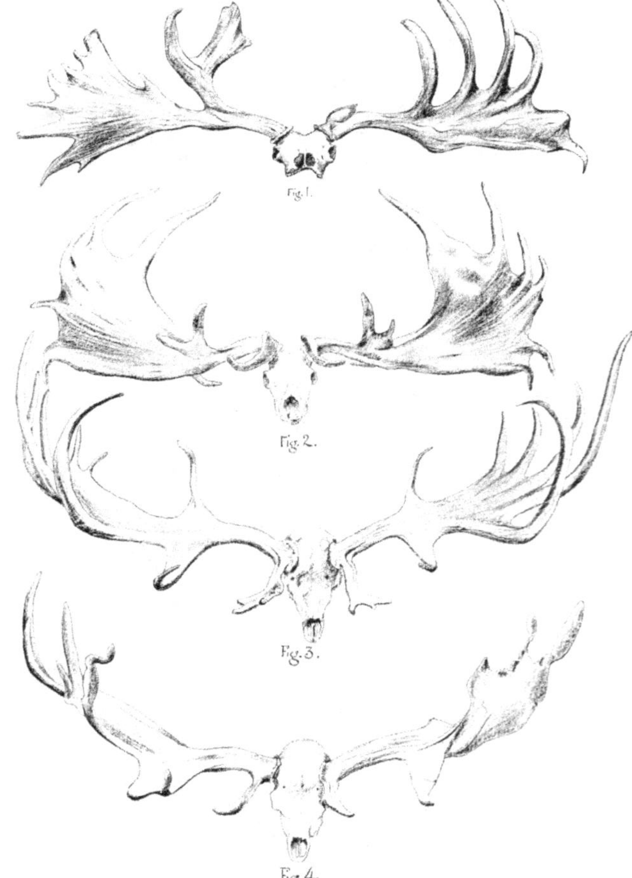

A149

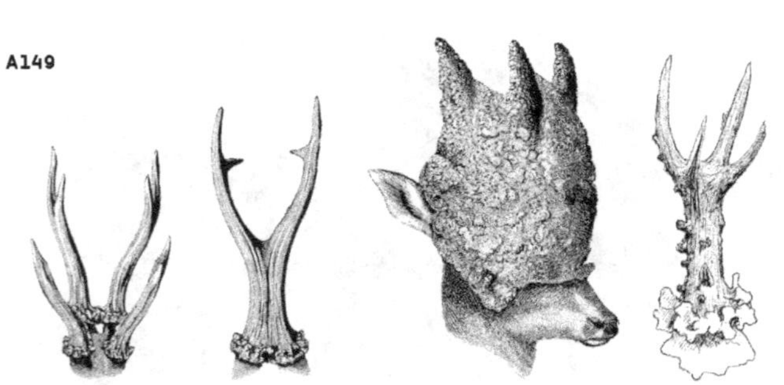

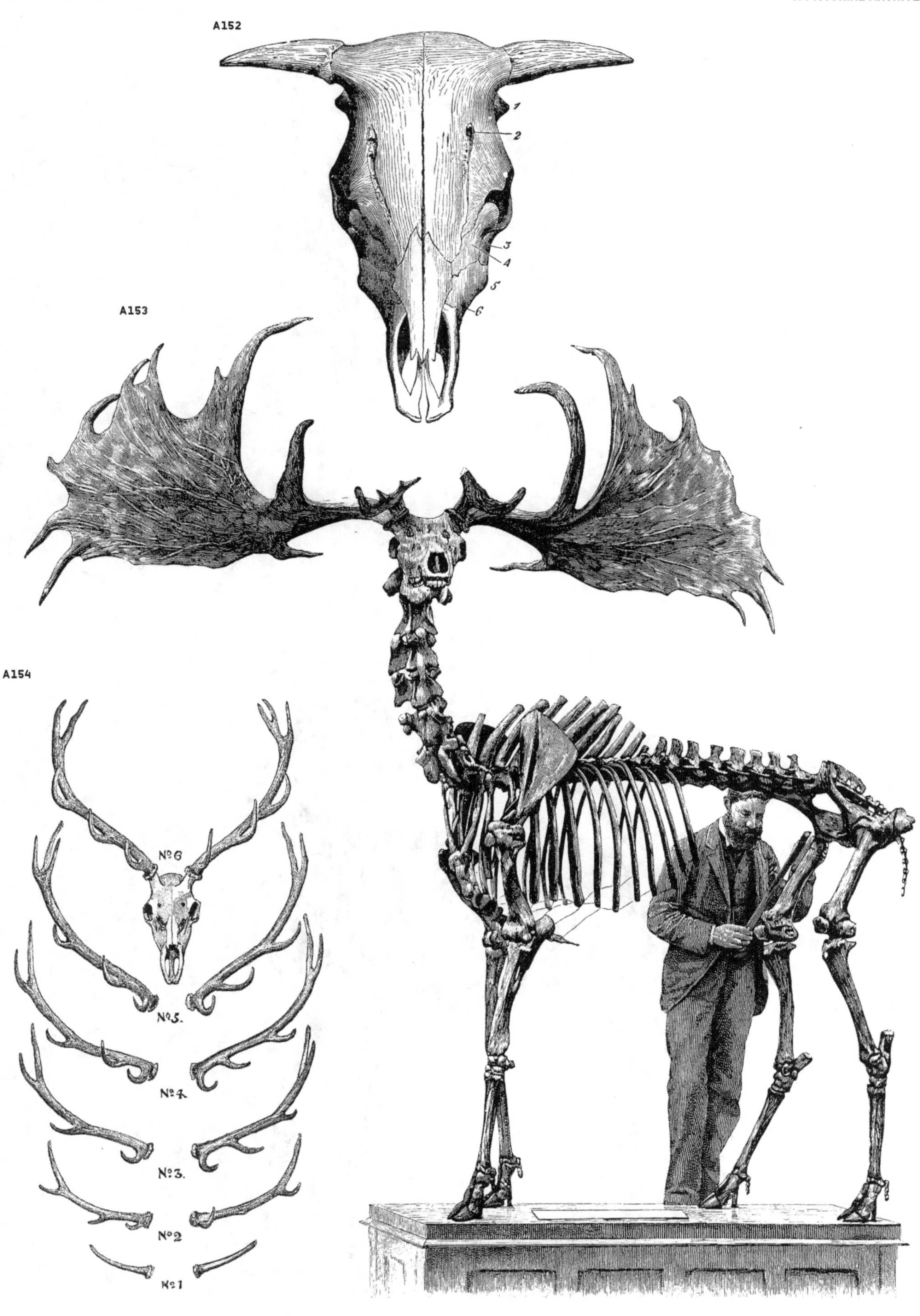
A152
1
2
3
4
5
6
A153
A154
NºG
Nº5.
Nº4.
Nº3.
Nº2
Nº1

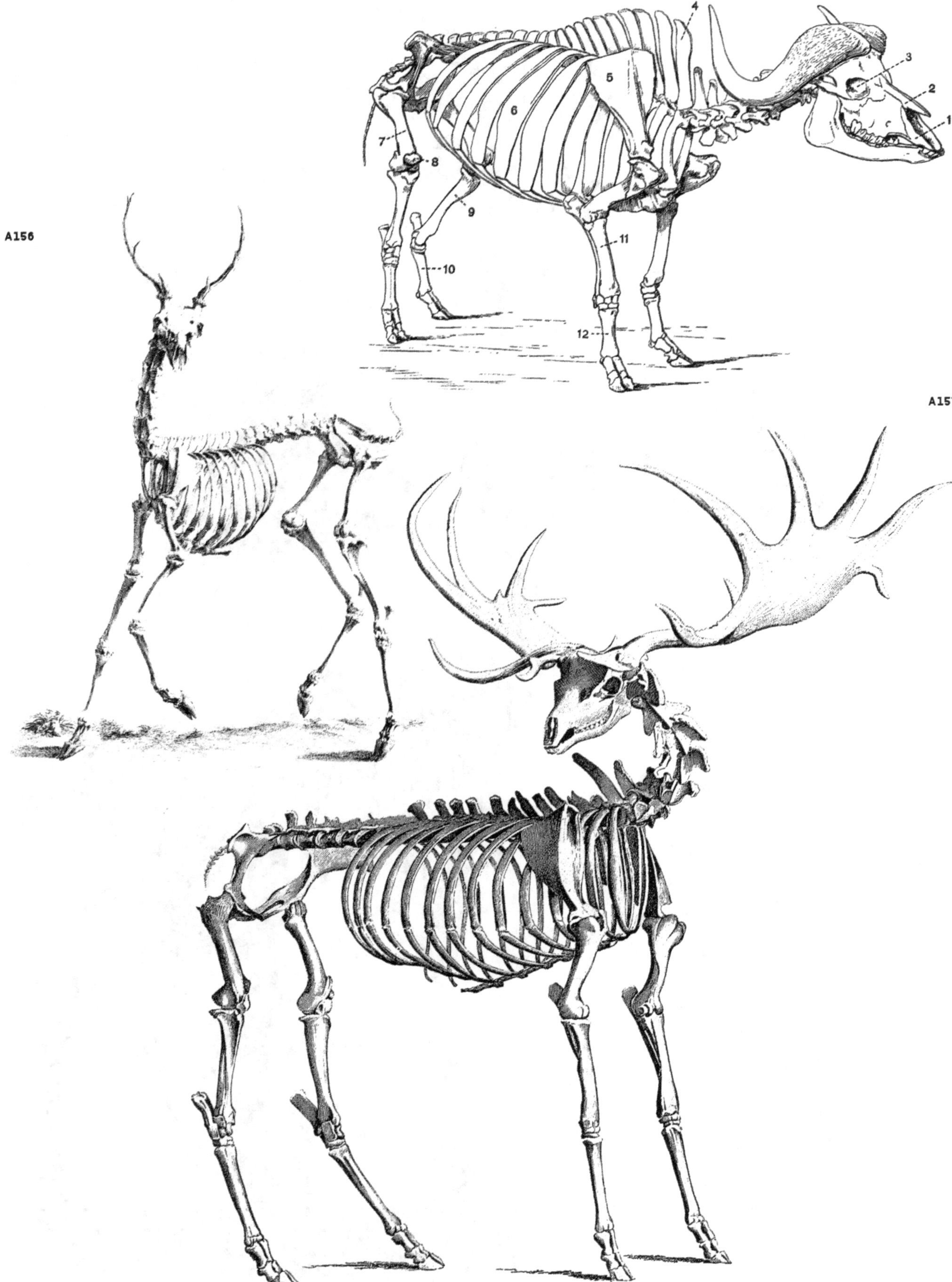
A155
A156
A157
1
2
3
4
5
6
7
8
9
10
11
12

A158

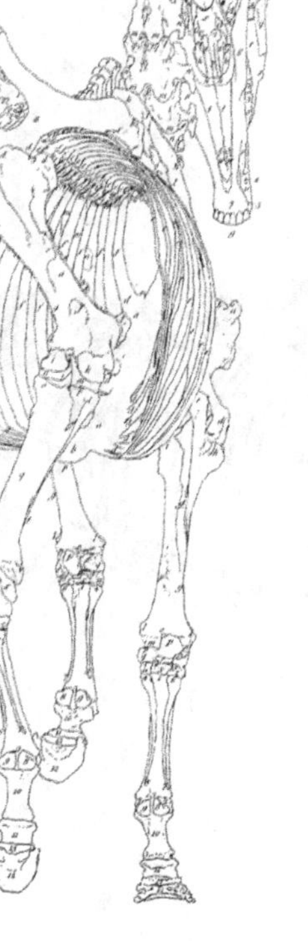 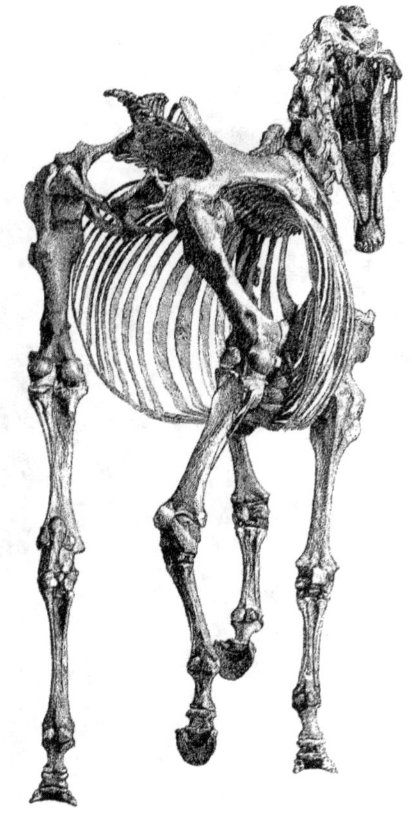

A159

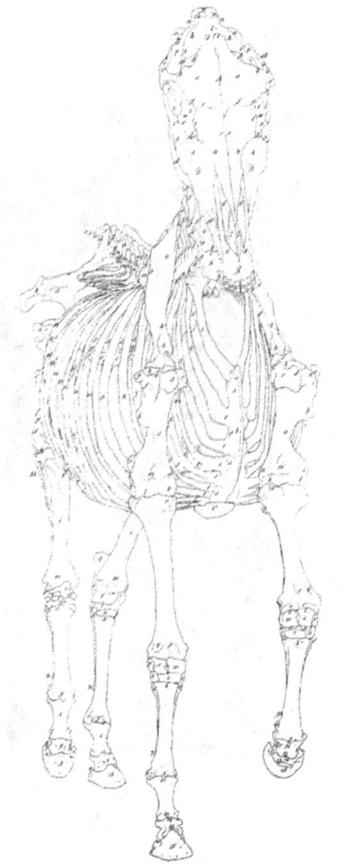 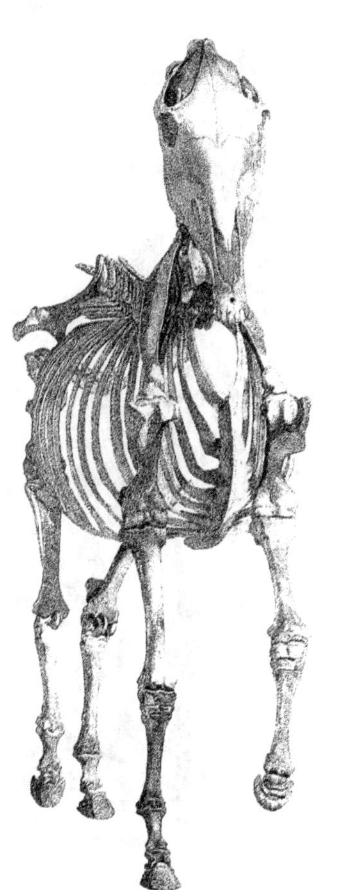

A160

Anatomy of the Horse, representing the Osteology in three Views.
See System of Farriery.
Fig.1
Fig.1 Side View of the Skeleton.
Fig.2
Fig.3
Fig.2 Front View of the Skeleton.
Fig.3 Back View of the Skeleton.
Plate 1

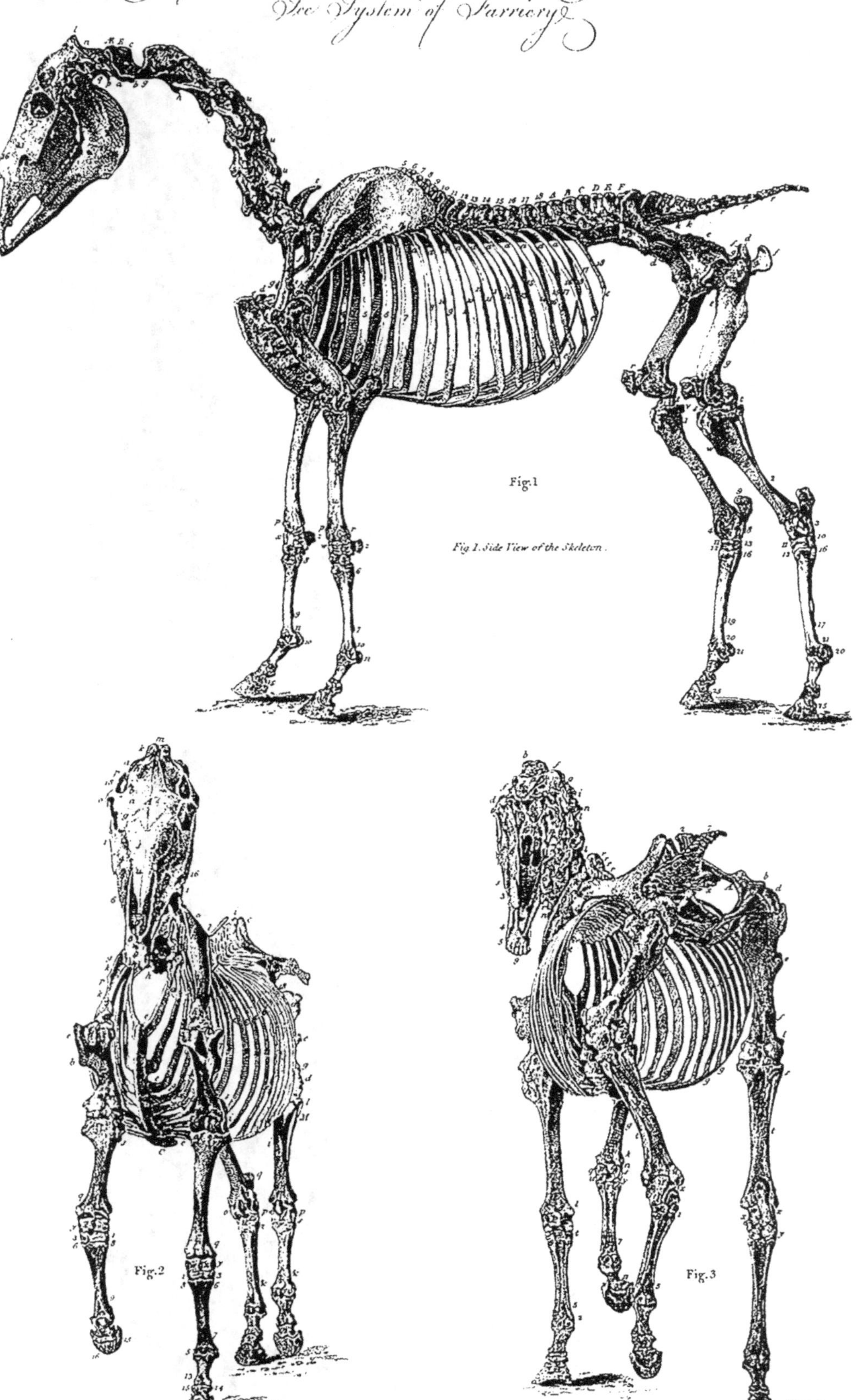

A161

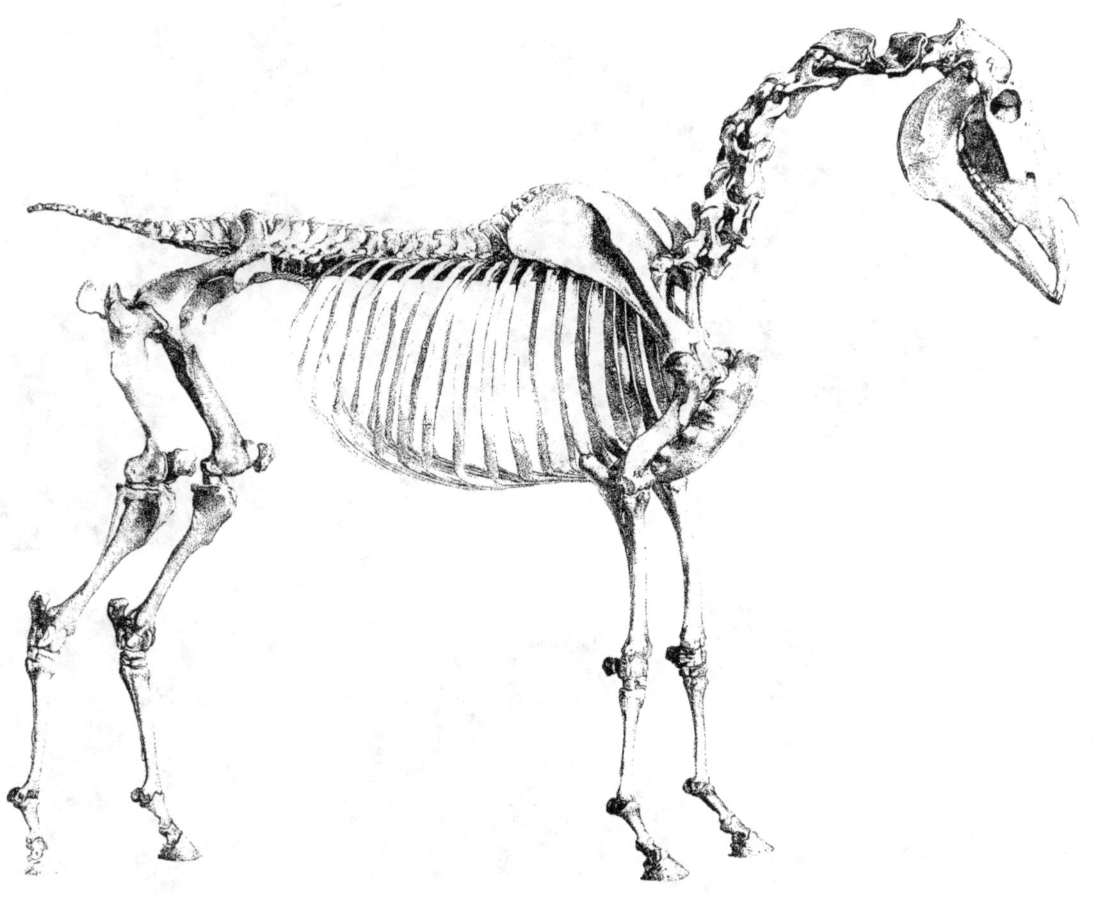

A162

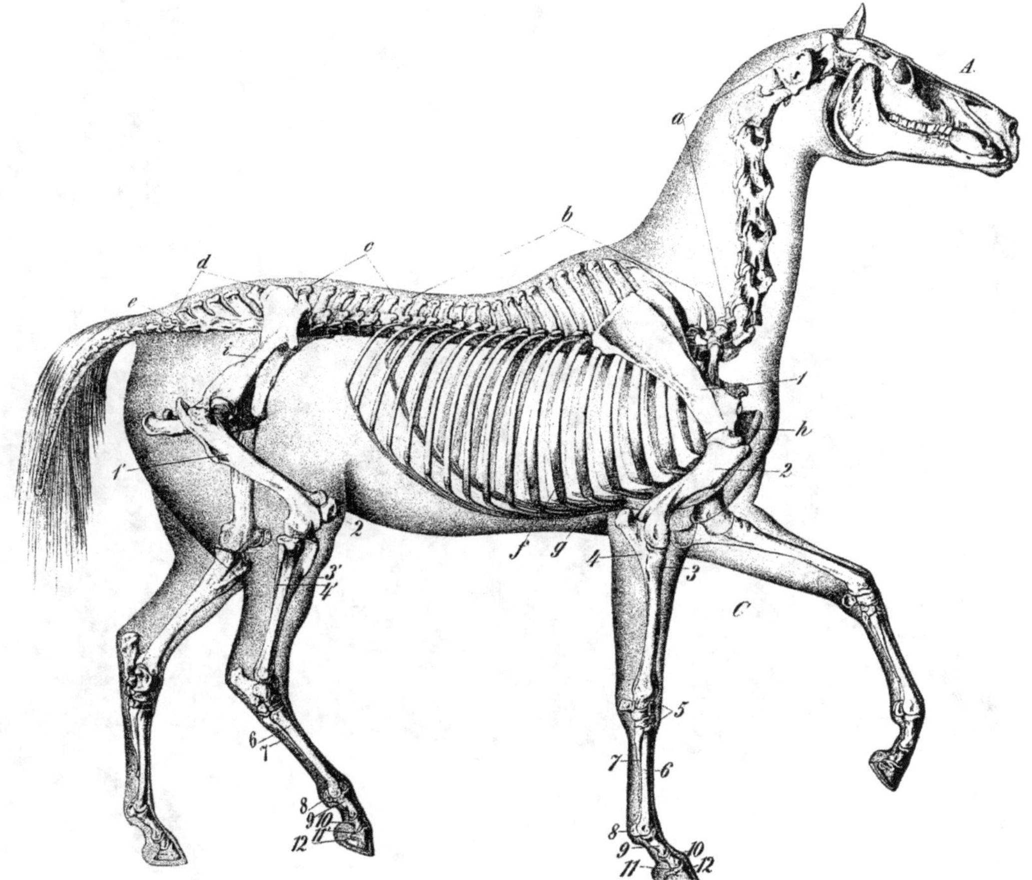

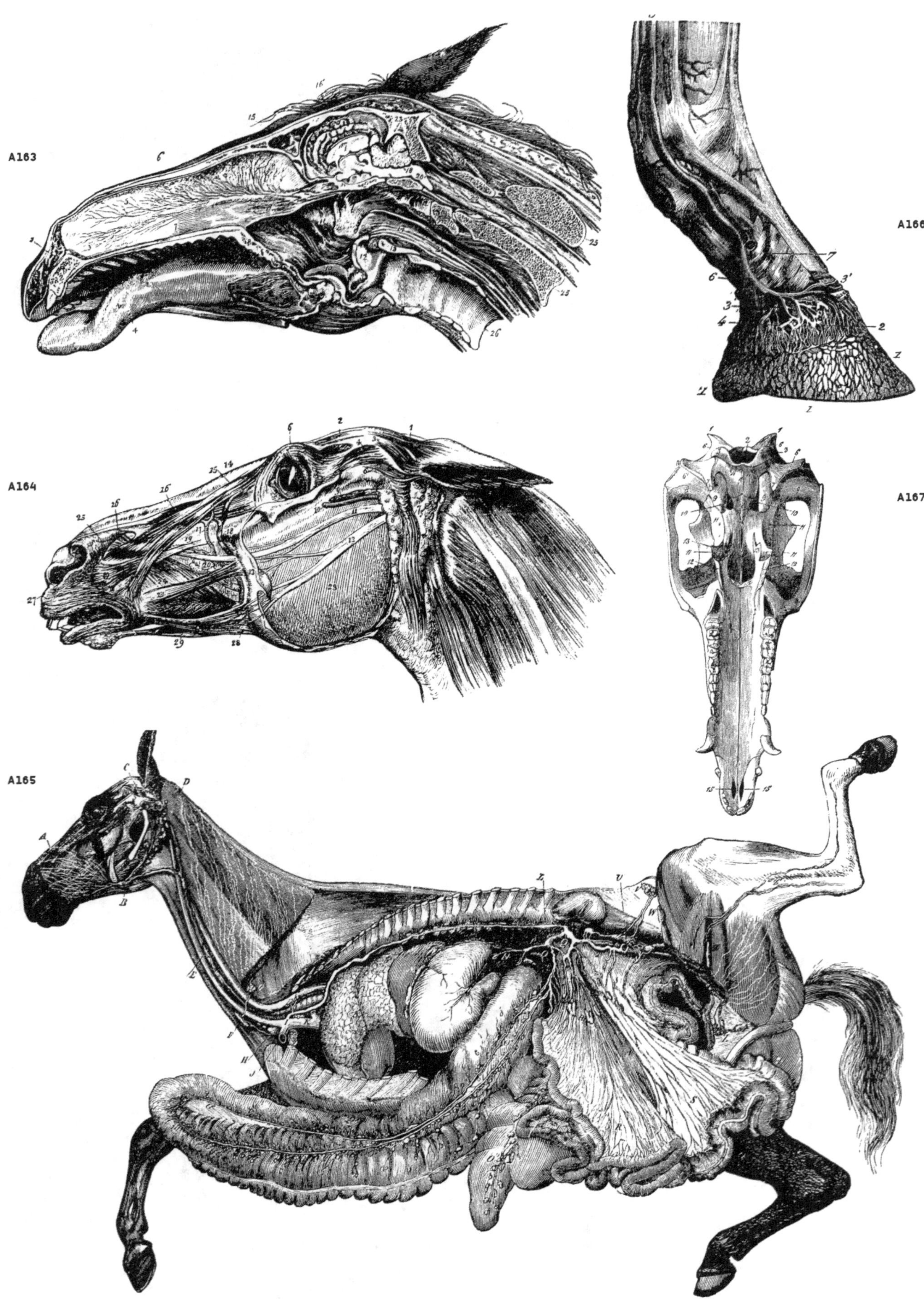

A163

A164

A165

A166

A167

A168

A171

A169

A172

A170

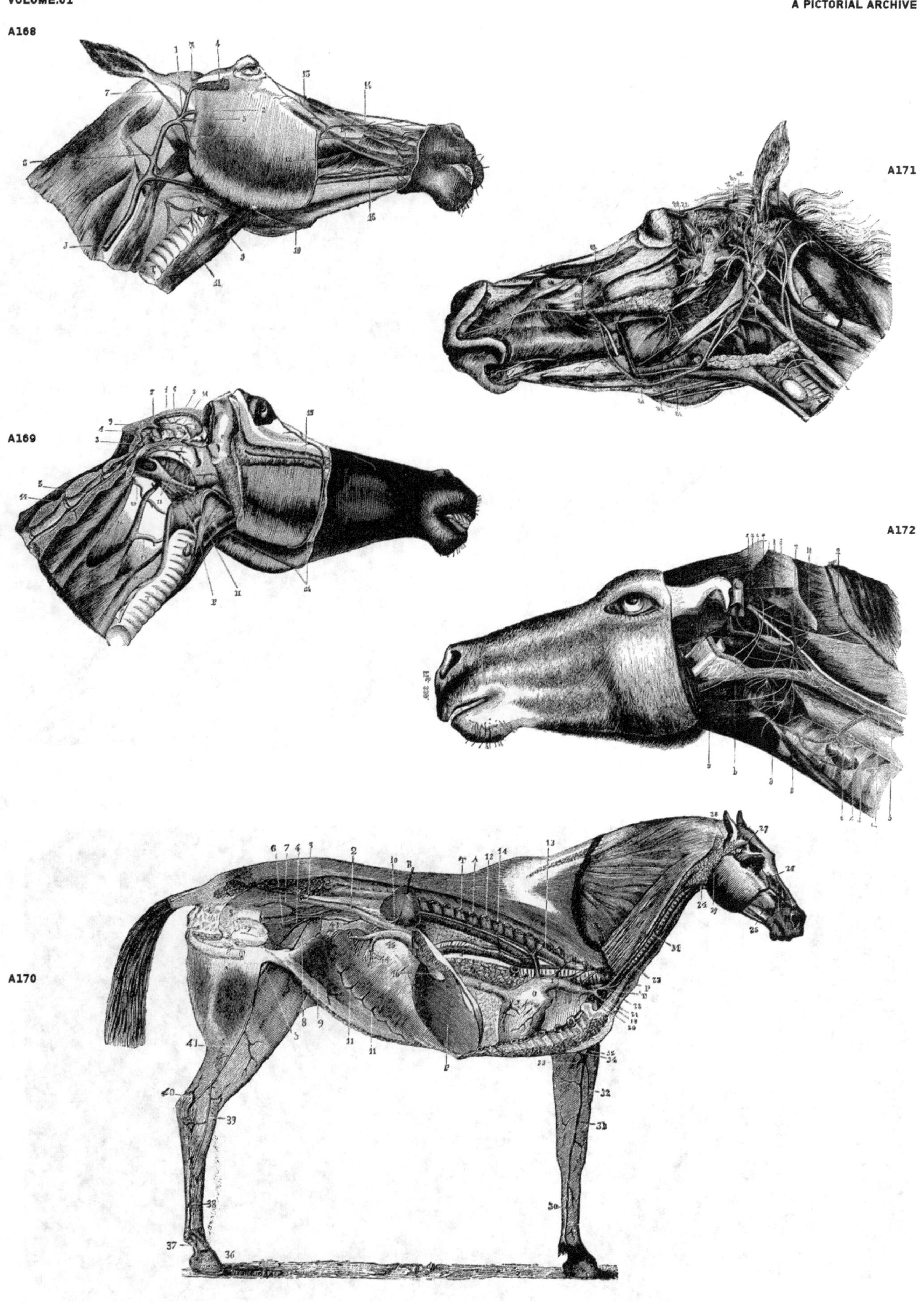

A173

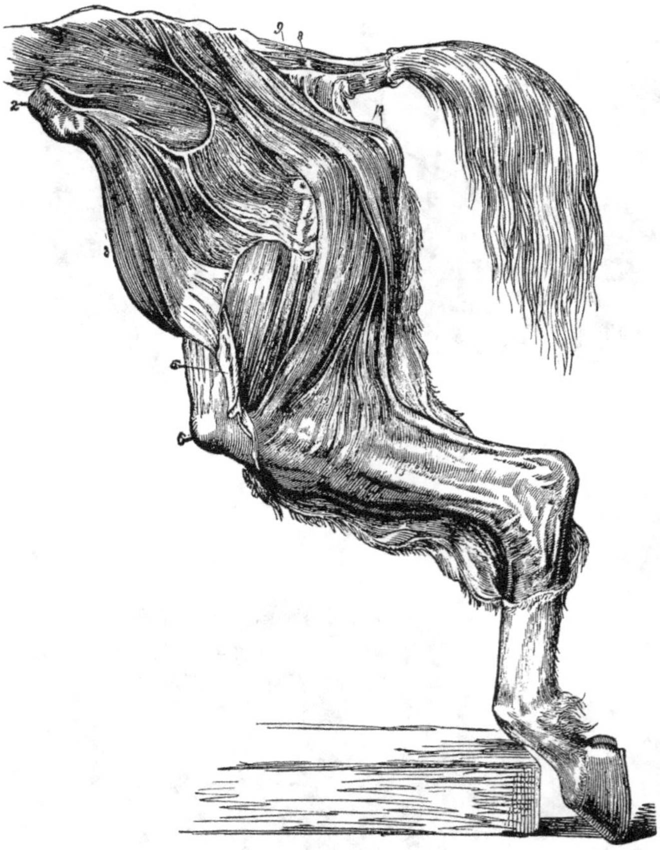

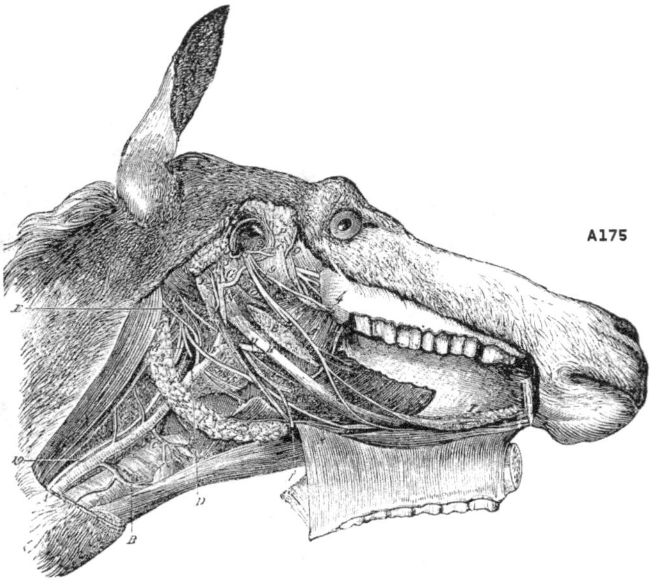

A175

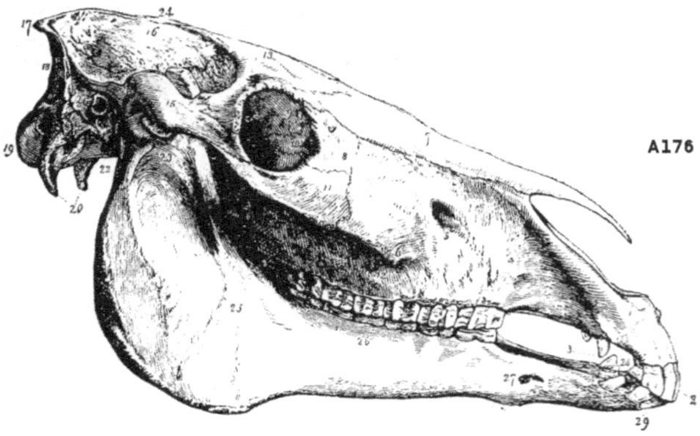

A176

A174

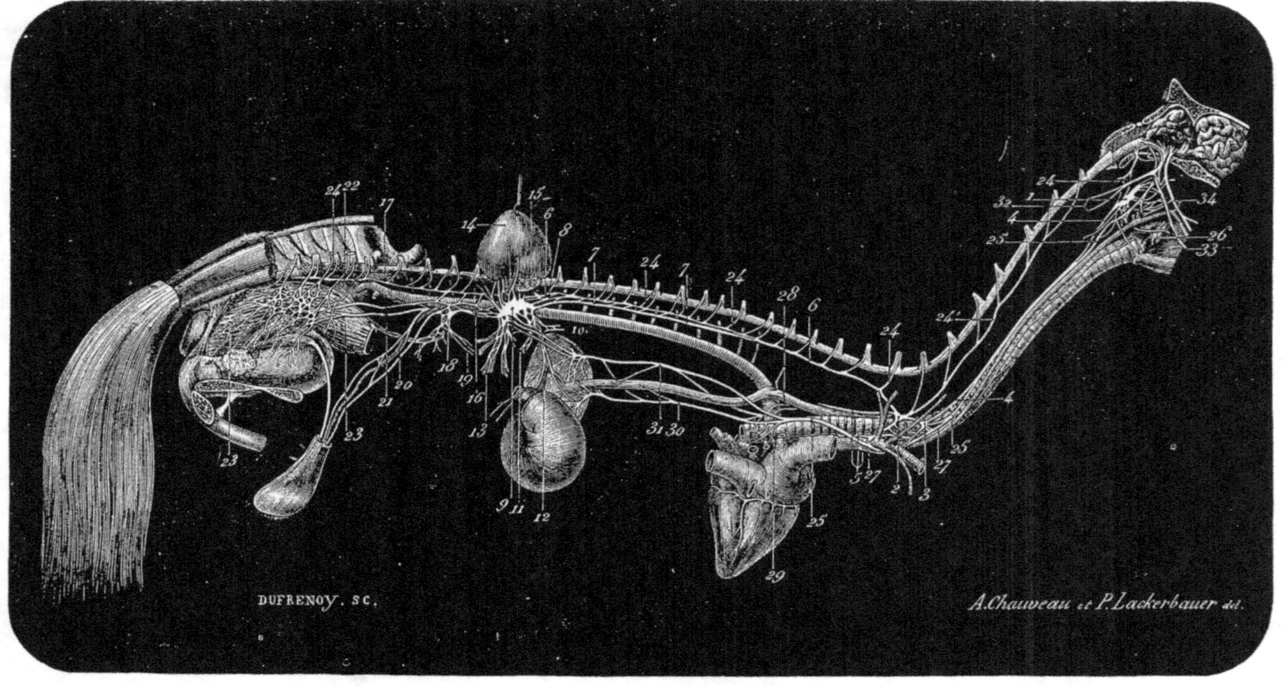

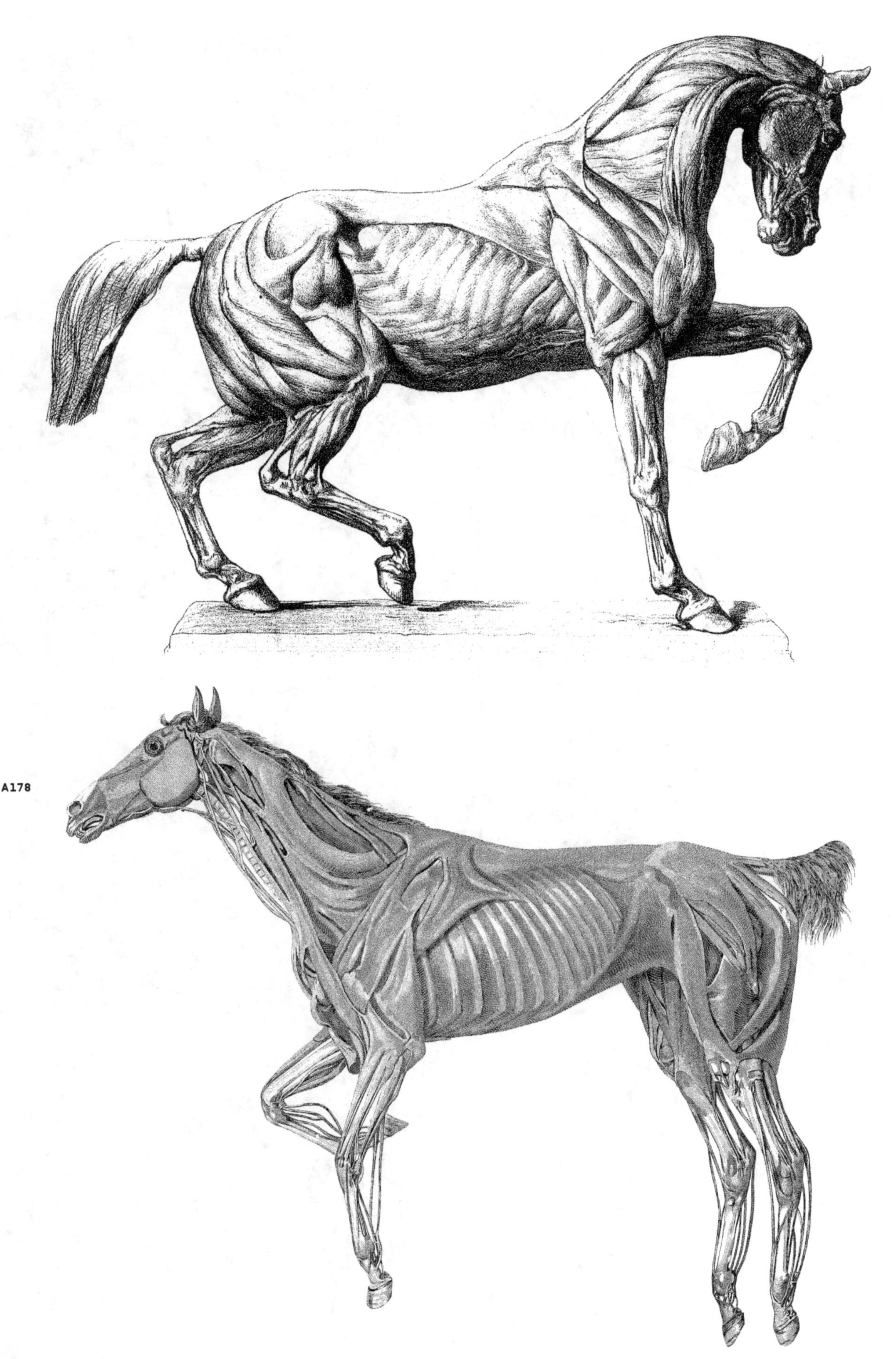

A177
A178

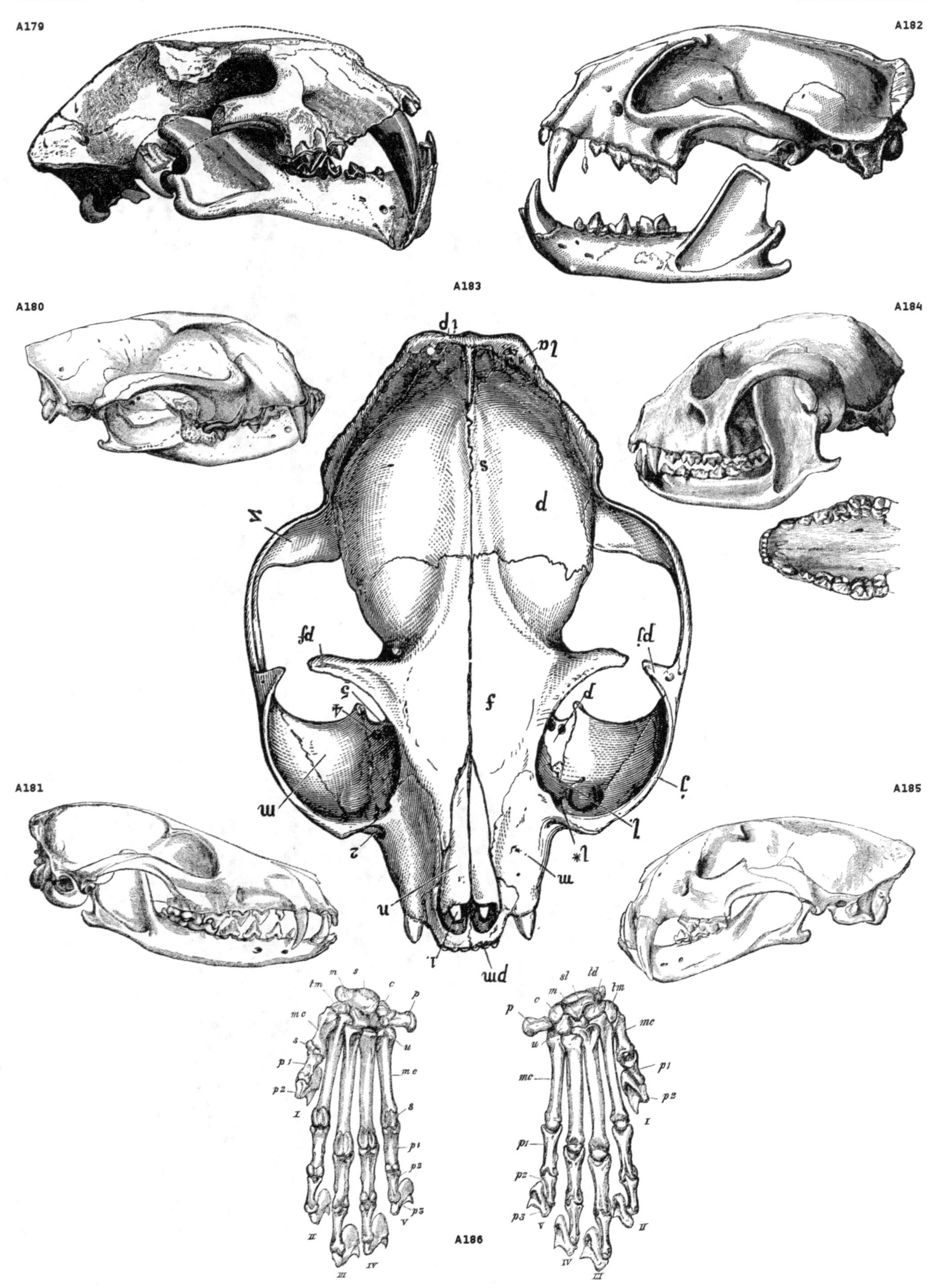

A179

A182

A180

A183

A184

A181

A185

A186

A187

A188

A189

A190

A191

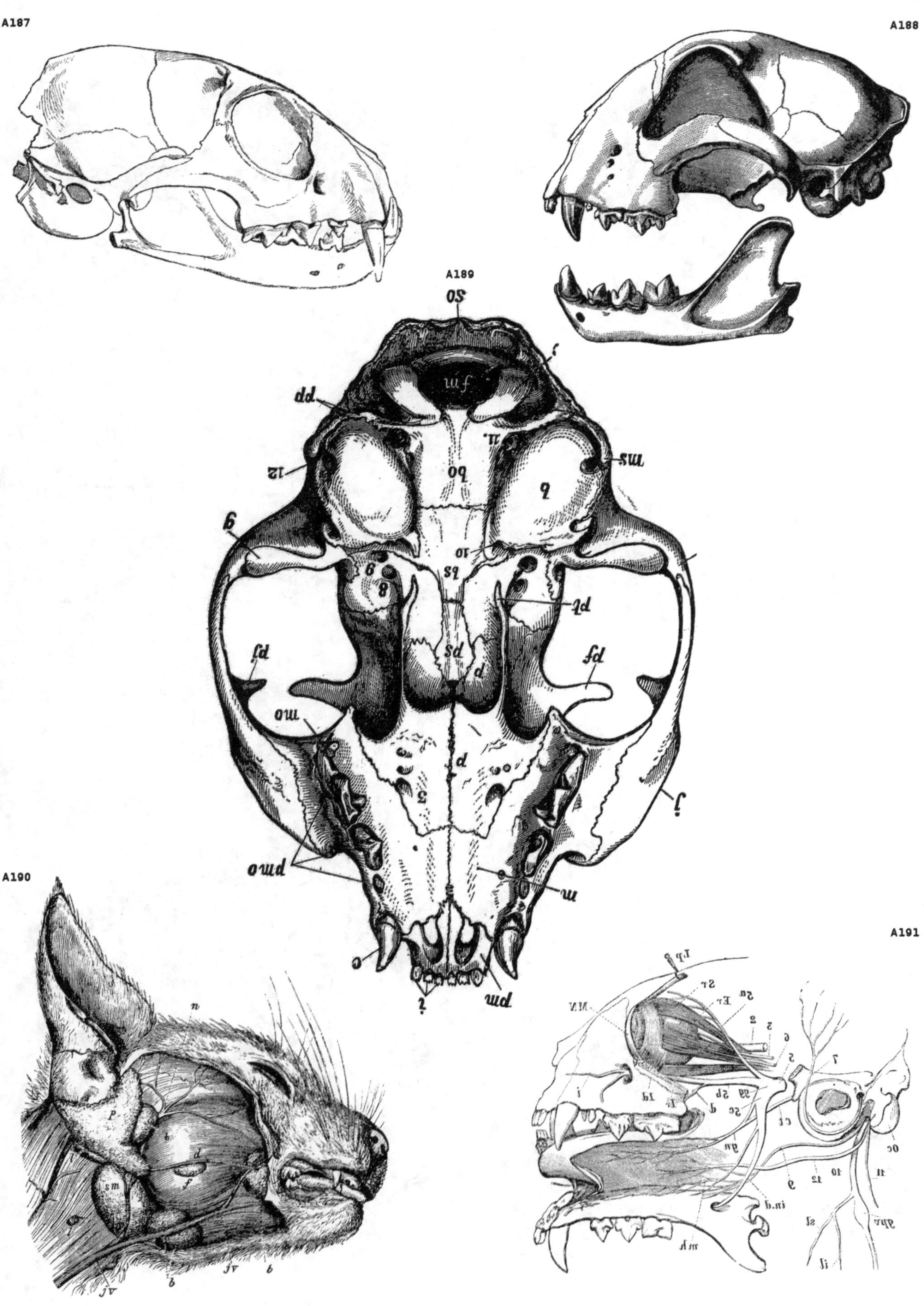

A192

A193

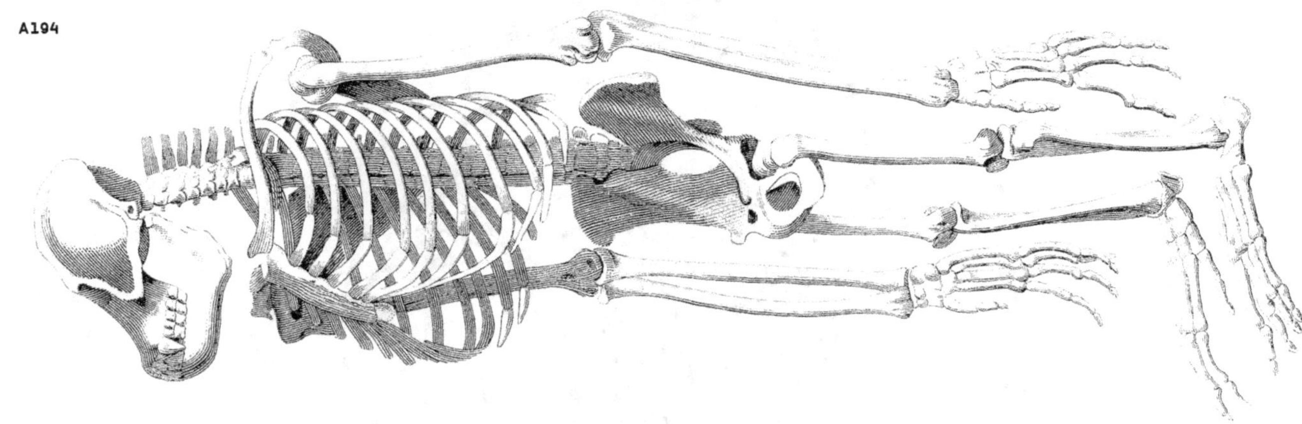

A194

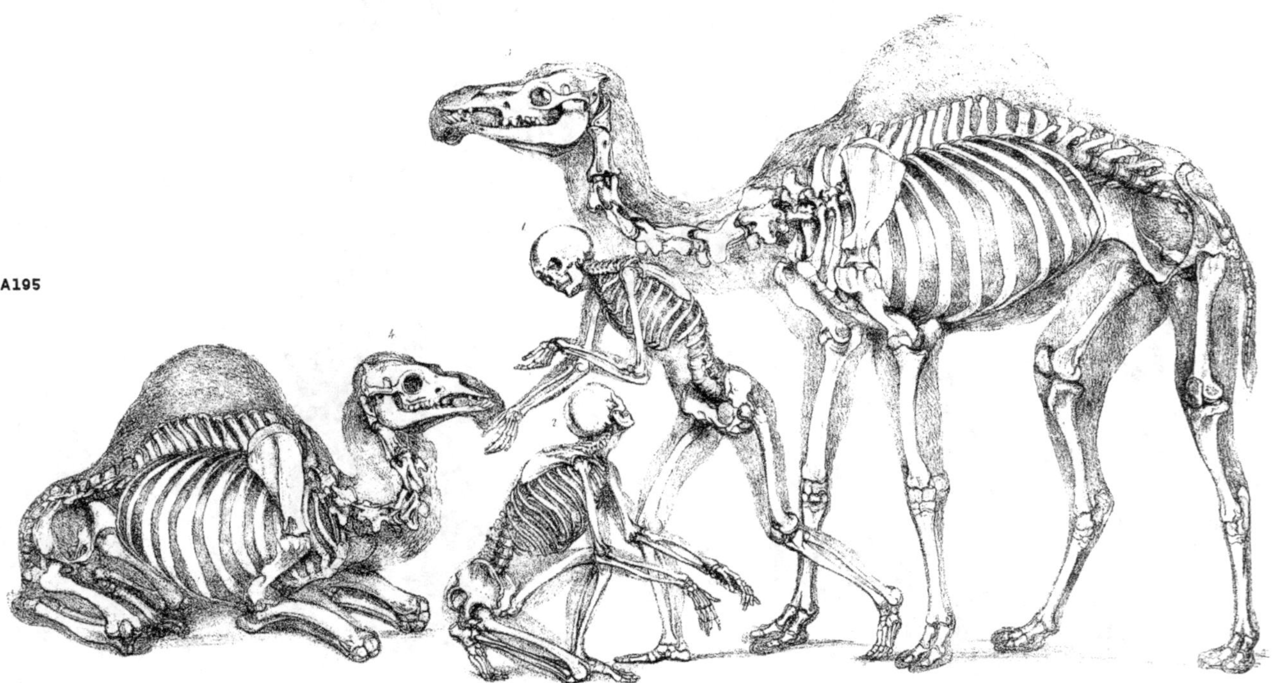

A195

WATERHOUSE HAWKINS' COMPARATIVE VIEW OF THE HUMAN AND ANIMAL FRAME.   *Plate VII*

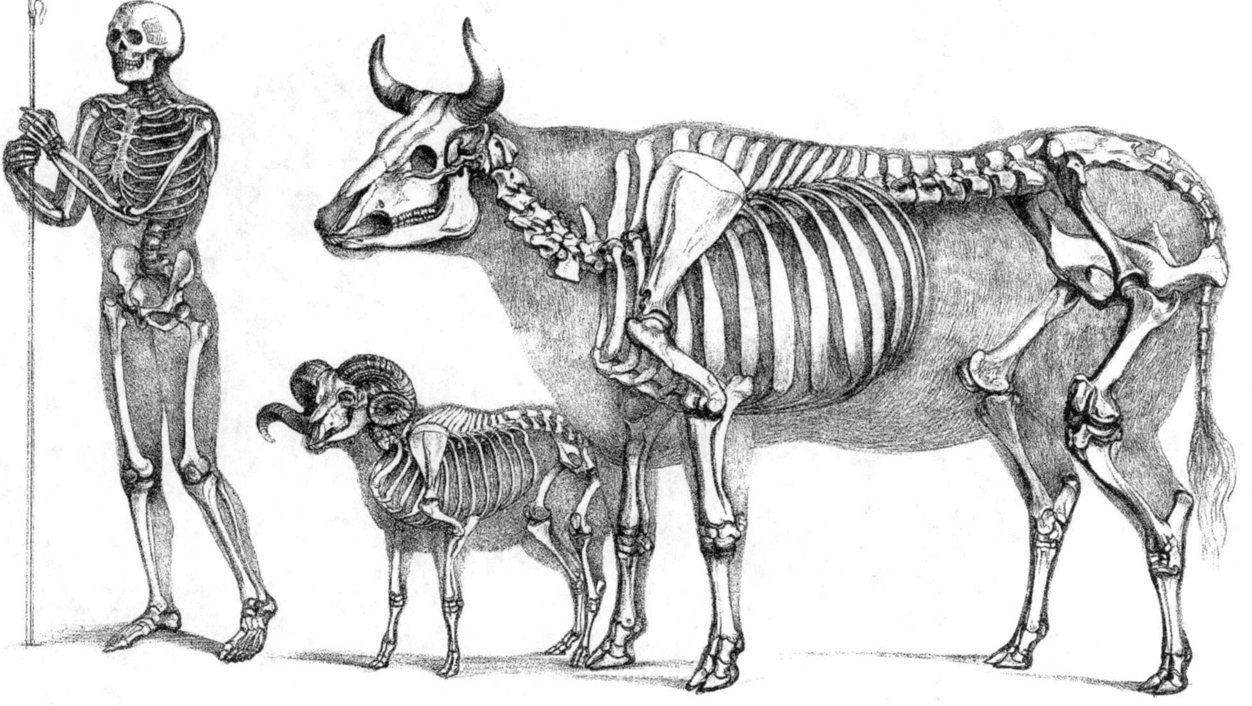

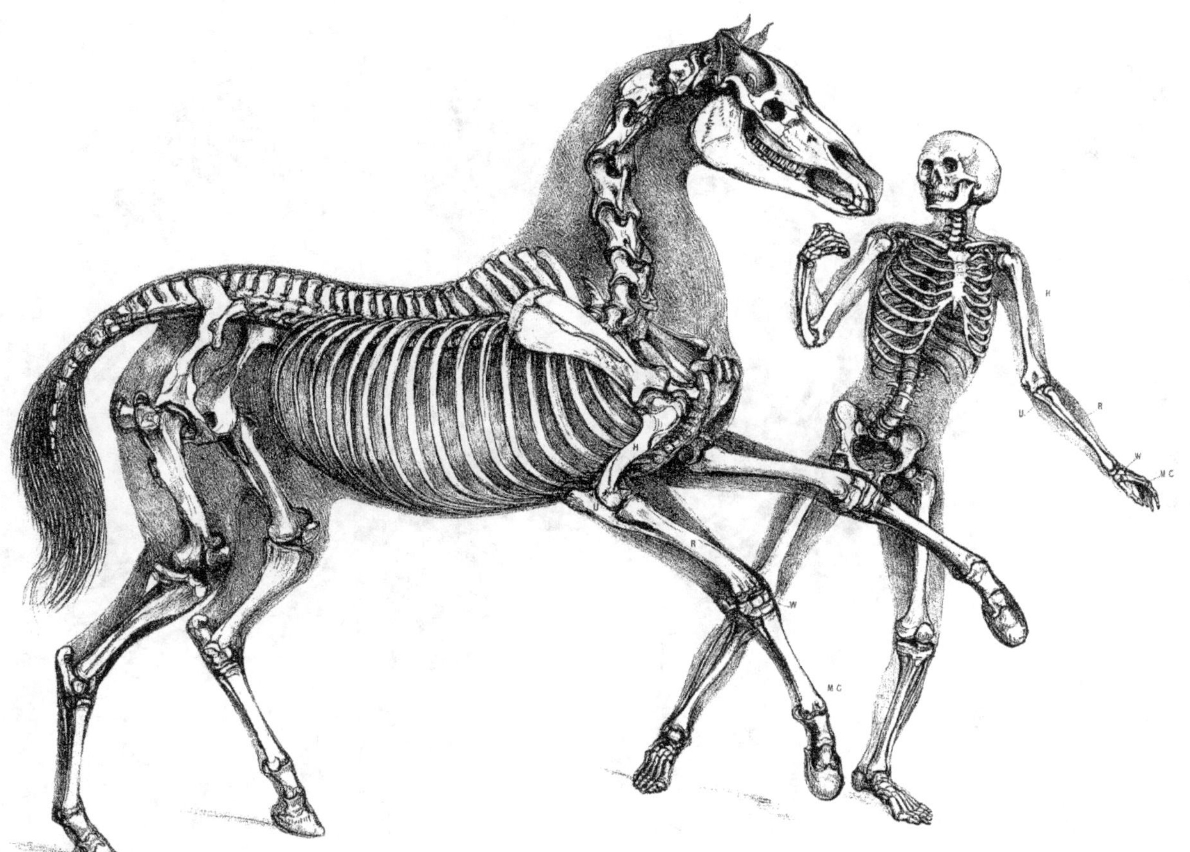

A198

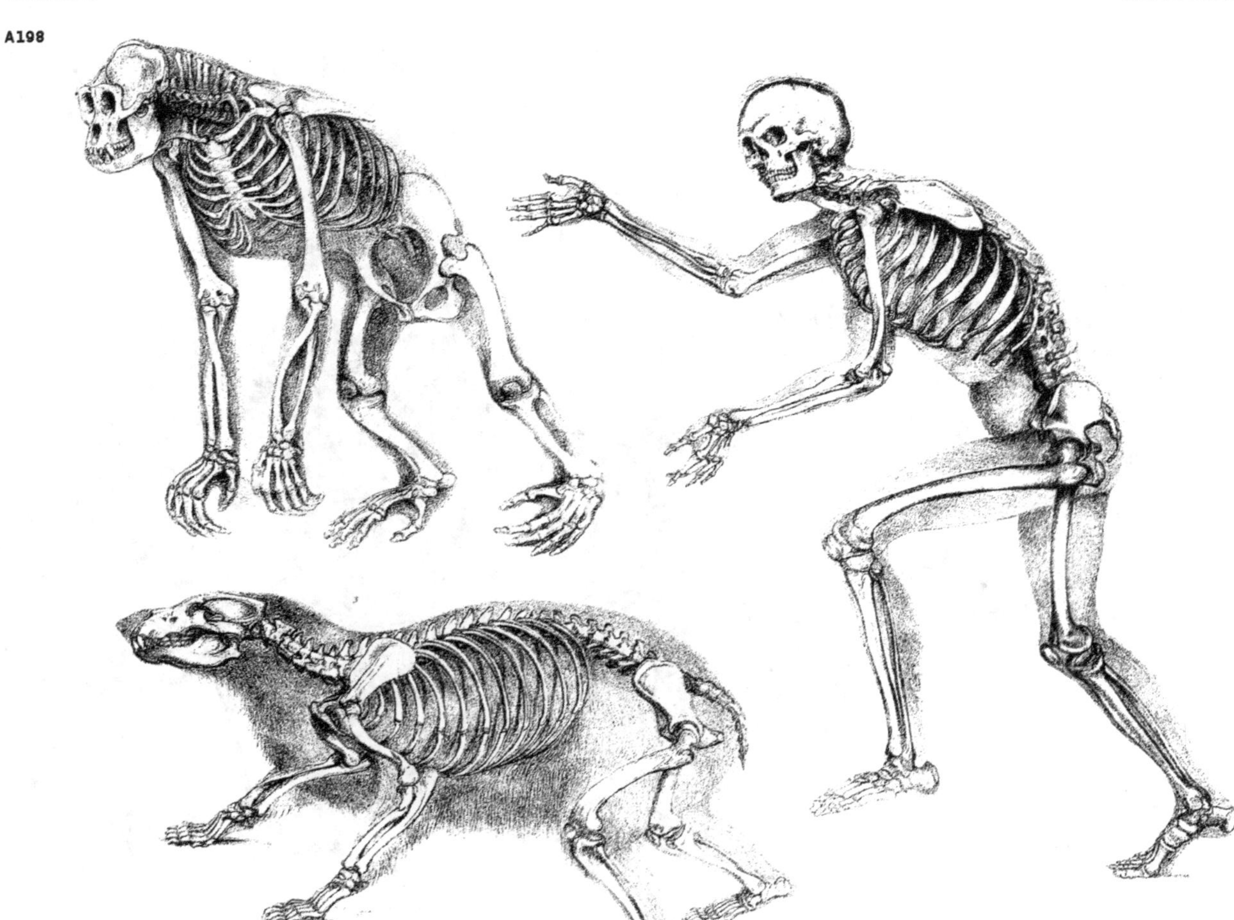

A199

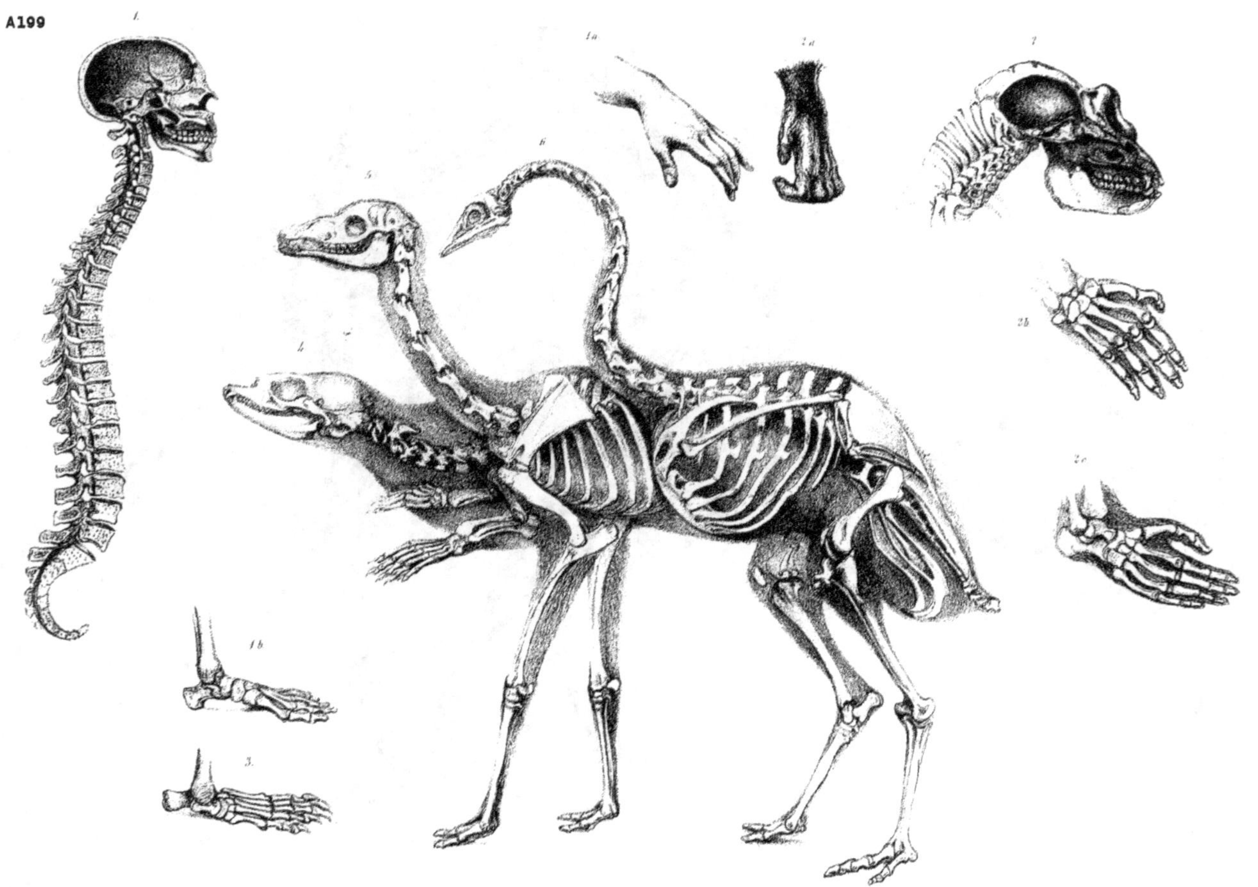

A200

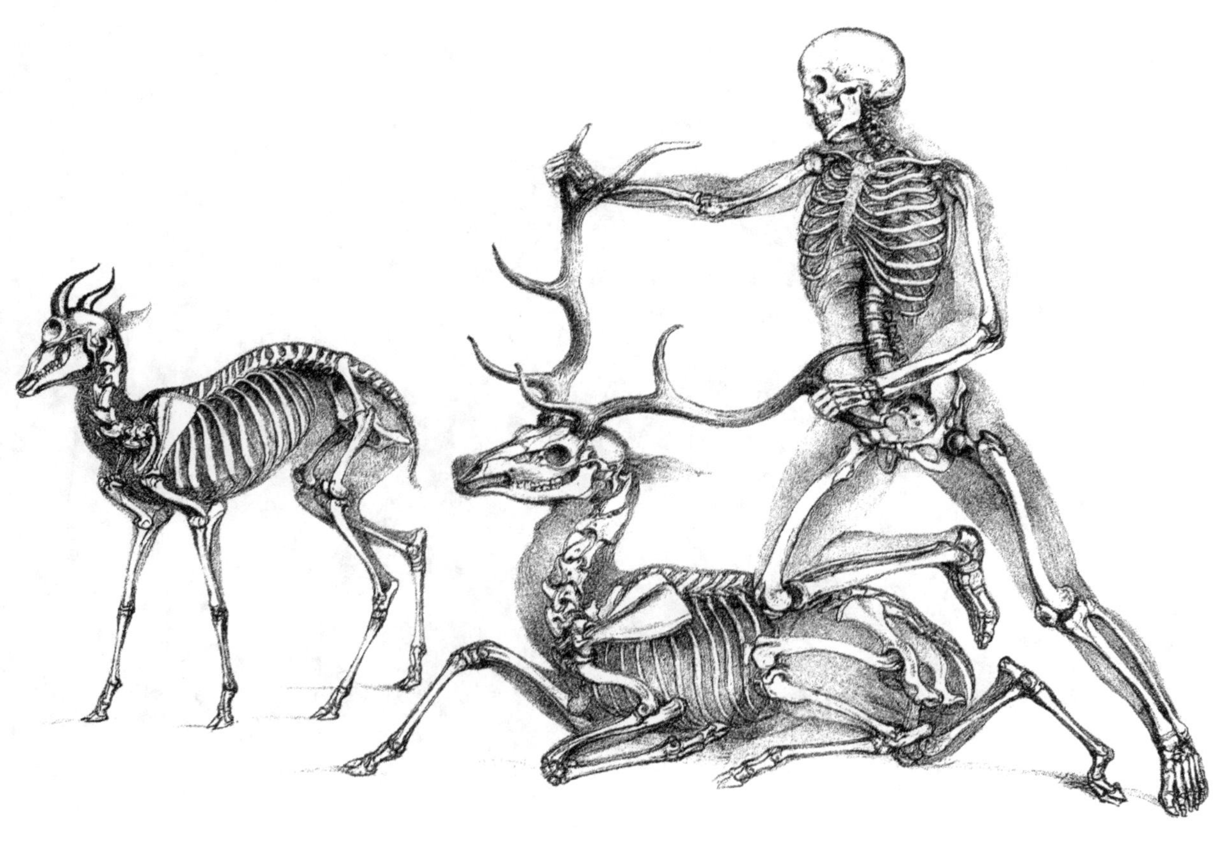

A201

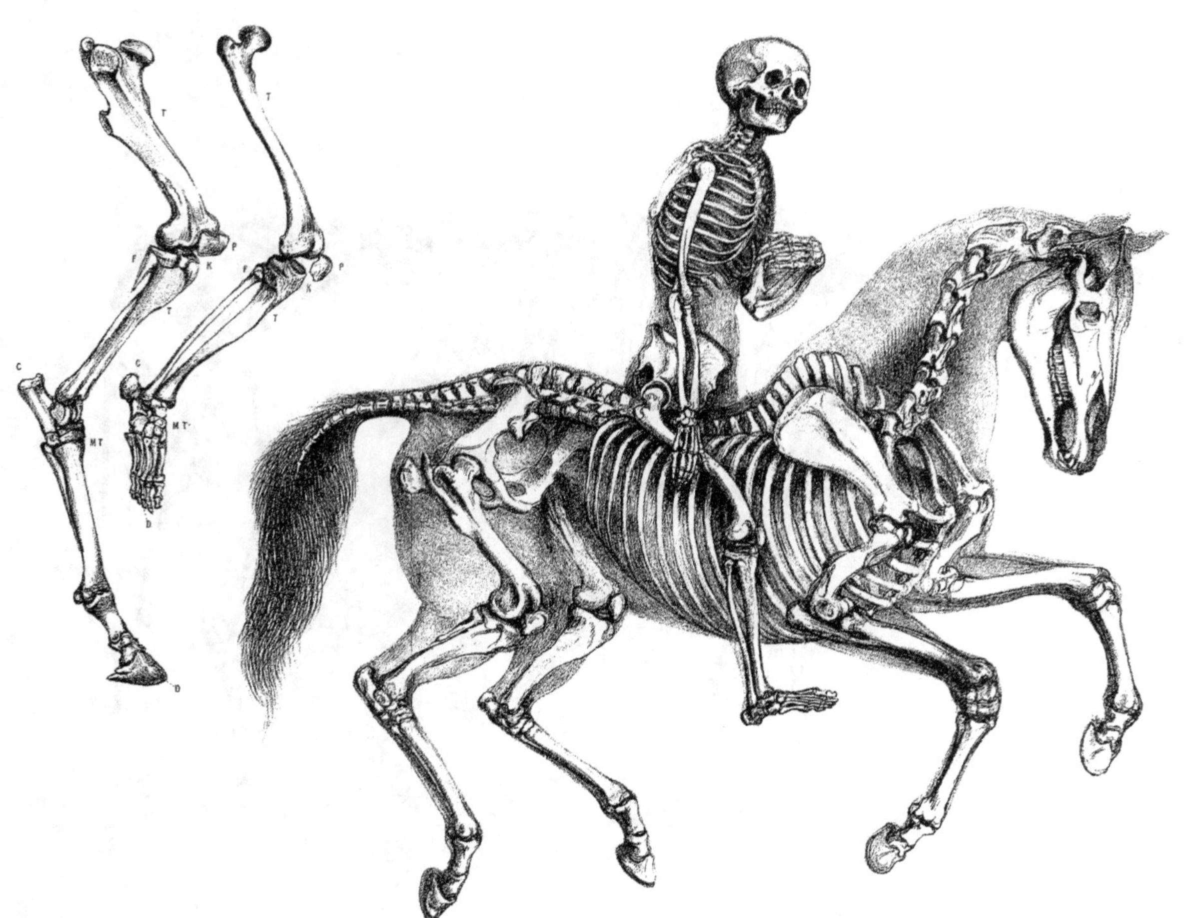

A202

ELEPHANTI.
TAB.XVII.
Fig.V.
Fig.I.
Fig.IV.
Fig.VI.
Fig.II.
Fig.III.

A203

Fig.1.
1
2
3
4
5
6
7
21
Round or
Beef Bone
26
Ribs of Brisket begin
27 Leg Bone
Shin Bone 23
24
28
29

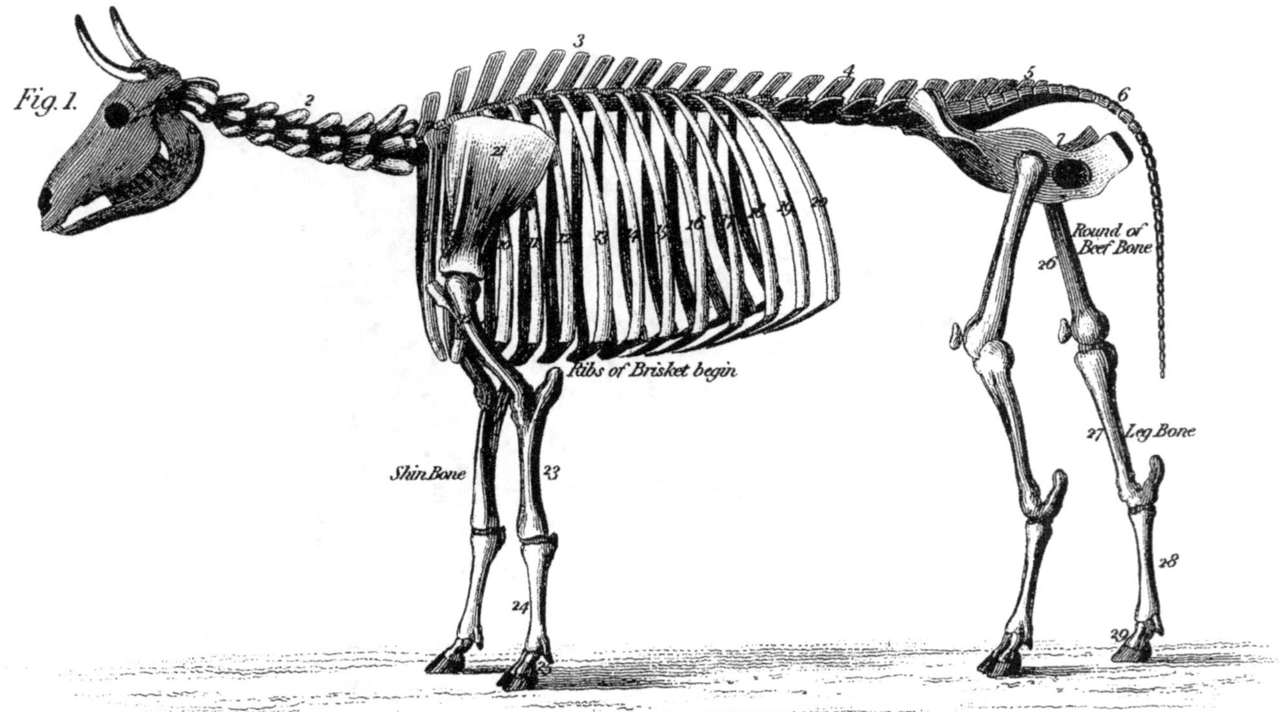

Plate XXVII.

A204

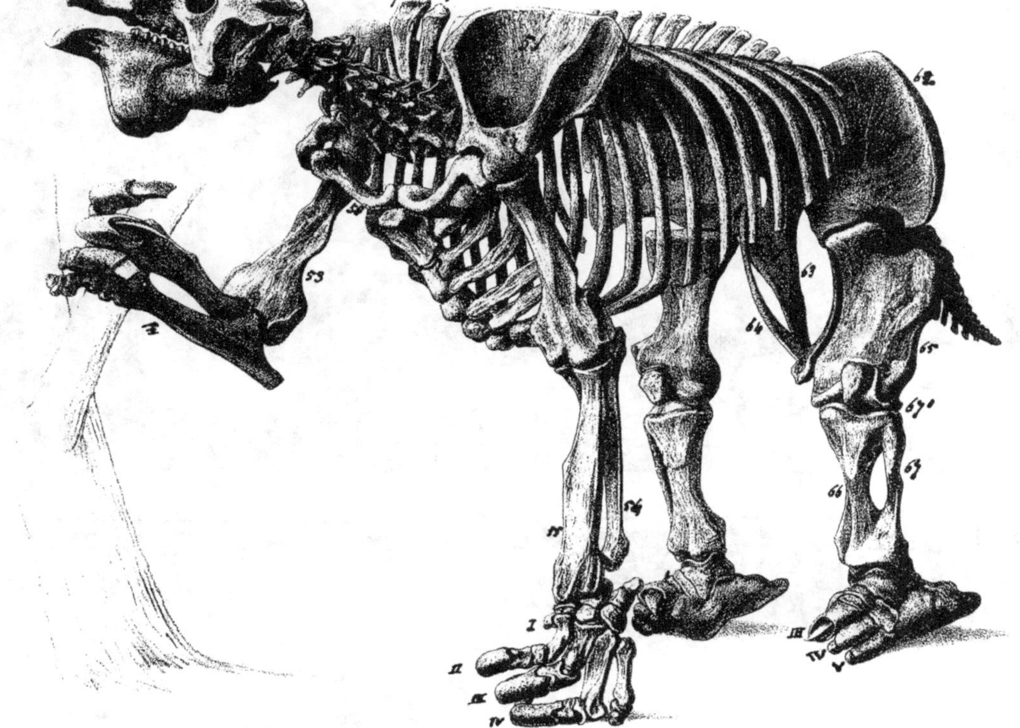

A205

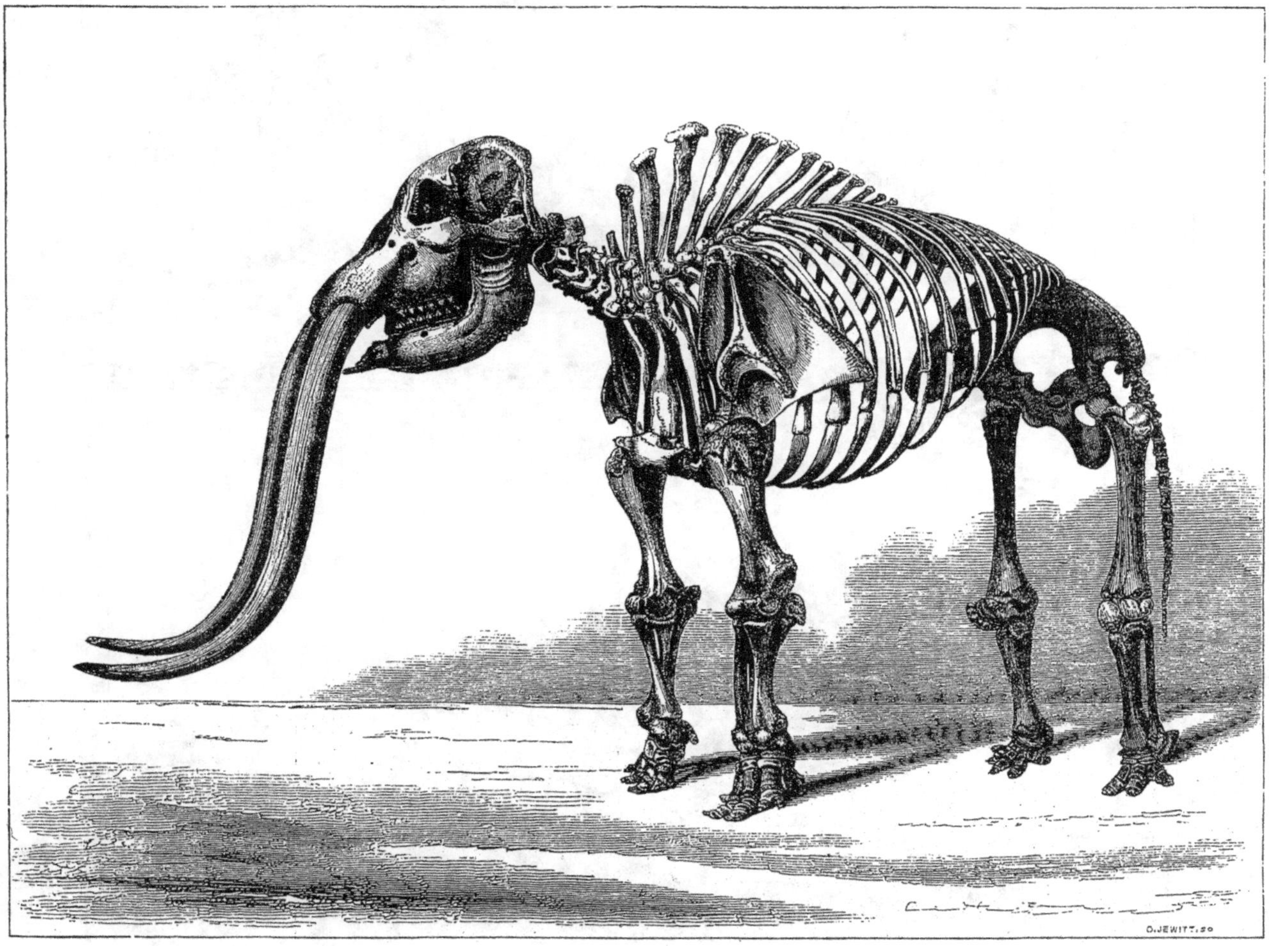

A206

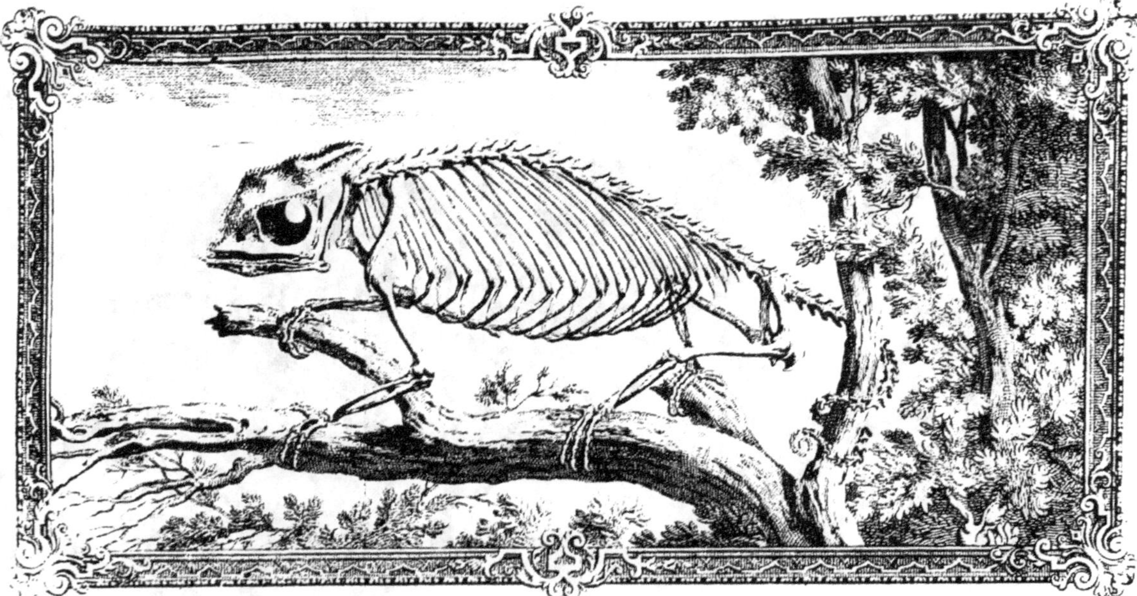

A207

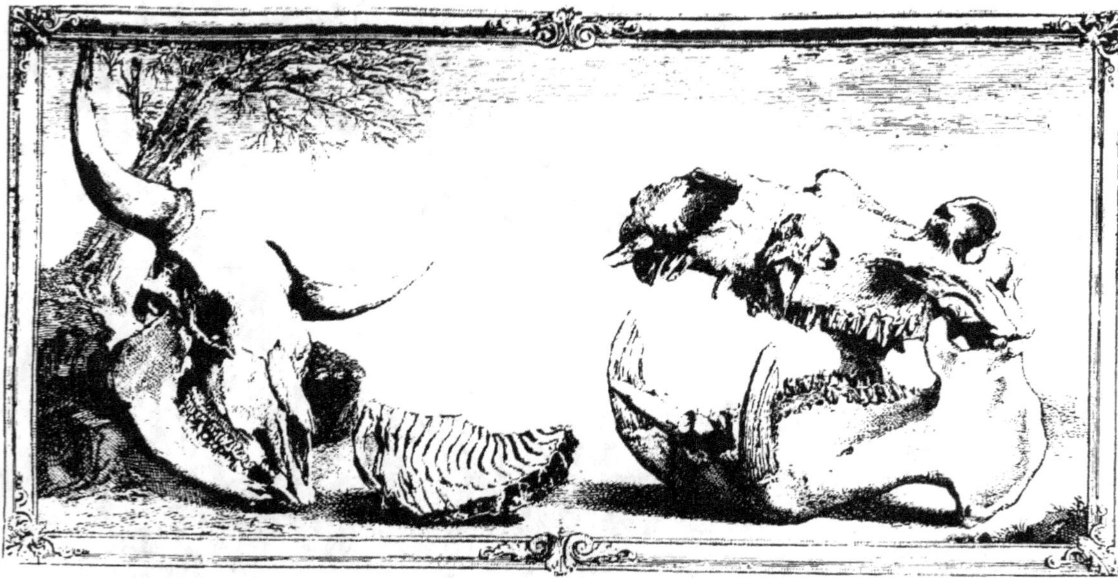

A208

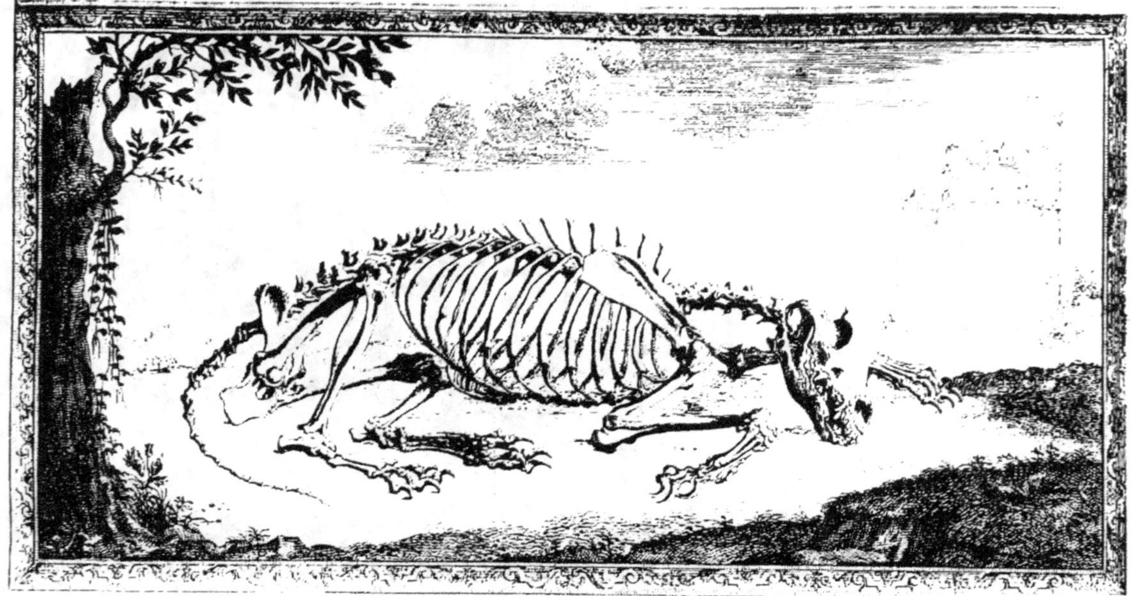

A209

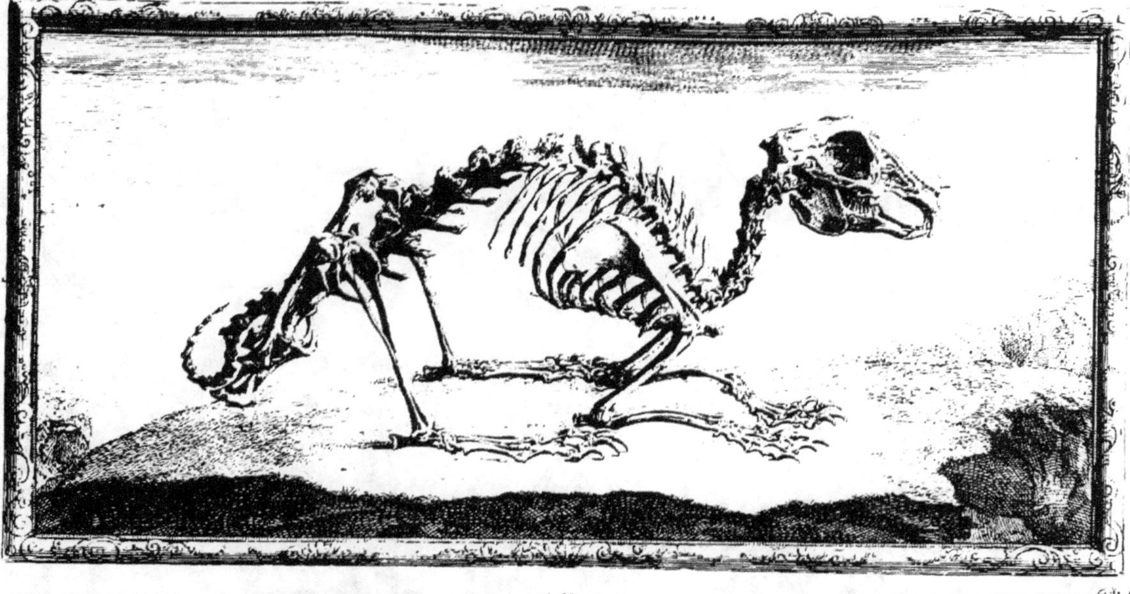

A210

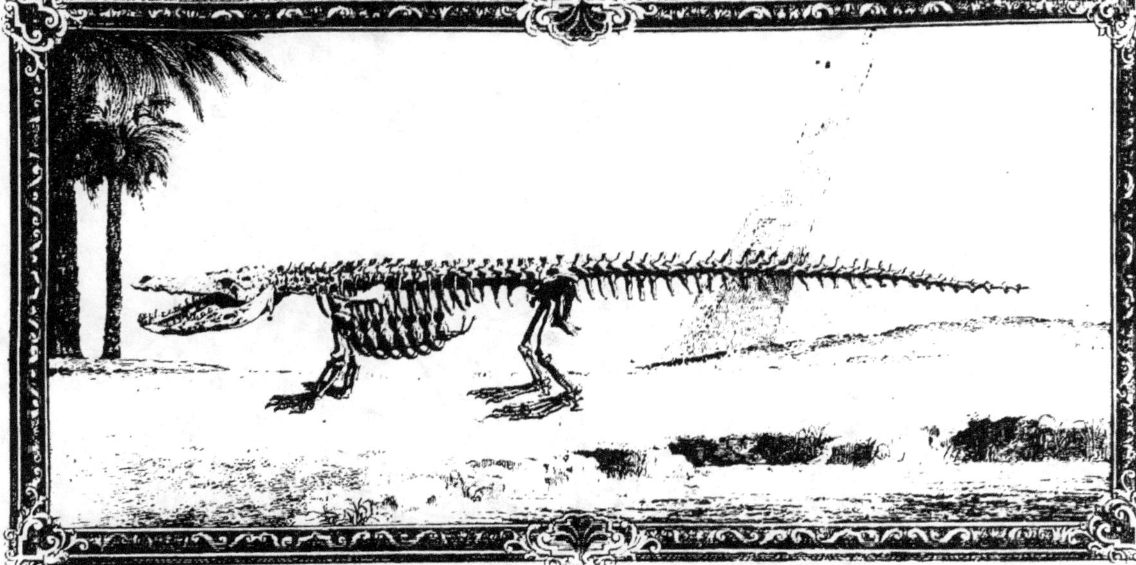

A211

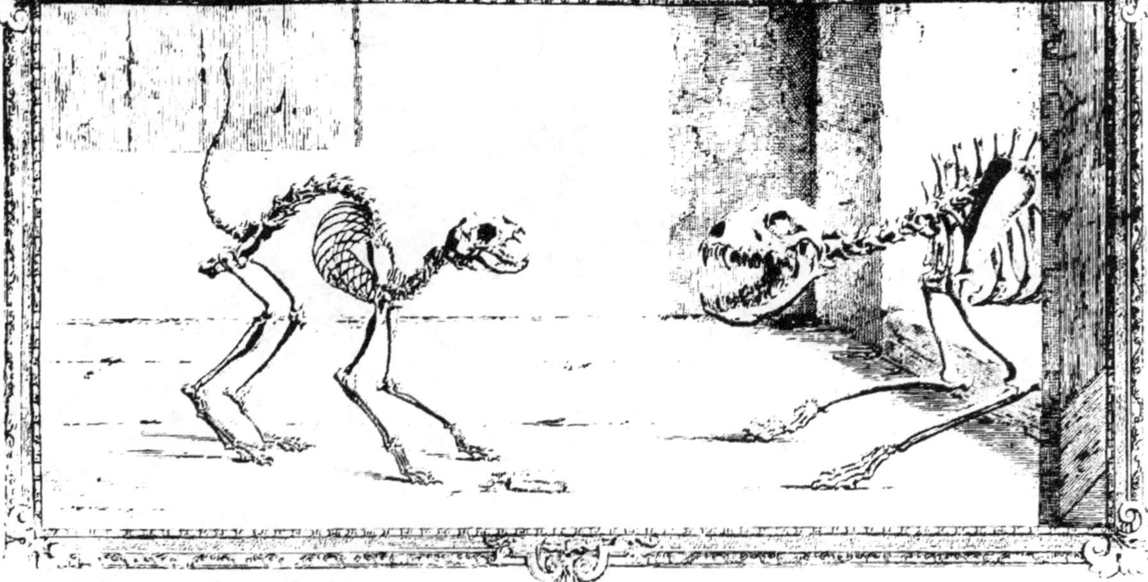

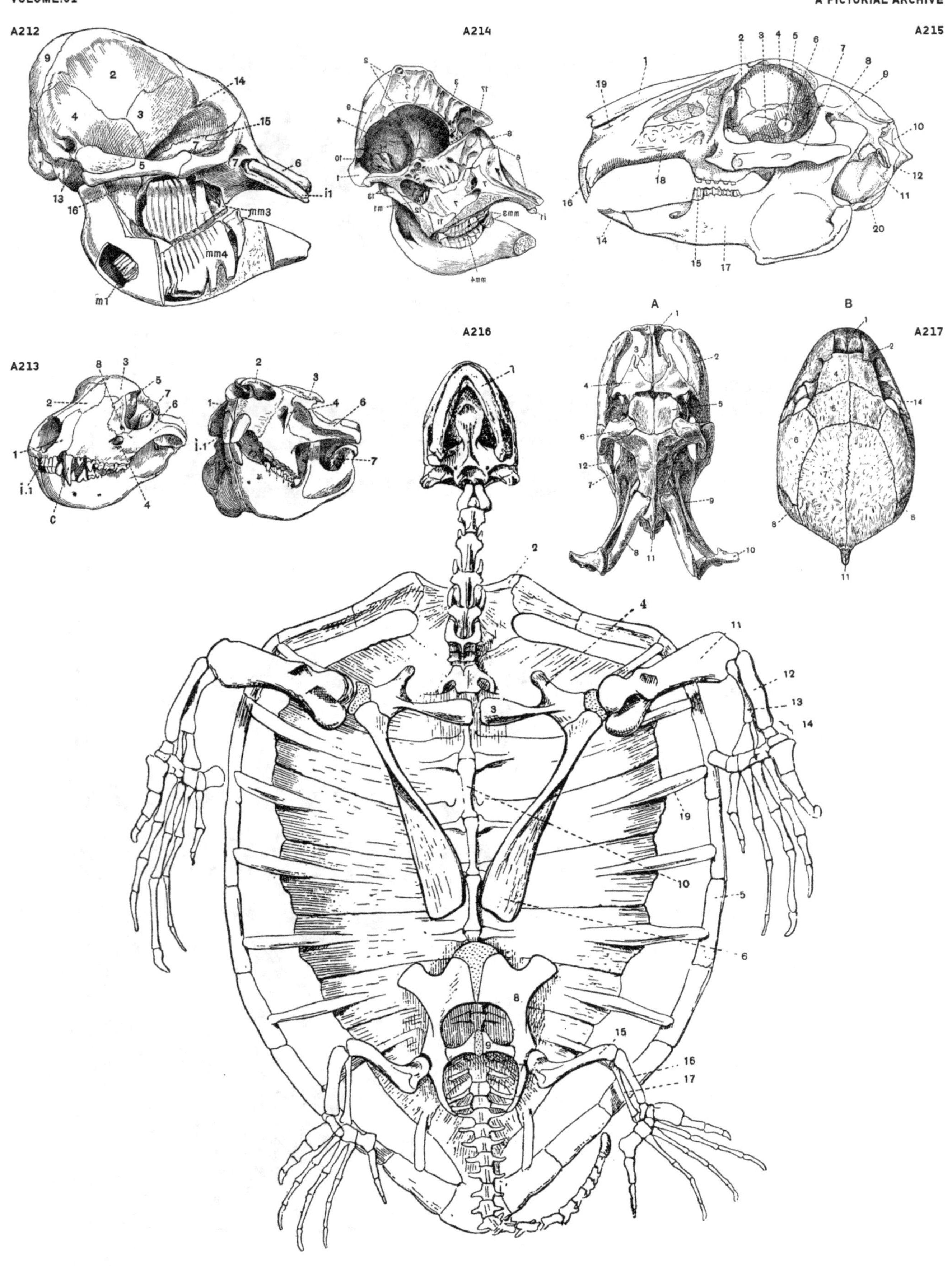
A212
A213
A214
A215
A216
A217
A
B

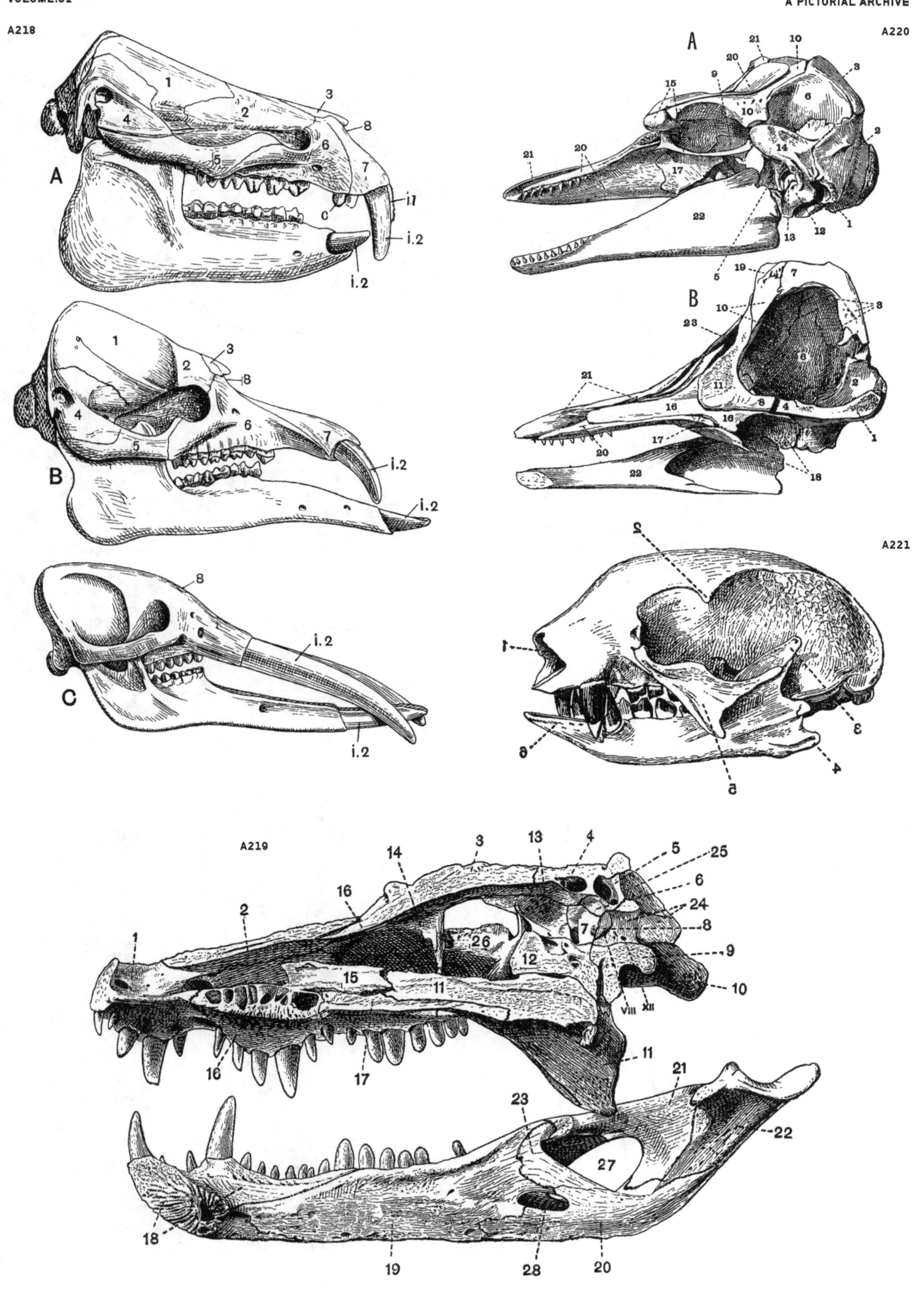
A218
A
B
C
A219
A220
A
B
A221

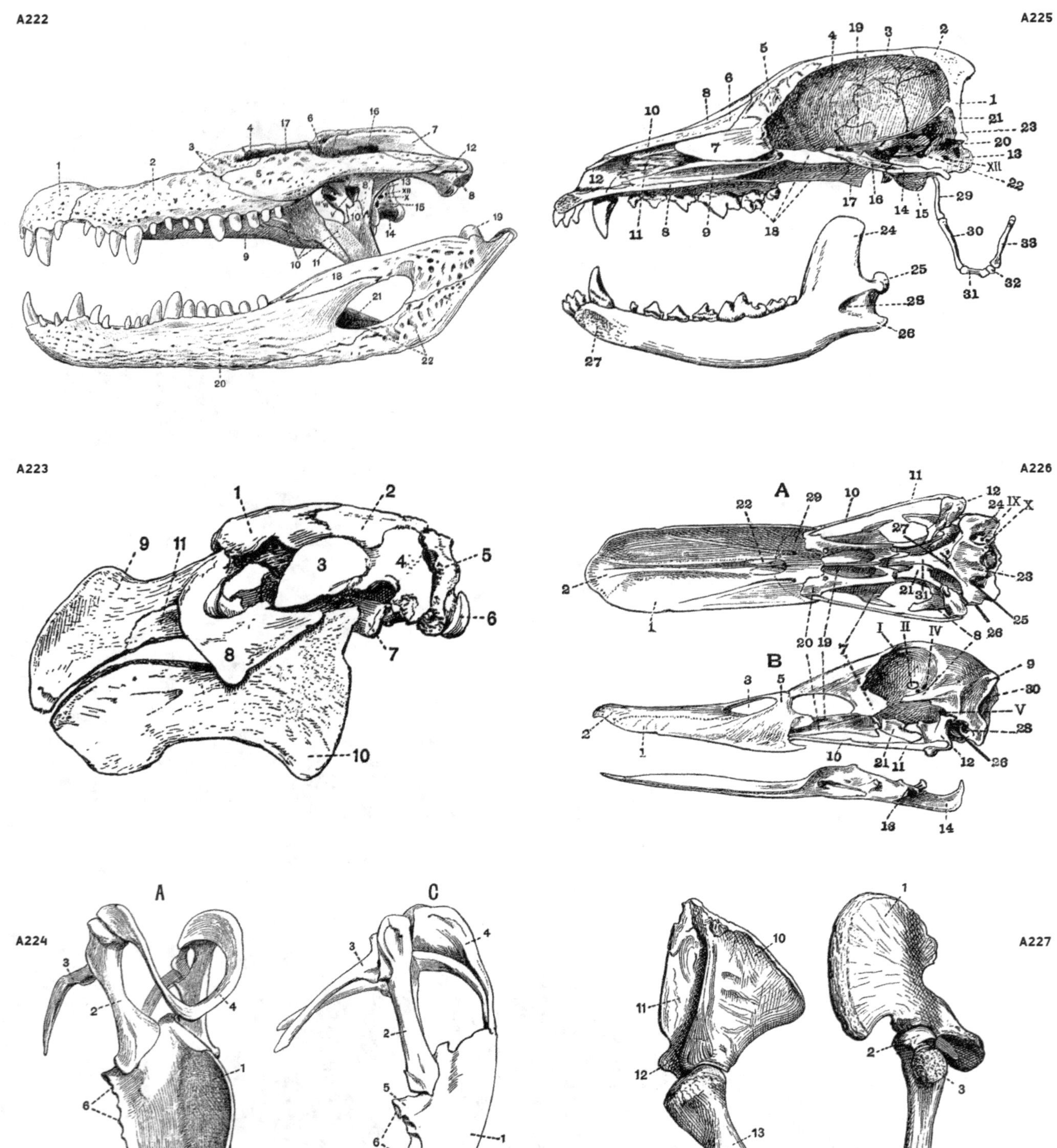
A222
A225
A223
A226
A224
A227
A
B
C
ANIMAL SKELETONS & ANATOMY

A228

A231

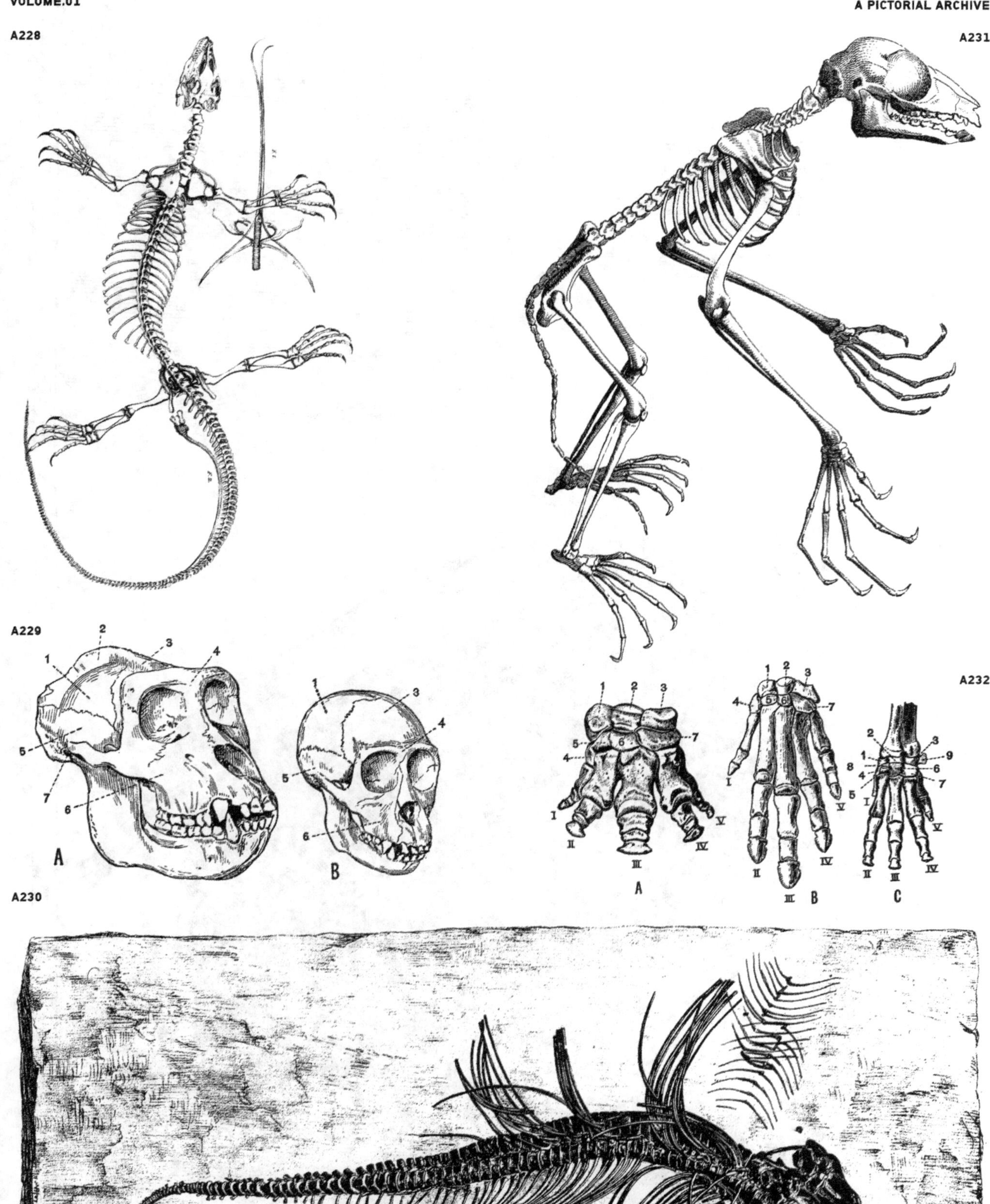

A229

A232

A230

A233

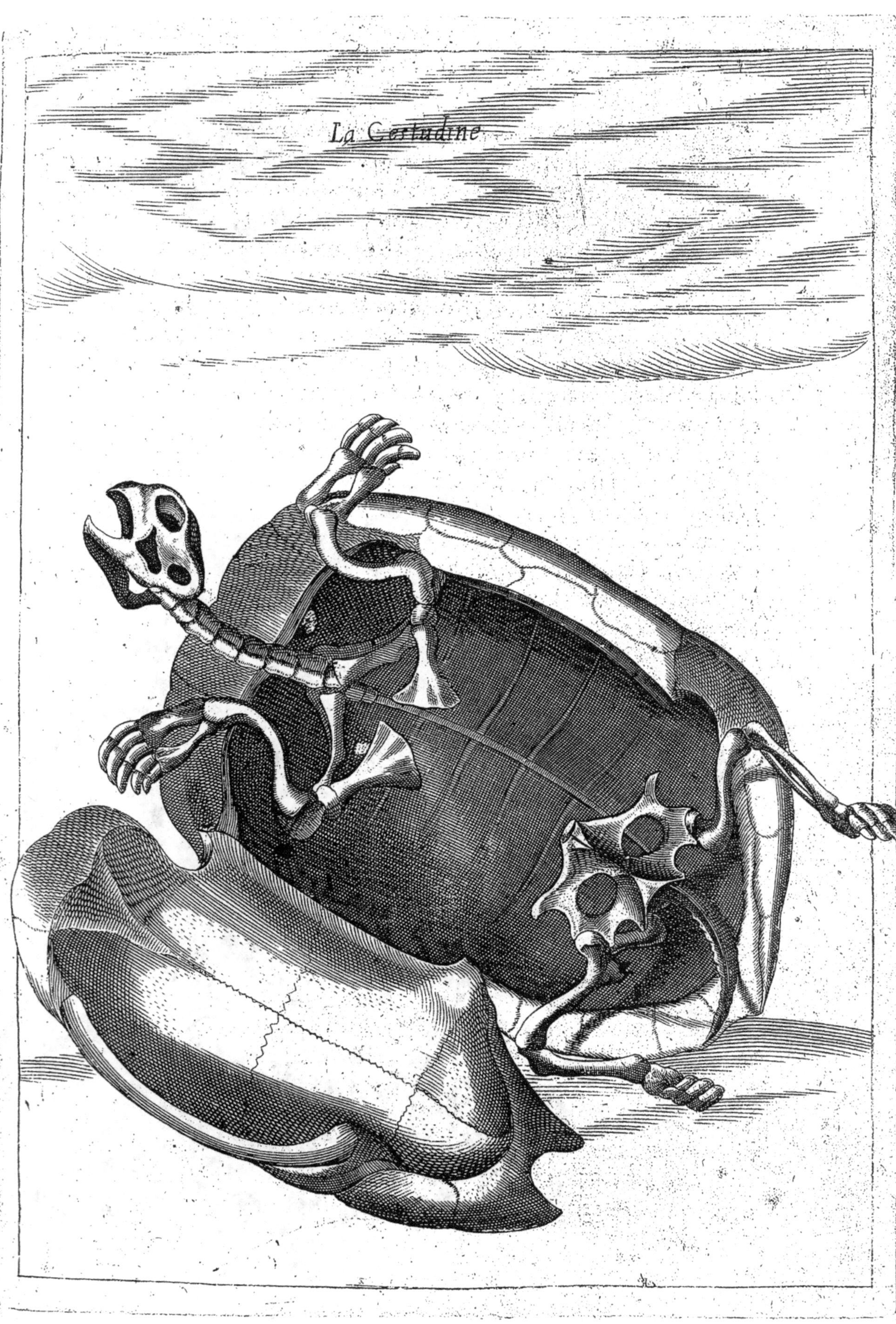

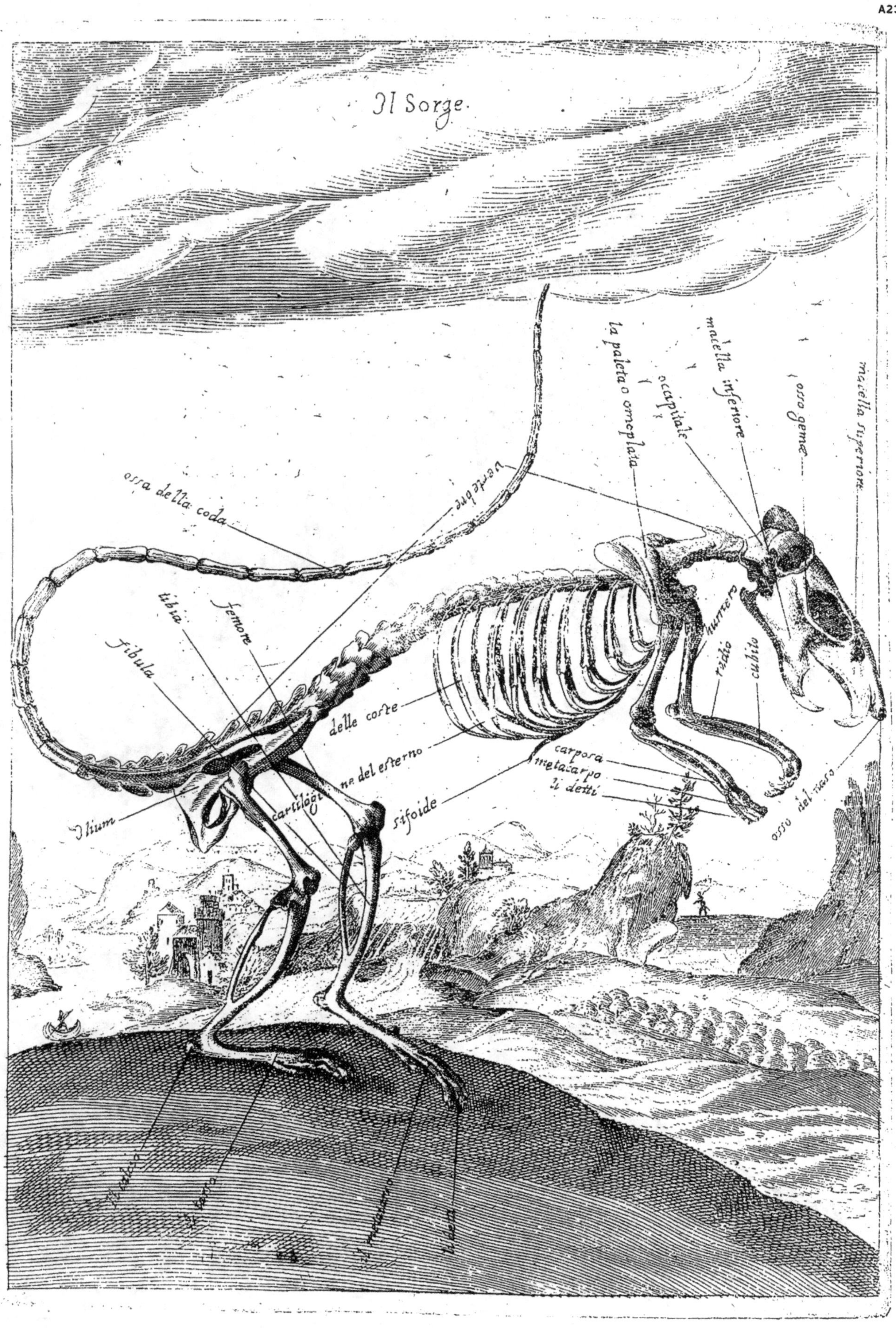
Il Sorge.
ossa della coda
tibia
femore
fibula
Ilium
delle corte
na del esterno
cartilagi
sifoide
vertebre
la paleta o omoplata
occipitale
macella inferiore
osso geme
macella superiore
humero
radio
cubito
carpora
metatarpo
li detti
osso del vicaro

A235

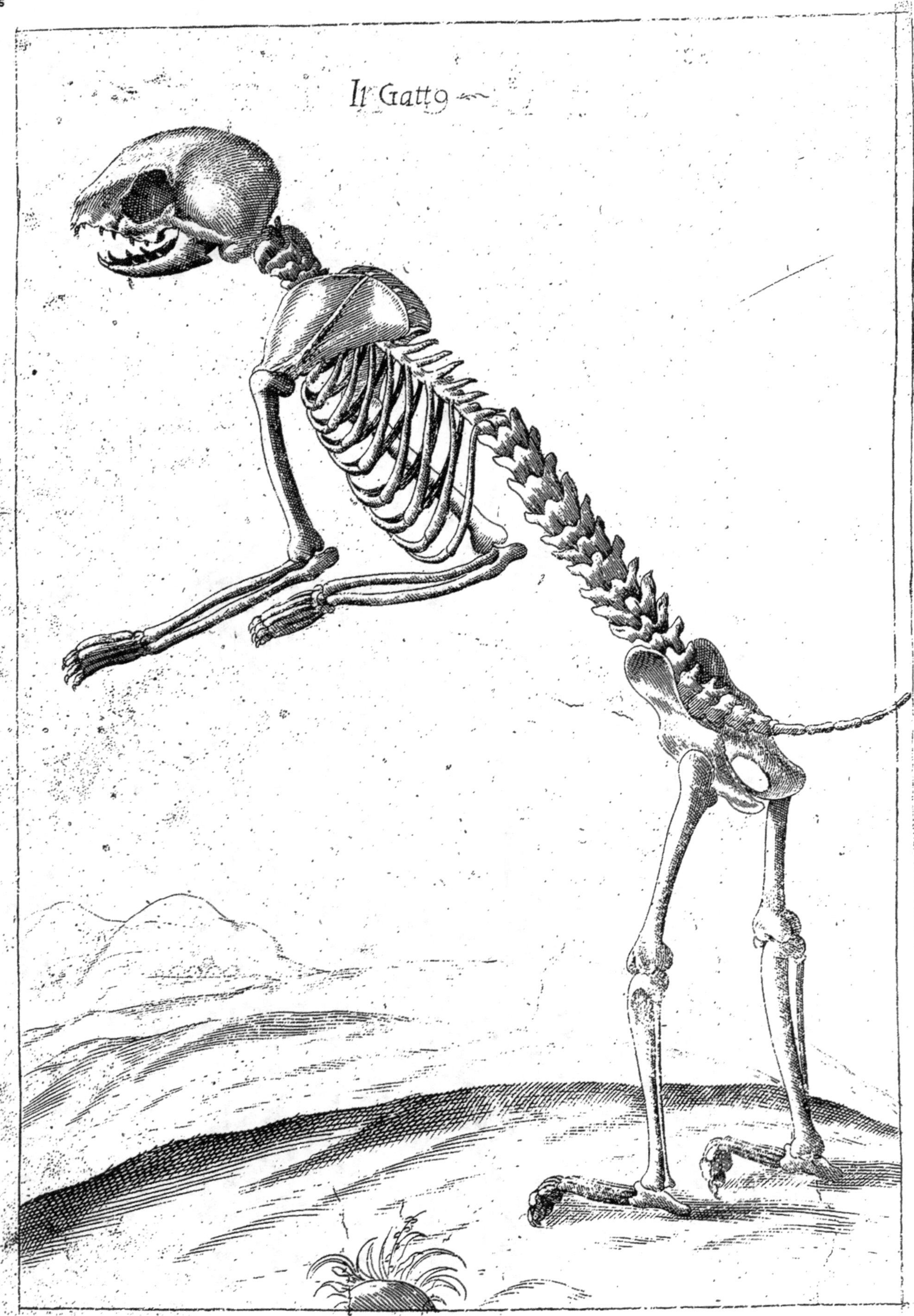

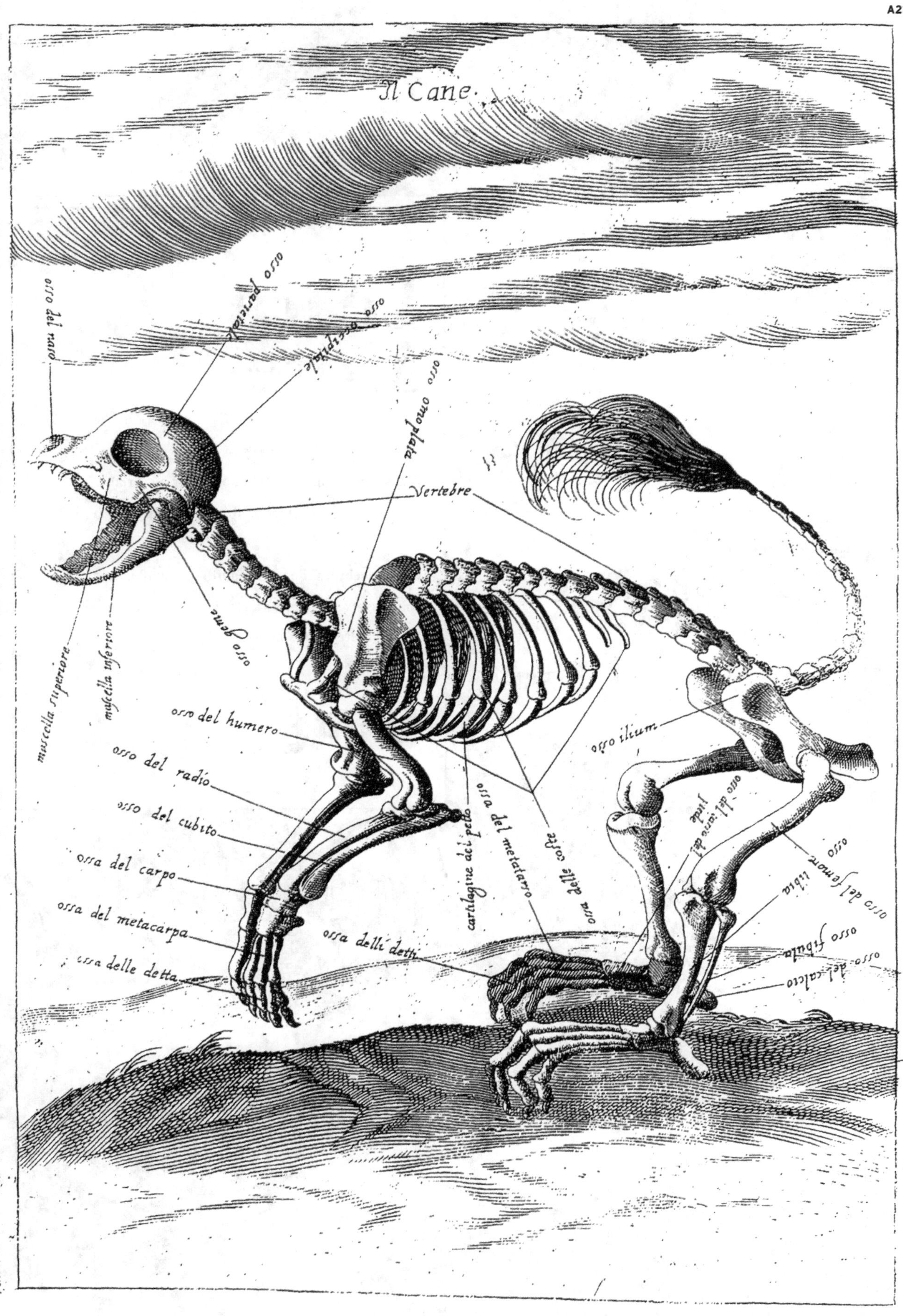
Il Cane.
osso del naso
osso parietale
osso occipitale
osso omoplata
osso del femore
Vertebre
mascella superiore
mascella inferiore
osso della gena
osso del humero
osso del radio
osso del cubito
ossa del carpo
ossa del metacarpa
ossa delle detta
ossa delli detti
cartilagine dei petto
ossa del metatarso
osso ilium
ossa delle cosfe
osso del femore
osso del marcello
osso tibia
osso fibula
osso del calcio

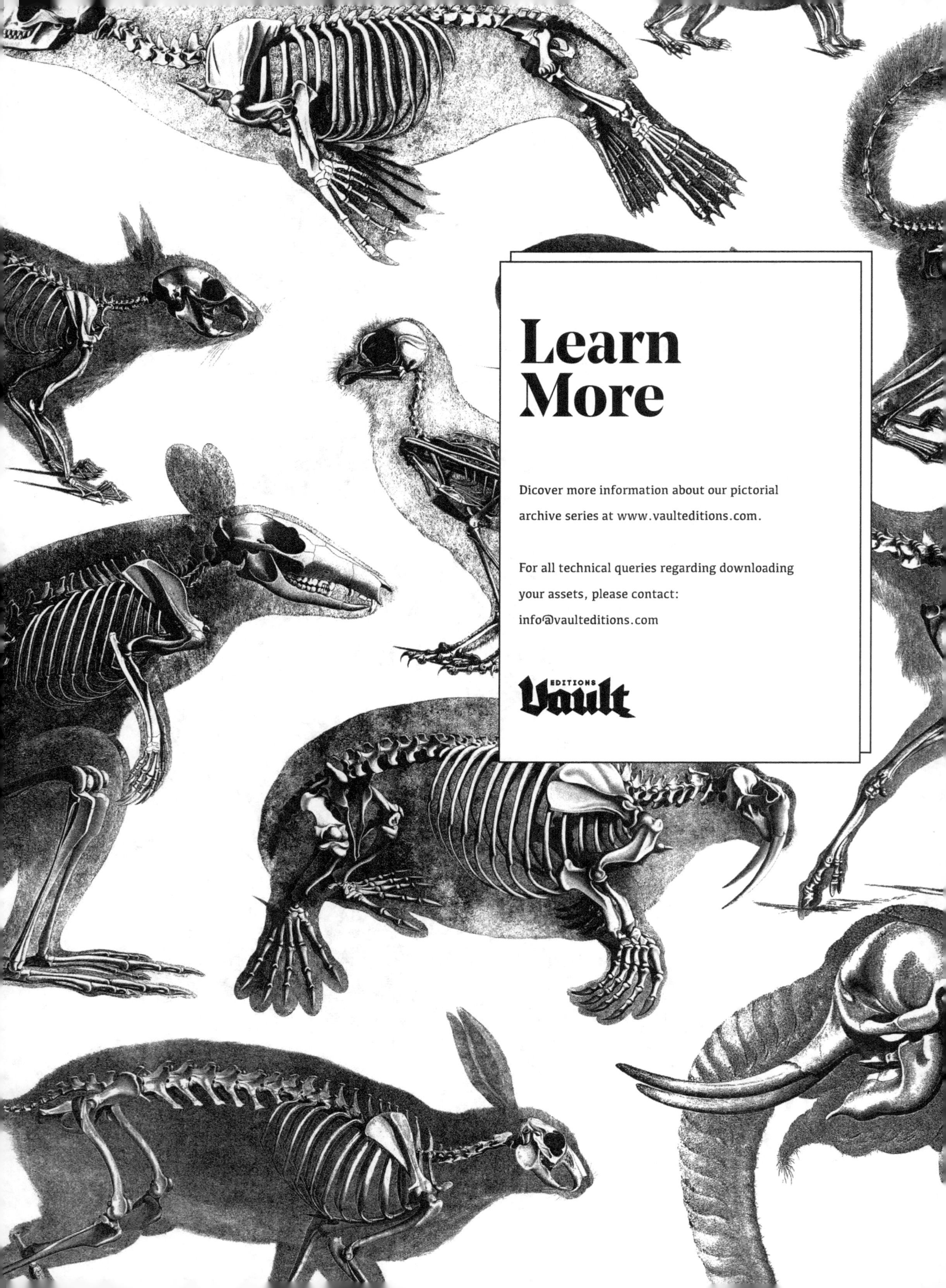
Learn
More

Dicover more information about our pictorial
archive series at www.vaulteditions.com.

For all technical queries regarding downloading
your assets, please contact:
info@vaulteditions.com

EDITIONS
Vault

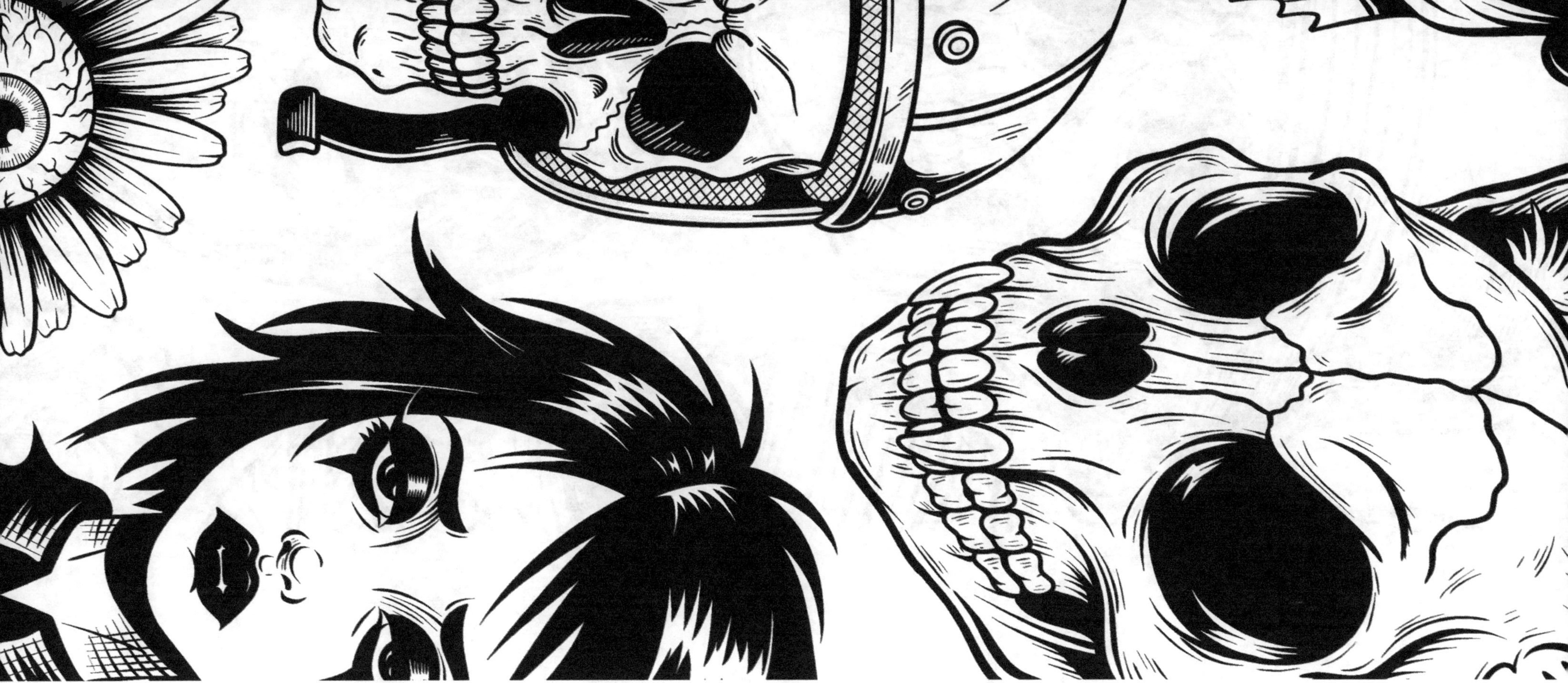
EDITIONS Vault

HAND DRAWN
UNIQUE 40 DESIGNS
BEST QUALITY

STEP BY STEP

A HELPFUL MANUAL FOR ARTISTS AND DESIGNERS

HOW TO DRAW
COOL THINGS

THE VAULT EDITIONS GUIDE TO
MASTERING
THE ART OF
DRAWING

INTRODUCTION

The aesthetic of the designs in this book has roots in punk, fashion, skateboarding, street culture, and pop art. It's graphic and bold, built around strong silhouettes, clear shapes, and high-contrast finishes. These are the kinds of images you'd expect to see on posters, patches, stickers, skate decks, and tees.

How to Draw Cool Things: An Adult Step-by-Step Drawing Guide introduces the foundations behind this style through the Vault Editions 12 step drawing method. Each design is broken into simple, guided stages, showing you how to build a finished illustration from basic shapes, clean construction, and clear proportions. The aim is to remove guesswork and help you build confidence through repetition.

To support your progress, the book begins with essential practice pages covering gradient value scales, mark-making, and rendering. From there, you'll move through a curated set of subjects that develop your skills while keeping every page fun to draw. You'll learn how to create bold outlines, control shape design, and add depth using straightforward shading techniques that suit a graphic look.

Clear, intentional artwork makes each step easy to follow, helping you understand not just what to draw, but why it works. Whether you're returning to drawing after years away or starting from scratch, this book provides a structured, accessible way to develop your skills and create illustrations with style, attitude, and impact.

Download Your Files
This book includes downloadable files to support your drawing practice. You'll find instructions on how to access them on the final pages of this book.

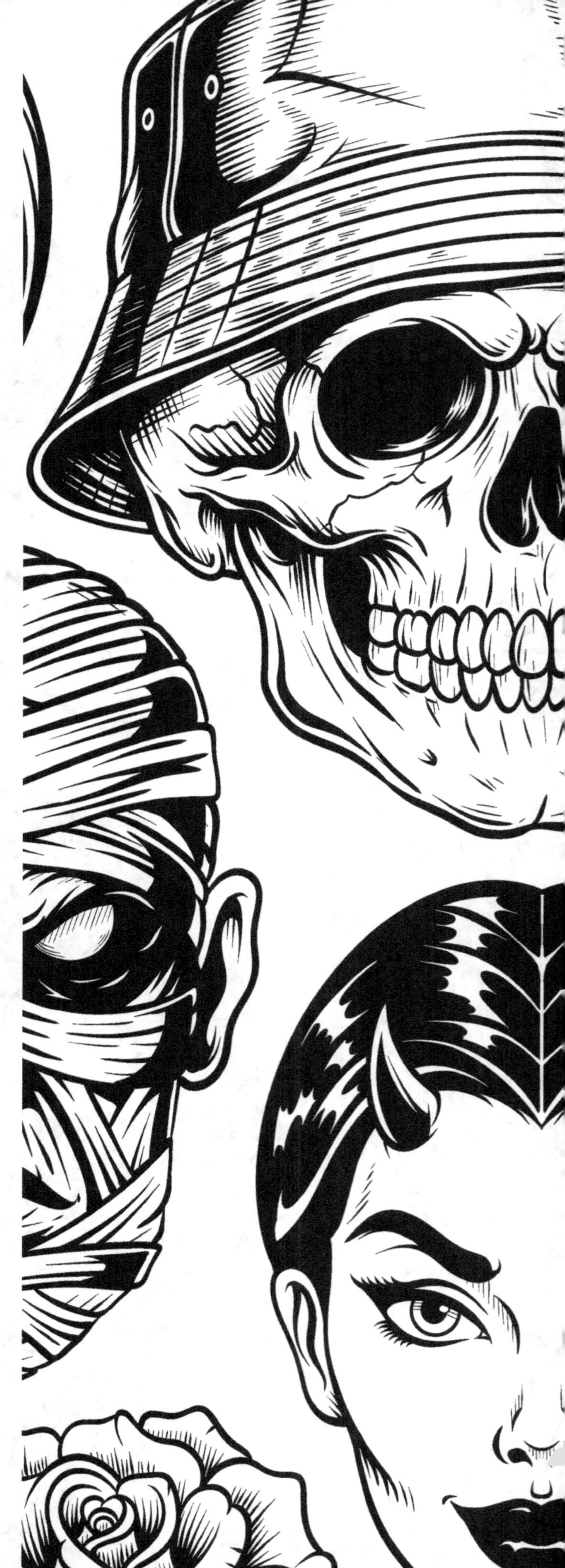